ROBERT LOUIS STEVENSON

AND ROMANTIC TRADITION

ROBERT LOUIS
STEVENSON

AND

ROMANTIC TRADITION

BY EDWIN M. EIGNER

PRINCETON, NEW JERSEY

PRINCETON UNIVERSITY PRESS

MCMLXVI

for Ruth

PREFACE

M O S T of the techniques used in the following chapters will need no special justifications, for they are those which readers have come to expect in critical books. There is perhaps one exception. Wherever I have seen an opportunity to relate a work of Stevenson's to fiction which was written before it, I have attempted to note the similarities and oftentimes to argue for an influence. The point I wish to make is not that Stevenson's fiction is unoriginal, but that it is closely related to an important literary tradition, that of the nineteenth century prose romance. Through the comparisons, I have attempted to define this tradition and at the same time to establish Stevenson's rightful place within it.

Very little must be said to demonstrate Stevenson's dependence upon past literature; Stevenson himself was always at great pains to make his debts known. In an age of realism, when most writers prided themselves on their redblooded originality, Stevenson was anxious to be known as a literary man, distinctly aware of the writers who had come before him and of those who were to follow. Thus he developed his famous prose style, he tells us, by playing "the sedulous ape to Hazlitt, to Lamb, to Wordsworth, to Sir Thomas Browne, to Defoe, to Hawthorne, to Montaigne, to Baudelaire, and to Obermann."[1] And the ideas for half of his stories, as he once wrote the editor of the New York

---

[1] "A College Magazine," *The Works of Robert Louis Stevenson: Vailima Edition*, 26 vols. (London, 1922-1923), XII, 50. Unless otherwise stated, all citations to Stevenson's works and letters will be to this edition and, in the notes, will be referred to as *Works*.

Tribune, were taken from the works of other men.[2] There is no reason to read such statements as bits of gallant modesty. Neither are they the confessions of a repentant thief, for the kinds of dependence Stevenson admits to were not at all uncommon in the romance tradition. As we shall see, such works usually took their beginnings from ideas rather than life experiences. Ideas are easily shared, and the works which derive from them are more apt than realistic novels to show something of a studio nature. It is for this reason especially meaningful to speak of a romance tradition.

Stevenson's official biographer, his cousin Graham Balfour, wrote that while the author took the best wherever he found it, "he rendered it to the world again with interest."[3] Such a statement may appear immodest, especially if we consider that the best from which Stevenson took included such masterpieces as *Wuthering Heights, The Marble Faun, Huckleberry Finn*, and *Crime and Punishment*. The partiality is understandable, though, for in 1901, when Balfour's book was published, Stevenson was almost as much overrated as he is neglected today. And while it is perhaps improper to regard Stevenson as having improved on these books, it is just as wrong to dismiss him as a mere copier of the ideas he took from the great masters of his tradition. Always, as we shall see, he modified their themes with his own insights and concerns, and he made their ideas fitter to be transmitted into our own century.

I have tried also to take account of the books, articles, and dissertations that have been written about Stevenson, but because Stevenson has been so long out of fashion most of this literature belongs to another generation of criticism from our own and reflects what one might call the unreconstructed view of romanticism. David Daiches' high in-

2 October 16, 1882, *Works*, XXI, 139.

3 *The Life of Robert Louis Stevenson*, 2 vols. (New York, 1906), II, 262.

telligence and excellent sense, of course, transcend critical styles. The only recent book, Robert Kiely's *Robert Louis Stevenson and the Fiction of Adventure* (1964), appeared after my own interpretations had been completed, and this is the only opportunity I shall have to explain how the present book and Mr. Kiely's differ from one another. For one thing, I deal with a larger body of the fiction than he has chosen to treat. And then, by relating Stevenson to the romance tradition, I have been able to argue that the same basic themes and techniques prevail in his early and his late works and that the whole of Stevenson's fiction contains more unity than Mr. Kiely and some previous critics have been willing to allow it. In short, I do not regard Stevenson as a case of temporarily arrested development, as an almost eternal boy who resisted coming of age, so to speak, until he wrote *The Master of Ballantrae* and *Weir of Hermiston*. I believe, as do all readers, that these two books are the author's most valuable products, but I maintain that the serious problems and fully adult themes treated in them can be found throughout Stevenson's fiction.

ACKNOWLEDGMENTS

I WISH to thank the Graduate School and the College of Liberal Arts at the University of Kansas for their generous support, in terms both of grants and of released time from teaching, which has made the completion of this work possible. I have to be grateful also to librarians at a number of institutions: Yale, Northwestern, Harvard, and the Universities of Iowa and Kansas.

Mr. W. H. Salter, Dr. Gardner Murphy, and Mrs. E. Q. Nicholson were most gracious in helping me to obtain copies of some unpublished and uncollected Stevenson letters.

My general approach to fiction derives from Professor Ralph Freedman of the University of Iowa. I was lucky enough, moreover, to get several key suggestions from Professor Freedman, which have guided many of my revisions. Professor Frederick P. W. McDowell, also of the University of Iowa, has been most helpfully concerned with every stage of this study. The finished product belongs in large measure to him, and my thanks for his assistance can never be adequately expressed in words.

Others who have read at least one draft and whose criticisms have been especially useful are Mr. Herbert S. Bailey, Jr., Professor Bergen Evans, Mr. Roy A. Grisham, Jr., Professor W. R. Irwin, Mr. Melvin Walker La Follette, Professor John C. McGalliard, and Professor George J. Worth.

My colleague, Professor John A. Meixner, has given unstintingly of his time and good sense to supply this book with whatever degree of focus it has attained. The failures in this respect as in all others are of course my own.

I want finally to thank my wife, to whom I owe for much more than the customary proofreading and advice, typing and forbearance, although she performed these feats patiently and with spirit. Beyond these, it was her fully adult appreciation for Stevenson which first sparked my own interest and made me question the neglect into which he had fallen.

EDWIN M. EIGNER

Lawrence, Kansas
February 1966

CONTENTS

ROBERT LOUIS STEVENSON

AND ROMANTIC TRADITION

CHAPTER I

THE BAD TRADITION AND
THE ROMANCE OF MAN

VIRTUALLY everyone is willing to say that Robert Louis Stevenson gave promise of becoming a great writer. He possessed a brilliant mind, a breathtaking skill with language, and a strong imagination. He had, moreover, what teachers of young writers consider the proper attitudes: a willingness and a disposition to spend long hours at the perfection of his craft, a deep interest in the traditions of prose fiction, and always a powerful ambition to create the compelling and significant books that would establish him as one of his country's major writers.

And, indeed, during his lifetime he was granted at least a measure of the reputation for which he seemed destined. Andrew Lang, Edmund Gosse, Sidney Colvin, and W. E. Henley were among his friends and admirers. "The intensest throb of my literary life," wrote Henry James, "as of that of many others, has been *The Master of Ballantrae*—a pure hard crystal, my boy, a work of ineffable and exquisite art."[1] Among the younger writers, Stevenson's reputation seemed even more secure, and in the last years of his life, when he lived on Samoa, he came near to setting up as something of a literary dictator to subjects residing in London, half a world away. On hearing of his death, Sir Arthur Quiller-

[1] Letter to Stevenson, March 21, 1890, *Henry James and Robert Louis Stevenson: A Record of Friendship and Criticism*, ed. Janet Adam Smith (London, 1948), p. 185.

Couch, one of the faraway disciples, commented that "surely another age will wonder over this curiosity of letters—that for five years the needle of literary endeavour in Great Britain has quivered towards a little island in the South Pacific, as to its magnetic pole."[2]

But Stevenson's reputation died soon after him, the victim of the same band of literary roughriders who kept his friend, Henry James, out of fashion for such a long time. When the violence of these critics had run its course, and artists were once again permitted to be artistic, James came back. He was revived, for one reason, because readers of fiction had become aware of a tradition in the English novel to which James' work was so central it could no longer be ignored. Stevenson's tradition, on the other hand, is not yet sufficiently understood, and so he remains outside. His enemies have been largely discredited, and no one actually bars the door to him anymore, but, by the same token, few critics pay him much attention. No voice protested when F. R. Leavis dismissed Stevenson from respectability in an eloquent footnote to *The Great Tradition*:

> Out of Scott a bad tradition came. It spoiled Fenimore Cooper, who had new and first-hand interests and the makings of a distinguished novelist. And with Stevenson it took on "literary" sophistication and fine writing.[3]

Dr. Leavis's judgment combines the two prejudices that have deprived Robert Louis Stevenson of a critical audience —that he was a mere romantic fabulist, writing in the Scott tradition, and that he composed English prose rather too well. The second of these strictures originated from George Moore, the professional young man. It belongs now to an old debate between manner and matter which few people take seriously anymore. We shall not rehearse it here. The other

[2] *Adventures in Criticism* (London, 1896), p. 184.
[3] *The Great Tradition* (New York, 1963), p. 6n.

objection, more basic and more serious, derives largely from our own and Leavis's nursery experiences, for it was in the nursery that most of us last encountered the works of Stevenson. Certainly the time has come for us to do them fuller justice.

Stevenson did not make excessive claims for his books. *Treasure Island,* as he stoutly maintained against Henry James, was an "elementary novel of adventure," intended for an audience of boys.[4] *The Black Arrow* he called "tushery."[5] And he dismissed the fragment *St. Ives* as "a tissue of adventures," with "no philosophic pith under the yarn."[6] But aside from these books and a handful of short stories there is little of the Walter Scott tradition of romance in the works of Stevenson. Nevertheless, I shall attempt to maintain that Stevenson was a Romantic writer, indeed, that he was much more seriously a Romantic than was Scott or any of Scott's true followers, the later nineteenth century fabulists who wrote exclusively in the picturesque tradition.

What we must realize is that English fiction contains two Romantic traditions. Stevenson has a place in both of them, while Scott belongs only to one, to the "bad tradition," as Leavis quite properly calls it. What is valuable in Walter Scott has, by virtue of his Fieldingesque techniques of characterization and his dominant theme of disillusionment, a firm and lasting place in the history of the realistic novel, which is still a third tradition. But the serious romance in England has little to do with Scott. Its tradition begins long before him, with Richardson, and it includes, besides Stevenson, such figures as William Godwin, Ann Radcliffe, Charles Maturin, Mary Shelley, Bulwer-Lytton, Dickens, Charlotte and Emily Brontë, Meredith, Hardy, Wilde,

---

[4] "A Humble Remonstrance," *Works,* XII, 216.
[5] Letter to W. E. Henley, May, 1883, *Works,* XXI, 180.
[6] Letter to R.A.M. Stevenson, June 17, 1894, *Works,* XXIII, 389.

Conrad, and D. H. Lawrence—important writers, many of whom we have forgotten how to value because they have been disinherited by the notion of a Great Tradition.

The serious romance is well understood and appreciated in the criticism of American literature. Richard Chase, for instance, acknowledges a "justly contemned,"[7] picturesque, American tradition, the legacy of Scott, but he insists equally on the existence of a more serious type of fiction, which is distinct nevertheless from what we have called the realistic novel. Along with a number of other American critics—most notably Harry Levin and Leslie Fiedler— Chase has established the serious romance as the most significant form of American prose fiction. But the dominance of the romance tradition was not always acknowledged. "For a long time," writes Fiedler, "American critics (influenced by Parrington among others) read the history of our novel as a melodrama with a happy dénouement in which a virtuous but harried realistic tradition, after resisting the blandishments of fantasy, romance, and allegory, was recognized as the true heir to the patrimony."[8] Nevertheless, today there are probably fewer courses in American literature victoriously entitled "The Rise of Realism" than there were a decade ago.

Critics (influenced by Leavis among others) still subscribe to such a melodrama so far as the history of English fiction is concerned. Perhaps there is more justice for it. Perhaps the romance was never dominant in England. In any event, it was a significant form, and we ought to begin at least to understand it and its English practitioners. The expense to literature is too great if we do not. The best beginning is to admit, as Chase does, that the serious romancers share with their more frivolous brothers a "penchant for the marvellous, the sensational, the legendary, and

7 *The American Novel and Its Tradition* (New York, 1957), p. 20.
8 *Love and Death in the American Novel* (New York, 1960), p. 141.

in general the heightened effect," but we must go on from this point by putting to *all* romances what Chase calls the critical question: "To what purpose have these amiable tricks of romance been used? To falsify reality and the human heart or to bring us round to a new, significant and perhaps startling relation to them?"[9] When we have done this, it will be again possible, I believe, to assess Robert Louis Stevenson at his true value.

Ironically, Scott himself was one of the first to make a distinction between the sensational and the serious romance. In his remarks on *Frankenstein* he pointed out the elementary fact that the tale of Tom Thumb and Gulliver's "Voyage to Brobdingnag" both turn "upon the same assumed possibility of the existence of a pigmy among a race of giants."[10] In novels, Scott disapproved of "any *direct* attempt at moral teaching,"[11] but he felt a didactic purpose was necessary to a romance if it wished to rise above simple entertainment. Thus he approved of *Frankenstein* because "the miracle is not wrought for the mere wonder, but is designed to give rise to a train of acting and reasoning in itself just and probable."[12]

The old sensational romances had the worst reputations as teachers of moral virtue. They had been blamed for the madness of Don Quixote and the damnation of Francesca da Rimini. Scott, who despite his admiration for the serious romance, became the chief inheritor of the old, heroic tradition, was eventually held responsible not only for the American Civil War,[13] but for the adulteries of Emma

9 Chase, p. 21.

10 "Remarks on Frankenstein, or the Modern Prometheus; a Novel," *Blackwood's Edinburgh Magazine,* II (Mar. 1818), 614.

11 Review: "*Northanger Abbey, and Persuasion,*" *The Quarterly Review,* XXIV (Jan. 1821), 358.

12 "Novels of Ernest Theodore Hoffmann," *The Miscellaneous Prose Works of Sir Walter Scott* (Edinburgh, 1835), XVIII, 291-292. First published in *Foreign Quarterly Review,* I (July 1827).

13 By Mark Twain in *Life on the Mississippi,* Chapter XLVI.

Bovary. But in the late eighteenth and early nineteenth centuries it was believed that the serious romance could be a force for good, a means of instructing the young.

Samuel Johnson had hoped that the emerging realistic novel of everyday life might better serve this educational function since its authors, as opposed to the writers of heroic romances, would have to be men of experience with a "knowledge of nature" and an "acquaintance with life." Yet he anticipated a danger and exhorted the new writers not to be primarily concerned with their role "as just copiers of human manners." He urged them to remember that their books "are written chiefly to the young, the ignorant, and the idle, to whom they serve as lectures of conduct, and introductions into life," and he warned them, therefore, not to mingle good and bad qualities in their heroes "for the sake of following nature."[14]

But this admonition of Johnson's was not long heeded, and critics very soon began to feel, perhaps in defense of such masterpieces as *Tom Jones,* that the novel's first obligation was to the truths of experience, not to the tenets of religion. And thus Clara Reeve in her *The Progress of Romance* (1785) could write about the novel much as Aristotle and Sidney had written about history, and could argue for the romance as a fitter vehicle of moral instruction than the novel, since it is free to present men as they should be, while the novel, bound to reality, is forced to draw them as they are.

In the next decade, the romance, as practiced by Godwin, Radcliffe, and Charles Brockden Brown, was heavily encumbered with its messages. Mrs. Radcliffe taught lessons of sensible sensibility throughout her first five works, and William Godwin was careful to explain that his message in the romance *St. Leon* differed from what he had previously stated in his chief philosophical work, *Political Justice,* be-

[14] *Rambler,* No. 4 (Mar. 31, 1750).

cause, quite simply, he had changed his mind.[15] Fiction, no matter how extravagant, did not afford him a vacation from philosophy. And as for the old, "Italian" romances, Godwin held them largely responsible for the false notions of pride which had corrupted and destroyed Falkland, the hero-villain of *Caleb Williams*. Meanwhile, in America, Charles Brockden Brown was writing serious romances, and announcing that his purpose was "neither selfish nor temporary," but aimed "at the illustration of some important branches of the moral constitution of man."[16] The psychology in *Wieland* and *Edgar Huntly* was perfectly current, and the romance *Ormond* is a dramatic comment on some of the ideas recently put forth in Godwin's *Political Justice*.

All this is not to say that the purely sensationalistic romance had by any means died away. On the contrary, Mrs. Radcliffe's successes had encouraged a whole school of translations from the German and of cheap and hastily put together entertainments in fiction. It is well known, for instance, that M. G. Lewis was, as he wrote to his mother, "induced to go on with" the writing of *The Monk* "by reading the 'Mysteries of Udolpho.'" In his opinion, Mrs. Radcliffe's romance was "one of the most interesting books that has ever been published."[17] But the difference between *Udolpho* and *The Monk* is basic to the distinction between the two traditions of the romance. Properly understood, *The Mysteries of Udolpho* is the story of a girl who has been nurtured by her philosophic father and by the simplicity and beauty of the Gascon countryside to possess exactly the right balance of sense and sensibility. Her ad-

[15] "Preface," *St. Leon: A Tale of the Sixteenth Century*, 4 vols. (London, 1799), I, ix.

[16] "Advertisement," *Wieland; or the Transformation* (Port Washington, 1963), p. 23.

[17] May 18, 1794, *The Life and Correspondence of M. G. Lewis*, 2 vols. (London, 1839), I, 123.

ventures and trials are like Clarissa Harlowe's: they prove the strength of her character and the value of her education. Clarissa had indeed been threatened with imprisonment in a moated castle, and Montoni is only Lovelace somewhat Gothicized. The delicate chills, of which critics and amateurs have made so much, the banditti, the nuns, the mysteries, are only bonbons, superadded to the basic plot for the sake of gaining length and interest. But for Lewis they opened up a whole new world of sensationalistic fiction. The intellectual backbone of *Udolpho* is formed in the early chapters when Emily St. Aubert travels with her father. Lewis recommended the book to his mother "by all means," but he warned her "that it is not very entertaining till St. Aubyn's [sic] death. His travels, to my mind, are uncommonly dull, and I wish heartily that they had been left out, and something substituted in their room."[18] And in his own fiction, *The Monk* and *The Bravo of Venice*, for instance, nothing so dull or so informative is ever permitted. Some of the stories from *Romantic Tales* could be republished today in the most mindless of men's adventure magazines, and while *The Monk* still has interest for serious readers, it is because Lewis had a fascinating warp in his own unconscious, not because he tried to communicate significant visions.

In the early years of the nineteenth century both romance traditions flourished: Mary Shelley and Charles Maturin developed from the serious romance; Charlotte Dacre and Walter Scott[19] wrote romantic entertainments. The difference is very wide indeed. Mrs. Radcliffe, for instance, regards the Inquisition the way a contemporary of our own might view Buchenwald; it gives her hero a new and surprising conception of the human soul:

18 *Ibid.*

19 Walter Freye demonstrates that the influence of Lewis on Scott was much greater than the influence of Mrs. Radcliffe. *The Influence of "Gothic" Literature on Sir Walter Scott* (Rostock, 1902).

Is this possible! . . . Can this be in human nature!—Can such horrible perversion of right be permitted! Can man, who calls himself endowed with reason, and immeasurably superior to every other created being, argue himself into the commission of such horrible folly, such inveterate cruelty, as exceeds all the acts of the most irrational and ferocious brute.[20]

When Scott describes the Invisible Tribunal in his Gothic play *The House of Aspen,* a love of medieval ceremony for its own sake converts what Radcliffe would have rendered as a hell of demons into a sort of Masonic ritual, as cheap and as gaudy as the Ku Klux Klan.

Needless to say, the realistic novel survived, as well as the romance, and it also developed along two lines. The one is frivolous, presenting ordinary life for its own sake, for the elemental pleasure of recognition. And we should note that Leavis rejects this type of novel as soundly as he does the romance. The other kind of novel uses realism as a means of getting at truth, for as serious novelists became influenced by the spirit of Romanticism, they accepted a world-view and an attitude towards art similar to those which Wordsworth had expressed in the "Preface" to *Lyrical Ballads.*

Like Wordsworth, the practitioners of the realistic English novel repudiated such "gross and violent stimulants" as were found in "sickly and stupid German Tragedies." They had instead a taste for "humble and rustic life," in Barchester or in Middlemarch, and they tried to describe such an existence "in the very language of men." But what is even more important is that the realistic novelist's conception of the artist was identical with Wordsworth's, who viewed himself as a "man speaking to men." The novelist, too, was the heightened ordinary man, and his wisdom usually pretended to be no more than a shrewdness born of

20 *The Italian,* 4 vols. (London, 1828), III, 17.

much experience. When he looked for truth, he looked in
sensible places—inwardly at his own clear motivations or
outwardly at the plain actions of men. Thackeray is a good
example. He writes in the first chapter of *Lovel the
Widower* that he is painting a portrait which hangs before
him every morning in the looking-glass when he is shaving.[21]
But it was also necessary on occasion to make pictures of
other men's faces, and here he was literally aided by his
ability as a draftsman. Geoffrey Tillotson writes that when
Thackeray "made notes for his fiction, some of them took
the form of drawings." And Tillotson comments on this
technique with a sentiment thoroughly Wordsworthian.
"No novelist," he adds, "gets straighter and deeper into the
mind, but it is by staying on the flesh."[22] Indeed it was
partly because of this kinship between Wordsworth and the
novel, that George Eliot, undoubtedly the greatest of
the realists, felt that with Wordsworth dead, there would
be no one besides herself who could be interested in her
fiction.[23]

The great opposing document of English romantic
criticism is, of course, Shelley's *A Defence of Poetry,* and
here we find expressed the attitudes towards man and art
with which the writers of the serious romance would have
felt more in sympathy.[24] For the truths of the romance are
usually more mystic, more inspirationally derived, more
visionary than those of the novel. The writer of the ro-

[21] *Lovel the Widower, Thackeray's Works,* 30 vols. (Boston, 1891),
III, 230.

[22] *Thackeray the Novelist* (Cambridge, England, 1954), p. 85.

[23] See letter to John Blackwood, 24 Feb. 1861, *The George Eliot Letters,* ed. Gordon S. Haight, 6 vols. (New Haven, 1954), III, 382.

[24] Of all the great Romantic poets, Shelley owed the largest debt to
the romance tradition. In his youth he had read Gothic stories avidly
and written them enthusiastically, though inexpertly. Later he became
related by marriage to two of the most important Gothic writers, his
wife Mary and her father, William Godwin.

mance, at least apparently, is more intellectual than the novelist; and rather than striving to go deep by staying on the flesh, he tries to capture an internal vision, never expressed on the surface of the real world or, indeed, in the conscious portion of the writer's mind. Moreover, the romancer believes with Shelley that "when composition begins, inspiration is already on the decline, and the most glorious poetry that has ever been communicated to the world is probably a feeble shadow to the original conception of the poet." He expects to discover no new truths through recollection or in the process of writing.

Always the writer of the romance *begins* with his conception. Those writers we have so far been looking at started oftentimes with a thesis, but more ususally the romancer begins with a vision or an overpowering truth which he feels incapable of holding back. Charlotte Brontë, for instance, apologizes for her sister's creation of Heathcliff by stating that "the writer who possesses the creative gift owns something of which he is not always master." And she goes on to say:

> Be the work grim or glorious, dread or divine, you have little choice left but quiescent adoption. As for you—the nominal artist—your share in it has been to work passively under dictates you neither delivered nor could question—that would not be uttered at your prayer, nor suppressed nor changed at your caprice.[25]

And the vividly symbolic, almost surrealistic pictures which Charlotte's Jane Eyre draws seem indeed to have been so inspired and executed. *The Castle of Otronto, Zanoni, Frankenstein,* and the *Strange Case of Dr. Jekyll and Mr. Hyde* are each attempts to recreate visionary and significant dreams which their authors claimed actually to have

[25] "Editor's Preface to the New Edition of Wuthering Heights," *Wuthering Heights* (New York, 1960), p. xxxv.

dreamed. By way of contrast, the realist, if he begins his work with any preconception stronger than a general attitude towards experience, will probably distort the phenomenal world he is trying to portray. He finds the kernel of truth within his real or imagined experiences, while the writer of romance fabricates experience to illustrate a truth which in his vision or his theory he has already apprehended. Conrad expresses this difference admirably in "Heart of Darkness" when he compares the kind of story Marlow tells with the downright yarns of typical seamen, where "the whole meaning . . . lies within the shell of a cracked nut." To Marlow, on the other hand, "the meaning of an episode was not inside like a kernel; but outside, enveloping the tale which brought it out only as a glow brings out a haze, in the likeness of one of these misty halos that sometimes are made visible by the spectral illumination of moonshine."[26] Marlow himself says that it seems he is trying unsuccessfully to relate a dream.[27]

Most realistic novelists and realist-oriented critics have had little patience with this other, less proper side of fiction. Writers of romance are described as "incurably romantic," as though a chosen method were a disease, and many great books have been condemned because of their subject matter. Thus one of Emily Brontë's first critics wrote that "the power evinced in Wuthering Heights is power thrown away. Nightmares and dreams, through which devils dance and wolves howl, make bad novels."[28] But more basically, realists have attacked the very presumption on the part of the writers of romance to special knowledge *before the act of creation.* Men of common sense, "nothing differing in kind from other men, but only in degrees," they utterly re-

<hr>

[26] *Youth* (New York, 1927), p. 48.
[27] *Ibid.*, p. 82.
[28] "Novels of the Season," *North American Review*, LXVII (October 1848), 359.

ject the notion of truth based on visions. Mrs. Barbauld simply could not understand how Rousseau, who as a writer of fiction "has so little to do with nature, should have so much to do with the heart."[29] And George Gissing speaks for many of the realists when he states that the writer of fiction

> may not pretend to do much more than exhibit facts and draw at times a justifiable inference. He is not a creator of human beings, with eyes to behold the very heart of the machine he has himself pieced together; merely one who takes trouble to trace certain lines of human experience, and, working here on grounds of knowledge, there by aid of analogy, here again in the way of bolder speculation, spins his tale with what skill he may till the threads are used up.[30]

But the writers of romances, in England and in America, were hardly content with so strict a limitation on their art. Charlotte Brontë rejected *Pride and Prejudice* as merely an "accurate daguerreotype portrait of a commonplace face," and she dismissed its author as "only shrewd and observant."[31] Poe called realism "pitiable stuff," the truthful depiction of "decayed cheeses."[32] And Edward Bulwer-Lytton, who, more than most mid-century writers, saw the tide of realism rising, bitterly attacked both the realistic novel and the critics who were its champions:

> The artist of the higher schools must make the broadest distinction between the Real and the True,—in other

[29] "On the Origin and Progress of Novel-Writing," *The British Novelists*, 8 vols. (London, 1810), I, 21.

[30] *Isabel Clarendon*, 2 vols. (London, 1886), I, 230.

[31] Letter to G. H. Lewes, Jan. 12, 1848, *The Brontë Letters*, ed. Muriel Spark (London, 1954), p. 143.

[32] "Marginalia," *The Works of Edgar Allan Poe*, eds. Edmund Clarence Stedman and George Edward Woodberry (New York, 1914), VII, 426.

words, between the imitation of actual life, and the exultation of Nature into the Ideal. The one . . . is the Dutch School, the other is the Greek. . . . The Dutch is the most in fashion. . . . Our growing poets are all for simplicity and Betty Foy[33] and our critics hold it the highest praise of a work of imagination to say that its characters are exact to common life. . . . People make the adoration of Shakspeare the excuse for attacking everybody else. But then our critics have discovered that Shakspeare is so *real!* Real! The poet who has never once drawn a character to be met with in actual life—who has never once descended to a passion that is false, or a personage who is real![34]

Truth to the writer of romances could mean only one thing: truth to the human heart. He saw realism as an unpleasant modern fashion, which he hoped would pass quietly away. Like Stevenson, "in this age of the particular," he remembered and took comfort in remembering "the ages of the abstract, the great books of the past, the brave men that lived before Shakespeare and before Balzac."[35]

Many of the great mid-century writers of romance—Melville and Dickens, for example—have been condemned at one time or another as sensationalists, as mere entertainers. Generally, these writers regarded themselves as the real intellectuals of fiction, and they believed that their own romantic subject matter was much more suitable for the communication of meaning than was the typical subject matter of the realists. As we have seen, they had good justification for this in the tradition that had preceded them. Turning again to Bulwer, who was perhaps the chief

[33] A character from Wordsworth, we should note.

[34] "Introduction to *Zanoni*," *The Works of Edward Bulwer-Lytton*, 9 vols. (New York: P.F. Collier, n.d.), VIII, 470. Subsequent references to this edition will be to *Bulwer's Works*.

[35] "A Humble Remonstrance," *Works*, XII, 221.

apologist for his school, we find him describing his work *Zanoni* as "a romance, and . . . not a romance. It is a truth for those who can comprehend it, and an extravagance for those who cannot."[36] Elsewhere he quotes from Proclus' "Apology for the Fables of Homer" to show the suitability of romantic subject matter for the transmission of intellectual material:

> It appears to me . . . that whatever is tragical, monstrous, and out of the common course of nature in poetical fictions, excites the hearers in all imaginable ways to the investigation of the truth, attracts us to recondite knowledge, and does not suffer us through apparent probability to rest satisfied with superficial conceptions, but compels us to penetrate into the interior parts of the fables to explore the obscure intention of their authors.[37]

In the same vein, Shelley, writing the "Preface" to *Frankenstein* in his wife's name, said that the author did not consider herself "as merely weaving a series of supernatural terrors," but that the Gothic elements afforded "a point of view to the imagination for the delineating of human passions more comprehensive and commanding than any which the ordinary relations of existing events can yield."[38]

Many writers of romances require not only strange circumstances and abnormal psychology to portray their visions, but exotic scenery, as well. But their imaginary landscapes provide a way to reality, not an escape from it, and their faraway islands are not discoverable on any map only because, as Melville says, "true places never are."[39] Blake felt that he "must Create a System, or be enslaved by another Man's." Unlike Wordsworth, he and Shelley

---

[36] "Introduction to *Zanoni*," *Bulwer's Works*, VIII, 472.
[37] "A Word to the Public," *Bulwer's Works*, VI, 719.
[38] "Preface" to *Frankenstein* [1817] (Garden City, N.Y., n.d.), p. 5.
[39] *Moby Dick* (Boston, 1956), p. 62.

sought to escape from the world around them, from physical nature, in order that they might free their imaginations. Similarly the serious romancer seeks a never-land where his mind will be released from the common sense of his neighbors and the truths of the sociologists. Visions oftentimes require a clean canvas. Thus Hawthorne explains that he has chosen Brook Farm as the setting for *The Blithedale Romance*

merely to establish a theatre, a little removed from the highway of ordinary travel, where the creatures of his brain may play their phantasmagorical antics, without exposing them to too close a comparison with the actual events of real lives. In the old countries, with which fiction has long been conversant, a certain conventional privilege seems to be awarded to the romancer; his work is not put exactly side by side with nature; and he is allowed a license with regard to every-day probability, in view of the improved effects which he is bound to produce thereby. Among ourselves, on the contrary, there is yet no such Faery Land, so like the real world, that, in a suitable remoteness, one cannot well tell the difference, but with an atmosphere of strange enchantment, beheld through which the inhabitants have a propriety of their own. This atmosphere is what the American romancer needs.[40]

But Hawthorne was wrong in thinking that his problem was relevant only to American writers, for many English romancers felt also that they must set their stories in the middle ages, or in the Apennines, or in the South Seas in order to free themselves from the limitations of the novel. Nevertheless, exotic scenery and characters are not essential to the romance, for they are a means to vision and

[40] "Author's Preface," *The Complete Writings of Nathaniel Hawthorne*, 22 vols. (Boston, 1900), VIII, xxix-xxx.

not an end in themselves. George Meredith, like Hawthorne, was a writer of intellectually oriented fiction. "If we do not speedily embrace philosophy in fiction," he warned, "the Art is doomed to extinction under the shining multitude of its professors."[41] But Meredith did not see a natural conflict "between realism and idealism" in fiction, although he felt that "little writers should be realistic" so that they might "at least do solid work." For great geniuses, however, "this completes that," he believed. "Men to whom I bow my head (Shakespeare, Goethe; and in their way, Molière, Cervantes) are Realists au fond. But they have the broad arms of Idealism at command. They give us Earth; but it is earth with an atmosphere."[42] Still, Arthur Symons is right to place Meredith squarely in the romance tradition. Symons explains:

> A style conceived in verse, and brought up on Arabian extravaganzas and German fantasies, could scarcely be expected to adapt itself to the narration of the little, colourless facts of modern English society. With such style, above all things literary, life recorded becomes, not a new life, but literature about life; and it is of the essence of the novel that life should be reborn in it, in the express image of its first shape.[43]

Perhaps here we find the key difference between the novel and the romance. To be sure, when it has value beyond entertainment, the novel not only creates new life; it also expresses a significant attitude towards it. Wordsworth, we must recall, insisted that each of his poems had "a worthy *purpose.*" He did not, however, as he explains, "always begin to write with a distinct purpose formally conceived."

[41] *Diana of the Crossways* (New York: Modern Library, n.d.), p. 17.
[42] Letter to Augustus Jessopp, Sept. 20, 1862, *Letters of George Meredith*, ed. William Meredith, 2 vols. (New York, 1912), I, 156-157.
[43] "Introduction," *Diana of the Crossways*, p. xiii.

And neither does the realistic novelist. In the romance, on the other hand, the statement *about* life is primary; *then* comes the picture. The truth, for which, as Conrad says, "you have forgotten to ask," comes distinctly first in the romance; and indeed, oftentimes, when you *do* forget to ask for it, you do not comprehend, and for you the romantic story must almost certainly seem a mere piece of extravagance.

Northrop Frye reminds us that "the romancer does not attempt to create 'real people' so much as stylized figures which expand into psychological archetypes. It is in the romance," he writes, "that we find Jung's libido, anima, and shadow reflected in the hero, heroine, and villain respectively."[44] And certainly an emphasis on psychology is basic to the entire genre. Elsewhere Frye notes that "the central form of the romance is dialectic: everything is focussed on a conflict between the hero and his enemy."[45] Such a duality exists in the romance because its writers almost always followed some sort of analytic psychology. That is, analysis, the division of the mind into component, oftentimes contrary parts, as in George Meredith's well-known division of the soul into the elements of blood and brain, was the characteristic method which these writers found of describing human nature. Such a method became, if not the essence, then at least the vehicle of their most significant visions.

The nineteenth century, of course, generally took its reality in terms of antitheses. At the higher levels of thought the century's habit of mind is reflected by the philosophies of Hegel and Kant; and on the lower, by the typical citizen's conception of good men and villains, of pure and scarlet women. In romantic fiction, the century's practice of splitting reality into convenient halves is expressed time

[44] *Anatomy of Criticism* (Princeton, 1957), p. 304.
[45] *Ibid.*, p. 187.

and again through the technique of the *Doppelgänger,* or double, and by the philosophies and psychologies of dualism which surround this device. We must explore the technique and its informing thought at some length before we can hope to come to an understanding of the themes of Robert Louis Stevenson or of the romance in general.

From as early as the Romantic period itself, critics have been aware of the concept of double mindedness in the works of serious writers. Coleridge spoke of this theme in a discussion of *Don Quixote.*[46] Hazlitt found doubles in the romances of William Godwin.[47] J. J. Ampère noted the *Doppelgänger* technique in *Faust.*[48] Modern criticism, too, has shown an active interest, so active, it appears, that to make a list of the writers whose use of the double and of dualistic psychology has been studied in recent years would be little less than to compile a catalogue of the German, French, Russian, Italian, English, and American romancers and romantic poets and dramatists of the last two hundred years.[49] Certainly we are dealing here with one of the most significant themes of nineteenth century literature, and undoubtedly with one of the most frequently repeated. By the end of the century it had spread so widely that, as Richard Ellmann writes, the concept of the self had become

[46] "Don Quixote," *Coleridge's Miscellaneous Criticism,* ed. Thomas Middleton Raysor (Cambridge, 1936), pp. 102-103.

[47] Hazlitt calls Caleb "a second conscience" of his patron. "William Godwin," *Spirit of the Age, The Complete Works of William Hazlitt,* ed. P. P. Howe, 21 vols. (London, 1930-34), XI, 24.

[48] Johann Eckermann, *Conversations of Goethe with Eckermann,* trans. John Oxenford (London, 1930), p. 199.

[49] Perhaps the most significant of these studies are Richard Chase, *The American Novel and Its Tradition* (New York, 1957); J. Hillis Miller, *Charles Dickens: The World of His Novels* (Cambridge, Mass., 1958); Mario Praz, *The Romantic Agony,* trans. Angus Davidson, 2nd edition (London, 1951); Peter Thorslev, *The Byronic Hero* (Minneapolis, 1962); Ralph Tymms, *Doubles in Literary Psychology* (Cambridge, England, 1949); Edmund Wilson, "Dickens: The Two Scrooges," *The Wound and the Bow* (Cambridge, Mass., 1941), pp. 1-104.

"binary or double-decked; whatever one's conception of the two parts may be, we may expect writers to anthropomorphize each part as Stevenson, Wilde, Valéry, Beerbohm, and others did."[50]

Ellmann goes on to note that we must not expect the psychologies behind these uses of the double to be identical. Indeed, there are many ways to divide reality, and each dichotomy expresses a different vision. Moreover, there are a great number of nineteenth century books in which the doubles express no psychology at all, where they are included purely for the purpose of sensation. The weirds of Walter Scott and the disguises of M. G. Lewis are of this discription. But in the serious works belonging to the romance tradition, the doubles carry most of the intellectual burden, and they usually reflect systems of psychology, some of which were considered quite respectable and even sound in a scientific sense. Both Shelley and Goethe believed that they saw their own doubles and spoke about the experiences in much the same way a modern writer might describe his Oedipus complex.

The works of E. T. A. Hoffmann demonstrate very clearly the relationship between the literature of the double and contemporary psychology. As Ralph Tymms points out, Hoffmann firmly based his own dualism on the theories of the mesmerist psychologist G. H. Schubert, *Die Symbolik des Traumes* (Bamberg, 1814). Schubert's theory that man is made up of a reasonable waking self and an evil shadow self, which are always in conflict with one another, is certainly reflected in many of the German Romantics and perhaps most clearly in Hoffmann's own "Fräulein von Scudere," where a respectable jeweler commits knife murders in his second existence.[51]

[50] *Yeats: The Man and the Masks* (New York, 1948), p. 73.
[51] My own research has indicated that the influence of Schubert upon Hoffmann is quite as strong as Tymms represents it to be. Hoffmann's

But this German psychology is older even than Schubert; it finds expression, for instance, in Kant, who perceived a constant struggle between man's radically evil heart and his Reason, the good element in his nature. Here we find overt theological connections, for the romantic dualism of the end of the eighteenth century and the beginning of the nineteenth is oftentimes an answer to the skeptical optimism of the perfectabilitarians. It does not always speak in Christian terminology, but it represents nevertheless something of a return, with a change of emphasis, to Christian dualism, which had seen man after the Fall as wholly corrupt and morally depraved, but still with a redeeming spark from God, a capability of receiving salvation through grace. Calvin had allowed this capability to only a fraction of mankind, to the elect. A century of common sense, however, had changed this estimate, and at the beginning of the Romantic movement, most Europeans thought of themselves as civilized beings, essentially benevolent and rational. What the Romantic dualists had to re-emphasize was that this man, who had emerged from the Enlightenment as a rather fine fellow, capable of infinite improvement if only corrupting and hindering institutions would get out of his way, kept a snarling and untamable demon in his breast. Indeed, Kant is quite specific in first stating the Enlightenment and Pre-Enlightenment attitudes, which he sums up in the disjunctive proposition: *"Man is* (by nature) *either morally good or morally evil,"*[52] and then contrasting them with his own theory that *man is essentially both evil and good.* "To become morally good," Kant writes, "it is not enough merely to allow the seed of goodness

---

Serapion Brethren, for instance, discuss Schubert's "Glances at the Nightside of Natural Science," *The Serapion Brethren*, trans. Alexander Ewing, 2 vols. (London, 1892), II, 99.

[52] *Religion within the Limits of Reason Alone*, trans. Theodore M. Greene and Hoyt H. Hudson (Chicago, 1934), p. 17.

implanted in our species to develop without hindrance; there is also present in us an active and opposing cause of evil to be combatted."[53]

In light of this relationship between Christianity and the new psychology, it is interesting that one of the earliest works of the romance tradition in Great Britain, James Hogg's *The Private Memoirs and Confessions of a Justified Sinner* (1824), is something of an attack on the Calvinist doctrine of election. Hogg's book owes almost as much to the eighteenth as to the nineteenth century. In one way it is a sort of *Tom Jones*, told through the point of view of Blifel. This is the eighteenth century aspect. The nineteenth century difference is that Hogg's villain—Robert, the justified sinner—is not a conscious hypocrite, but a pious Christian who has been taught to believe that he has been predestined for salvation, while his amiable brother has been cast away. This sincere conviction certainly justifies all the many sinful actions against his brother which Robert's jealousy prompts him to take.

Another prompter to evil is Robert's double, his exact lookalike, who enters into his dreams and accompanies him during his waking hours. Soon Robert begins to think of himself as two people, and actually to perceive his second self in the physical world. This other identity, moreover, tempts him to murders and, it appears, sometimes usurps his body, for although Robert has no memory of it, he is accused of continual drunkenness and of the seduction of a young girl. He is also conscious of much less time than has actually passed.

I was a being incomprehensible to myself. Either I had a second half, who transacted business in my likeness, or else my body was at times possessed by a spirit over which it had no control, and of whose actions my own soul was

[53] Kant, p. 50.

wholly unconscious. . . . To be in a state of consciousness and unconsciousness, at the same time, in the same body and same spirit, was impossible. I was under the greatest anxiety dreading some change would take place momently in my nature; for of dates I could make nothing; one-half, or two-thirds of my time, seemed to me totally lost.[54]

Slowly Robert begins to believe that this *alter ego,* which he had at first welcomed as his good angel, is in fact the Devil or perhaps a diabolical element within his own nature. But when he wishes to free himself from the evil influence, he is told that he is speaking of an impossibility. "I am wedded to you so closely," says the second identity, "that I feel as if I were the same person. Our essences are one, our bodies and spirits being united, so that I am drawn towards you as by magnetism, and, wherever you are, there must my presence be with you."[55]

The idea of a man driven to murder by a diabolic voice from within, which he mistakes for God's voice, might have come from Charles Brockden Brown's *Wieland; Or, the Transformation* (1798). More likely, however, the influence was from Hoffmann's romance, *The Devil's Elixir,* a translation of which was published in Edinburgh by Hogg's friend, John Ballantine, in 1824, the year *Confessions* was written.[56] Not only are the central conceptions of the two books identical; but Hogg has chosen to borrow characters, incidents, and even bits of dialogue from Hoffmann's great masterpiece of double identity. Nevertheless, David Daiches has justly called Hogg's book "one of the greatest pieces of imaginative prose produced in Scotland in modern

[54] *The Private Memoirs and Confessions of a Justified Sinner* (London, 1926), p. 208.

[55] Hogg, p. 259.

[56] The simultaneous London publication was printed by Robert Cadell, who had published Hogg's poems two years earlier.

times."[57] Its obvious relationship to German mesmerist theories, on one hand, and to such later works as *Eugene Aram, Crime and Punishment,* and *Dr. Jekyll and Mr. Hyde,* on the other, make *Memoirs of a Justified Sinner* one of the most important works in the romance tradition. It reflects, moreover, a literary interest in abnormal psychology which was shared by Lockhart and many others of the influential *Blackwood's* group.

Charles Dickens was an accomplished mesmerist, and certainly the divided man of mesmerist psychology is a frequent figure in his fiction. According to the critic Taylor Stoehr, Sydney Carton and Charles Darnay of *A Tale of Two Cities,* Eugene Wrayburn and Bradley Headstone of *Our Mutual Friend,* and Lady Dedlock and Mademoiselle Hortense of *Bleak House* are sets of "symbolic twins, projections onto separate characters of . . . conflicting impulses."[58] In *Great Expectations,* Mr. Wemmick, who marks an absolute separation between his public and his private lives, is very nearly a split-personality. John Jasper of *The Mystery of Edwin Drood* and Jonas Chuzzlewit, murderers with peaceful, even dull *alter egos,* belong clearly to the Mesmer–Schubert tradition of psychology. They are both *Doppelgänger* in the full sense of the term—Jonas thinks he is his own ghost, and Jasper keeps two separate diaries—and, as we shall see, they were important influences on the writings of Stevenson.

But such obvious doubles are rather difficult to find in mid-century England. Following the mesmerist fad of the 1840's, dualistic psychologies were considered occult and, as the literary historian Ralph Tymms writes, "the scientific character of the theories of animal magnetism was to a

---

[57] "The Writing of Scottish Literary History," *Literary Essays* (Edinburgh and London, 1956), p. 152.
[58] *Dickens: The Dreamer's Stance* (Ithaca, 1965), p. 167. See also J. Hillis Miller, *Charles Dickens: The World of His Novels,* p. 248.

great extent lost."[59] Positivism and meliorism certainly did not encourage a psychology of demons, and the new scientists of the mind, men like Francis Wayland and Herbert Spencer were introspective by technique, whereas doubles psychology, unless the psychologist were himself a somnambulist, depended upon an interest in clinical cases. The psychology of dualism, therefore, passed into the hands of quacks like A. L. Wigan, an amateur physiologist who argued for man's double nature on the basis of his observations of the two hemispheres of the brain.[60] And the attendant literature was consequently forced to the frontiers —to New England, to Russia, and to Yorkshire, where the Brontës wrote.

In such works as *The Woman in White* and *The New Magdalen,* Wilkie Collins continued to use the double, but ususally for the purposes of pure sensationalism. When Charles Reade describes a double life in *Griffith Gaunt,* his aim is merely to set up a series of stagey effects. Nevertheless, despite this cheapening, the two sides of man's character, as the German Romantics had seen them, did not disappear altogether from the best literature; they simply went separate ways for a while. Two books by Mario Praz, *The Romantic Agony* and *The Hero in Eclipse in Victorian Fiction,* attest to the separate continuance of both lines, and Praz makes us aware of the relationships between the two kinds of characters he discusses, the demonic and the *Biedermeier.* He writes that "the century's subconscious stratum was a turbid one; and when in 1866 Swinburne flustered the Victorians with the sadistic cruelty of *Anactoria* and the *Dolores* litanies, instead of being astonished by the contrast between such daring expressions

59 *Doubles in Literary Psychology,* p. 72.
60 *A New View of Insanity: The Duality of the Mind: Proved by the Structure, Functions, and Diseases of the Brain, and by the Phenomena of Mental Derangement* (London, 1844).

and the atmosphere out of which they arose, we should on the contrary, see in them a clear verification of the intimate and profound relation between the two."[61]

Nevertheless, this "subconscious stratum" was beginning to find little serious, direct expression in mid-Victorian England. Most of the important writers dealt exclusively with the other side of the duality. Thackeray, Trollope, and George Eliot had only the most qualified beliefs in heroism and villainy. Arnold thought that men of action—the Hebraists of *Culture and Anarchy*—were often over-zealous, but he certainly did not represent them as evil. Even the moral activists—Tennyson, Carlyle, Charles Kingsley, Macaulay—believed that heroic energy was derived from God, not the devil. And certainly none of these writers saw the heart of man as "radically evil," as Kant had. "Sir Galahad's strength was the strength of ten," Jerome H. Buckley reminds us, "*because* his heart was pure."[62]

One of the results of these changes in attitude and taste was that the literature of the double—and all Romantic literature for that matter—was no longer considered quite respectable. Bulwer-Lytton had contributed significantly to the romance tradition in 1832 with *Eugene Aram* and interestingly in 1842 with *Zanoni*, which he considered "to be the loftiest conception in English prose fiction."[63] When he tried again twenty years later, the title of his book, *A Strange Story*, unintentionally reveals how unconventional the literature of the double had become.

Nevertheless, *A Strange Story* is worth pausing over not only because it was an influence on Stevenson, but because the psychology in it is presented with perfect seriousness.

[61] *The Hero in Eclipse in Victorian Fiction*, trans. Angus Davidson (London, 1956), p. 139.

[62] *William Ernest Henley: A Study in the "Counter-Decadence" of the 'Nineties* (Princeton, 1945), p. 15.

[63] Letter to Forster, 1842. *The Life of Edward Bulwer, First Lord Lytton by his Grandson*, 2 vols. (London, 1913), II, 35.

Indeed, the book reads in parts like some of the most dry-as-dust works of psychology, morality, and medicine, complete with footnotes and references. Bulwer, following the doctrines of the German mesmerist Jung-Stilling, divides man into three segments—the animal, the intellectual, and the spiritual—and psychological disturbance is described in terms of an over-ascendancy of, or a deficiency in, any one of the three elements. Thus Dr. Fenwick, the hero, is weak in his spiritual nature and must pray. Lilian, the heroine, has too much soul and is advised to spend more time regarding the world. And Margrave, the moral monster of the story, would delight a modern psychologist, for he is a psychopath and has no spiritual nature at all.

A Strange Story is at least as much a treatise on mid-century psychological and animal-magnetism theory as it is a romance, but the psychology is mixed with very strange, fantastic matter which obviously escaped from Bulwer's control, and the result is a bad confusion of the two traditions of romance, the serious and the picturesque. Margrave, who at his best reads like Hawthorne's Donatello before his fall from innocence, turns out in the end to be an evil magician who projects his double to execute wicked designs on helpless females. The story, moreover, is filled gratuitously with alchemy, secret passages, giants, and magic elixirs. Romanticism may be "literary mysticism," as Montague Summers writes,[64] but *A Strange Story* is an extravagance even to the reader who comprehends.

And yet Bulwer's separation of man's mind into the animal, the intellectual, and the spiritual parts is almost the same as George Meredith's division of the soul into the blood, the brain, and the spirit—the very analysis with which we began this consideration of the Romantic conception of the psyche. And while Meredith has quite rightfully been thought doctrinaire, he has not, in his mature

[64] *The Gothic Quest* (London, 1939), p. 18.

works at least, been called fantastic. As we have noted, Meredith saw no contradiction between the themes of the idealists and the subject matter of the realists. Thus he wrote thoroughly reasonable and solid romances. Perhaps what enabled him to do so was the new respect which the psychology of dualism, largely free now of Browning's Mr. Sludge, had in the meantime recaptured.

It was Taine who brought the concept of double personality back into good psychological repute. In his work, *On Intelligence,* published in 1870, he wrote,

> Our images, by connecting themselves, make up the group which in literary and judicial language we call the moral personality. If two groups are distinctly severed, so that no element of the one calls up any element of the other, we shall have . . . two moral personalities in the same individual.

Taine goes on to say that if "the passions take another degree and another direction, not only will these moral personalities be distinct, but there will be enormous disproportions and contradictions between them."[65]

The idea was taken up all over the world—by Max Dessoir in Germany, William James in America, Thomas Henry Huxley in England. The most systematic work on the concept, however, was performed in France itself by the doctors of abnormal psychology, Jules and Pierre Janet, Jean Martin Charcot, and Alfred Binet. Unlike the earlier introspective psychologists, these men dealt largely with patients in mental institutions, but they assumed always that by observing the insane, they were gaining insights into the normal mind. This in itself is a Romantic notion. As we have seen, it is one of the prime tenets of the romancer, and is in clear contrast to the practices of such pictorial novelists

[65] *On Intelligence,* trans. T. D. Haye (London, 1871), p. 97.

as Trollope and Thackeray, who based their characters' psychologies on their own minds and motivations.

Both Pierre Janet and Binet believed that a somnambulist was, in fact, two persons rather than one. Janet wrote that somnambulism was "a second existence,"[66] while Binet believed that "the person who rises in the night is entirely distinct from the one who is awake during the day."[67] These psychologists, moreover, saw the two alternate personalities of their patients as incessantly at war with one another, engaged in a constant battle for dominance. "Usually," Janet wrote, "the second state . . . finally takes possession of the whole life."[68] Such an outcome, however, far from ending the patient's derangement, usually went far to confirm it, for the normal state of the sane man's mind, they both believed, was radically double. Janet concluded that "all hysterical symptoms," are characterized by "disaggregation of the mind, undoubling of the personality."[69]

These theories are of course very much like Schubert's theory of the evil shadow-self, which had influenced Romantic literature at the beginning of the century, and the new psychologists were well aware of the similarity. Binet wrote, in fact, that "the old mesmerists were quite right" when they described somnambulism as "a second personality."[70] The principal difference between the two schools lay in the connections or lack of connections which they made between psychology and theology. The psychologists of the end of the century, as one might expect, fought shy of making moral value judgments. Influenced as they were by Darwin rather than Calvin, they never specifically condemned the second state as evil. Nevertheless, many of

[66] *The Mental State of Hystercals*, trans. Caroline Rollin Corson (New York, 1901), p. 450.
[67] *Alterations of Personality*, trans. Helen Green Baldwin (New York, 1896), p. 3.
[68] Janet, p. 435.   [69] Janet, p. 453.
[70] Binet, p. 80.

their cases would have made excellent grist for the mesmerist mills. Always the patient in his first identity is dull
and orderly. In his second he is gay and witty, oftentimes
even criminal. The most famous of the double personalities, Azam's patient Féleda X, alternated between dullness and vivacity.[71] One of Janet's cases was a poor country
girl in her first personality, but a malicious society wit in
her second. Binet had a patient who was a respectable
lawyer in one identity, while in the other a thief, a gambler,
and a swindler. Huxley, more than any of the others perhaps,
was aware of the similarity between the psychologies of the
beginning and the end of the century. Considering a patient
of the French doctor E. Mesnet, Huxley wrote:

> F's case is singularly instructive, for though, in his normal
> state, he is a perfectly honest man, in his abnormal con-
> dition he is an inveterate thief, stealing and hiding away
> whatever he can lay hands on, with much dexterity, and
> with an absurd indifference as to whether the property is
> his own or not. Hoffman's [sic] terrible conception of the
> "Doppelgänger" is realized by men in this state—who
> live two lives, in one of which they may be guilty of the
> most criminal acts, while, in the other, they are eminently
> virtuous and respectable.[72]

Thus during the last thirty years of the nineteenth century, the literature of the romance tradition was based
again—one could indeed say was based for the first time—
on scientific theory which was deemed thoroughly respectable. Writing in the early 1890's, Sigmund Freud and Josef
Breuer stated as a starting point for their psychology:

---

[71] Féleda X's case history was first published in *Revue Scientifique*
for May 26, 1876; it is recounted at length both by William James in
Principles of Psychology and by Binet.

[72] "Animal Automatism," *Animal Automatism and Other Essays* (New
York, 1884), p. 12.

The longer we have been occupied with these phenomena the more we have become convinced that *the splitting of consciousness which is so striking in the well-known classical cases under the form of "double conscience" is present to a rudimentary degree in every hysteria, and that a tendency to such a dissociation . . . is the basic phenomenon of this neurosis.* In these views we concur with Binet and the two Janets.[73]

It is true that these were also the heydays for the societies for psychical research, but the best psychologists, men like William James, belonged to them, and the journals of these organizations oftentimes published the most solid of psychological essays. The consequence of this new respectability was that Meredith, Stevenson, Hardy, James, Wilde, and Conrad did not, like Bulwer-Lytton and Charlotte Brontë, have to defend their psychologies. And therefore the serious and respected literature of the double which these men produced might almost have been predicted.

But as I remarked at the outset, Robert Louis Stevenson belonged to both Romantic traditions. His nurse, Alison Cunningham, and his father were enthusiasts of the ghost story; his wife, from all evidence, seems actually to have been a believer in occult matters. Stevenson himself was publicly scornful of superstitions, but, as his acquaintance H. J. Moors writes, at times a belief in the supernatural "seemed to grow on him; and he would remind me that there were 'more things in heaven and earth than are dreamt of in your philosophy.' "[74] Probably he always retained at least a half, though a somewhat shamefaced credence in the otherworldly. His wife describes him fleeing

[73] "Preliminary Communication," *Studies on Hysteria (1893-1895)* (London, 1956), p. 12.
[74] *With Stevenson in Samoa* (Boston, 1910), p. 31.

from *āitus* through the woods of Samoa,[75] and in one of his letters, Stevenson recounts with scientific seriousness a supernatural occurrence that he claims to have observed on the Pacific island of Apemama.[76]

This taste for the fantastic shows itself in a number of Stevenson's short stories and ballads—"The Waif Woman," "The Bottle Imp," "Tad Laprick's Tale," "The Body-Snatcher," "The Isle of Voices," and *Ticonderoga*. In several of these works a *Doppelgänger* appears, and in all of them the supernatural is used purely for sensational effects. In *Ticonderoga* a man meets his weird. In "Tad Laprick's Tale" a weaver is seen on a rock out at sea while he is known to be busily at work in Edinburgh. When the double is shot, the man falls dead at his loom.

But while Stevenson participated at times in the Scott and M. G. Lewis tradition of romance, he did not, like Bulwer, confuse this sort of diablerie with ideas belonging to the more serious romance tradition. Such stories as we have just mentioned, Stevenson called "crawlers" or "entertainments." He was even reluctant to take much money for them. In the writing that concerned him, on the other hand, he was very fearful of any gratuitous intrusion of the fantastic or the supernatural. He was afraid for instance that the "steep" conclusion of *The Master of Ballantrae* would ruin the book. "My novel is a tragedy," he wrote to Henry James:

> four parts out of six or seven are written. . . . Five parts of it are sound, human tragedy; the last one or two, I regret to say, not so soundly designed; I almost hesitate to

[75] *Our Samoan Adventure*, ed. Charles Neider (New York, 1955), p. 36.

[76] *RLS: Stevenson's Letters to Charles Baxter*, eds. DeLancey Ferguson and Marshall Waingrow (New Haven, 1956), p. 254.

to write them; they are very picturesque, but they are fantastic; they shame, perhaps degrade, the beginning.[77]

He worried for several days over the "willful . . . steep . . . silly," supernaturalism in *The Beach of Falesá* until he finally converted his real and terrible wizard into a cheap stage magician with Aeolian harps taken from *Ferdinand Count Fathom* and phosphorescent paintings from *Melmoth the Wanderer*. "The yarn is cured," he wrote. "No supernatural trick at all; and escaped out of it quite easily; can't think why I was so stupid for so long."[78] As we shall see, Stevenson referred to *Dr. Jekyll and Mr. Hyde* as a Gothic gnome and was least happy with what we would now call the science fiction aspect of the story. He retained it because the "business of the powders," as he explains, was a part of the dream which had inspired the story.[79] He did not add it for fantastic effect. It was itself the central idea that needed expression. Similarly the picturesque conclusion to *The Master of Ballantrae* was allowed to stand only because it was not *merely* picturesque, because, as Stevenson says, "that was how the tale came to me."[80] To suppress it would have meant to falsify the vision, as grave a sin to the romancer as the falsification of character is to the novelist.

Moreover, if Stevenson was connected to the sensationalists through his half-credence in things mystical, there were aspects in his background and of his interests which tied him much more securely to the more important tradition of romance. We have seen in this brief account of the romance tradition that the dualism it described was in-

77 Letter to Henry James, Mar. 1888, *Henry James and Robert Louis Stevenson*, p. 170.
78 Letter to Sidney Colvin, Sept. 1891, *Works*, XXII, 399, 405.
79 "A Chapter on Dreams," *Works*, XII, 247-248.
80 Letter to James, Mar. 1888, *Henry James and Robert Louis Stevenson*, p. 170.

formed either by the devil-haunted extremes of fevered Calvinism or by some sort of scientific psychology of double identity. Stevenson was in close connection with both of these sources.

When F. R. Leavis dropped *Wuthering Heights* out of the great tradition of the English novel because he thought it was "a kind of sport,"[81] Richard Chase was quick to appropriate it for America. "Suppose," Chase wrote, "it were discovered that *Wuthering Heights* was written by an American of New England Calvinist or Southern Presbyterian background."[82] Stevenson, of course, was not an American, although he married an American woman with an acutely inflamed Gothic sensibility. His religious upbringing in Edinburgh, however, was more Presbyterian than that of any of the major American writers. "About the very cradle of the Scot," Stevenson wrote, "there goes a hum of metaphysical divinity,"[83] and this divinity, in its crudest form, was not very far removed from Manicheism itself. Alison Cunningham, Stevenson's nurse, gives us a good example of her own Presbyterianism when she writes during her visit to France in 1863, "Here there is everything to please the unconverted heart of man—worldly pleasure of every kind, operas too! Is it not *waesome* to see mankind thus turning his back on his best Friend and *tramping* his honour in the dust? The great adversary does triumph here."[84] The influence of Alison Cunningham can be and, indeed, has been greatly overemphasized. Even in 1863, when he was only thirteen, Stevenson did not take either her or her prejudices very seriously.[85] But Cummy's theology, in

---

[81] *The Great Tradition*, p. 27.

[82] *The American Novel and Its Tradition*, pp. 3-4.

[83] "The Foreigner at Home," *Works*, XII, 17.

[84] *Cummy's Diary* (London, 1926), p. 41.

[85] Cummy recounts an instance of the thirteen-year-old RLS pulling her leg. While visiting in a Catholic church, Cummy noticed "some men like priests doing something in a corner curtained off, and when we came

a somewhat more sophisticated form, was what Louis heard every Sunday of his youth. Like the narrator of his own "Adventures of Henry Shovel," Stevenson was brought up to believe that "there were but two camps in the world; one of the perfectly pious and respectable, one of the perfectly profane, mundane, and vicious; one mostly on its knees and singing hymns, the other on the highroad to the gallows and the bottomless pit."[86]

And when, as he grew older, Stevenson rejected his religion, he accepted in its place a discipleship to Darwin, to Meredith, and to the psychologists of dualism. In the 1870's he was secretary of an Edinburgh psychical society. Towards the end of his life he was an associate member of the London Society for Psychical Research, as was his good friend from Davos, John Addington Symonds. Since 1886 he had been writing to the secretary of the society, F.W.H. Myers. Mr. Robert D. Stein, who has been working on a dissertation about Myers, reports that this correspondence gives evidence of Stevenson's familiarity with the classic cases of contemporary doubles psychology.[87] According to Fanny Stevenson, *Deacon Brodie*, "Markheim," and *Dr. Jekyll and Mr. Hyde* were inspired by a paper on "sub-consciousness" which her husband had read in a French scientific journal.[88] As Stevenson wrote in 1891, "I am at bottom a psychologist and ashamed of it."[89]

Much of Stevenson's nonfiction reflects his interest in the contemporary psychology he had been following. The accounts he sent to the Society for Psychical Research, for

out Lew said they were priests playing at cards for money. Is it not very melancholy?" (p. 46).

[86] *Works*, XXV, 317.

[87] Myers' side of the correspondence is available at the Beinecke Library. For one of Stevenson's letters see note 90.

[88] "Prefatory Note" to *Strange Case of Dr. Jekyll and Mr. Hyde*, *Works*, VII, 338.

[89] Letter to H. B. Baildon, Spring 1891, *Works*, XXII, 342.

instance, concern dream debates between the two parts of his own mind. Like the somnambulant patients of the French psychologists, he refers to the parts as *"myself"* and *"the other fellow."*[90] In the essay, "A Chapter on Dreams," which Myers accepted as a valuable contribution to experimental psychology,[91] he sees his own writing as a collaboration between the two sides of his ego. The "little people" provide him with a story, as they did in the cases of "Olalla" and *Jekyll and Hyde.* "I do most of the morality, worse luck! and my Brownies have not a rudiment of what we call a conscience." Elsewhere in the same essay he writes:

> For myself—what I call I, my conscience ego, the denizen of the pineal gland . . . the man with the conscience and the variable bank-account, the man with the hat and the boots, and the privilege of voting and not carrying his candidate at the general elections—I am sometimes tempted to suppose he is no story-teller at all, but a creature as matter of fact as any cheesemonger or any cheese, and a realist bemired up to the ears in actuality.[92]

Nevertheless it is this cheesemonger, the realist, who reads articles on psychology and who edits and selects the dream-tales for their significance and interest. Perhaps he goes so far even as to give the Brownies their somnambulant assignments, for at the time when the little people of "A Chapter on Dreams" created the incidents of *Dr. Jekyll and Mr. Hyde,* the conscious Stevenson, as he explains, "had long been trying to write a story on this subject, to find a body, a vehicle, for that strong sense of man's double being which must at times come in upon and overwhelm the mind of every thinking creature."[93]

[90] Printed in *Proceedings of the Society for Psychical Research,* IX (1894), 9-11. Binet noted this characteristic of divided personalities in *Alterations of Personality,* p. 148.
[91] Letter to Stevenson, 1892, in the Stevenson Library at Yale.
[92] *Works,* XII, 246-248. [93] *Works,* XII, 247.

E N O U G H has been said, perhaps, to establish two points: (1) that an intellectually, particularly a psychologically oriented Romantic tradition of English fiction flourished in the nineteenth century and (2) that Robert Louis Stevenson shared many of the attitudes of its practitioners. He had many of their virtues—perhaps most notably, he believed with them that fiction is an important and a serious art, not simply an entertainment; and that significance or meaning is at least as important to it as charm is. He believed that without significance, interest was impossible to maintain.

On the other hand, he shared to some extent the greatest fault of the romantics: thinness of characterization. It is as well to face this fact now at the very beginning. In writing fiction, it should be remembered, no effect is gained without a consequent loss. The writers of the pictorial or novel tradition specialize in characterization. To them nothing comes before the complete presentation and development of the rounded character. It is out of this delineation, in fact, that theme develops, and should the protagonist grow in a different direction from that which was at first contemplated, the novelist will alter his theme and his plot before he will molest his character. To the romancer, on the other hand, the theme or the vision comes first, and this priority occasions, we should not say a falsification of character, but certainly a less vital interest in it and oftentimes the resultant thinness.

Moreover, a work involving doubles must of necessity present us with un-rounded characters, since it gives us not full, but half-men. Muriel Spark speaks to another aspect of this problem when she writes that the dual heroes of *Frankenstein* are "so essentially complementary to each other, so engrossed one with the other, and in so many ways facets of the same personality, that they defeat powerful characterisation which demands a positive interplay of different temperaments."[94]

[94] *Child of Light*, p. 145.

But we are speaking here only of the serious romance. On the other hand, when characters from the Walter Scott-derived tradition of romance are thinly conceived or executed, it is usually due to the writers' ineptitude. For certainly there is nothing flat about the heroes and heroines Scott himself created. Characterization was indeed his greatest skill. It was a talent, however, that belonged to the realist side of his temperament, and like a true realist, Scott followed along in his novels wherever his characters wished to lead him. "I never could lay down a plan," he once wrote, "or, having laid it down, I never could adhere to it; the action of composition always dilated some passages, and abridged or omitted others; and personages were rendered important or insignificant, not according to their agency in the original conception of the plan, but according to the success or otherwise with which I was able to bring them out."[95]

As a countryman of Scott's, Stevenson always felt a sentimental fondness for the Waverley Novels, but he absolutely rejected Sir Walter as a model and an influence. We should be perfectly clear on the grounds for this disavowal. He dismissed Scott as "a great romantic" but "an idle child," because he was a "day-dreamer, a seer of fit and beautiful and humorous visions, but hardly a great artist; hardly, in the manful sense, an artist at all."[96]

Artistry for Stevenson did not mean, as Leavis implies, "fine writing"; it meant control over the materials of fiction. To gain this control he arduously developed his narrative prose style, which is lively and engaging mainly because of its lucidity. George Moore's attack on Stevenson's elegance was made at a time when Stevenson was known as an essayist, and it is true that in the essays and travel

[95] *The Journal of Sir Walter Scott*, ed. J. G. Tait, 2 vols. (Edinburgh, 1939), I, 100.
[96] "A Gossip on Romance," *Works*, XII, 205.

books Stevenson's sentences oftentimes play very interesting tricks, fascinating to watch, but not really essential to the argument. Such verbal juggling, however, does not appear in the fiction, where the narrators are usually matter-of-fact men with much more honesty than brilliance. Their style, at least apparently, strives to get the story told in as direct and immediate a fashion as can be contrived. In any event, the sentences do not call attention to themselves.

But artistry is not entirely a matter of prose style. Stevenson believed that his early narrative, *Prince Otto,* had been a failure because in it he had "tried to attain too clear a realisation, too full an embodiment; and that in the mass multiplicity of detail, the lineaments of my characters . . . have been lost." He had tried, he believed, to create more of a fictional world than he was capable of controlling. He goes on to say,

> Strong hand, it may be answered, can fashion, in one grasp, the whole conditions and detail of life, or so great a bulk of them at least, as gives us that illusion. But we are not all strong. In seeking after strength we may overlie and dissemble other qualities. A certain level of realisation fits a certain mind; and he will be the wise artist, and he only will accomplish things of beauty, that has the tact to discover and the courage to confine himself to that.[97]

Stevenson had also the good sense to suppress this admission of weakness, which he had intended as a preface to *Prince Otto.* But until very late in his career, he held it as a literary credo. He believed, as we shall see, that realism was not a very good way of getting at the truth about things, but he had also more aesthetic reasons for rejecting it. To be manageable, the world of his romances had to be kept relatively simple, without too much detail in its furniture or too much complication in its secondary characters.

[97] Unpublished manuscript in Yale University Library.

During the middle 1880's, when Stevenson was trying hardest to develop control over his material, he dispensed entirely with sub-plots, parallel plots, and digressions, so popular in his period.

But there was a second aspect of *Prince Otto,* which must also have dissatisfied Stevenson: the omniscient author method of narration. This technique is not common in the romance tradition, but Stevenson made two attempts early in his career to master it. *The Black Arrow* was also a failure, which went badly out of control, so badly, in fact, that the reader for *Young Folks,* the magazine in which it first appeared, had to remind the author that he was leaving two of his basic plot commitments unfulfilled: he had forgotten to account for the last black arrow and to arrange for the death of a principal villain. After *The Black Arrow* and *Prince Otto,* Stevenson did not publish a book-length work with an omniscient author until *The Ebb-Tide,* his last completed romance.

He retreated to narratives recounted directly by their heroes or by onlookers less immediately involved in the central action. He had used both kinds of narrators in *Treasure Island,* where the story-telling was managed with great success, and in the books which followed *Prince Otto,* the personalities of the narrators—Henry Jekyll, Loudon Dodd, Ephraim Mackellar, David Balfour—helped Stevenson measurably in his effort to rein his imagination. And if he had to restrain himself from giving too much detail to the world of his stories, he found a much safer outlet for his creativity in the depiction of his story-tellers. For the more particularity they attained, the more capable they became of providing the tale with a unifying center. Thus Stevenson prided himself in his ability to describe the sensations of his narrators—heat, cold, fear, exhaustion—in such detail, and with so much prosaic realism that the reader was forced to experience them as well.

The result of Stevenson's highly particularized narrators, with whom the reader identifies, and his sparsely furnished and therefore easily manageable representation of the real world is a degree of focus and artistic control which Scott never asked for or indeed thought possible. And since he did not, Stevenson could not accede to become Scott's disciple.

The other reason for the disavowal of Scott is made clear in Stevenson's essay on "Victor Hugo's Romances." There Stevenson praises Scott for the improvements he made on the Fieldingesque novel, but he rejects him ultimately because his works are not guided by central themes. Here Stevenson is asking for more than artistic control (although he is asking for that, too). The primacy of theme over incident and character is, as we have already seen, the distinguishing feature of the serious romance. Stevenson compares Victor Hugo and Walter Scott in the following terms:

> There never was artist much more unconscious than Scott; and there have been not many more conscious than Hugo. . . . He [Hugo] has, underlying each of the five great romances . . . two deliberate designs: one artistic, the other consciously ethical and intellectual. This is a man living in a different world from Scott who professes sturdily (in one of his introductions) that he does not believe in novels having any moral influence at all.[98]

Thus Stevenson reads his great countryman out of the romance tradition.

But neither criticism of Scott—that he is not an artist and not a romancer—bespeaks a distaste for Scott's heroic subject matter. Stevenson himself had committed a number of mindless stories of adventure, and while he blushed at them, he never conceded that there was any incompatibility

[98] *Works,* IV, 35.

between significance and charm in romantic fiction, between
intellectual burden and highly pitched incident. As Henry
James wrote of him:

> It is, indeed, my impression that he prefers the author of
> *The Three Musketeers* to any novelist except Mr.
> George Meredith. I should go so far as to suspect that his
> ideal of the delightful work of fiction would be the ad-
> ventures of Monte Cristo related by the author of
> *Richard Feverel*.[99]

We should also be perfectly clear on the grounds for
Stevenson's rejection of the realistic or pictorial tradition
of the novel. It was not an unthinking rejection. He was
very much aware of the tendency in writers of his own
school, with their eyes not on the world, but on their vision
of it, "to become merely null, and lose all grip of fact, particularity, or passion"; and he tried to guard himself from
this danger by living in the real world as much as his poor
health would allow him. On the other hand, he saw equally
and feared much more the realist's danger, which is "to
sacrifice the beauty and significance of the whole to local
dexterity, or, in the insane pursuit of completion, to im-
molate his readers under the facts."[100] He disagreed strongly
with William Dean Howells and others whose precepts he
felt would create an art "like mahogany and horsehair
furniture, solid, true, serious and as dead as Caesar."[101]
"The danger," he wrote, "is lest, in seeking to draw the
normal, a man should draw the null, and write the novel of
society instead of the romance of man."[102]

Stevenson's intentions, then, were highly ambitious. No

[99] "Robert Louis Stevenson," *Henry James and Robert Louis Stevenson*, p. 152.
[100] "A Note on Realism," *Works*, IV, 422.
[101] Letter to Trevor Haddon, Apr. 23, 1884, *Works*, XXI, 268.
[102] "A Humble Remonstrance," *Works*, XII, 223.

group of writers has ever taken art more seriously than the Romantics did. "Do not forget," says a character in Godwin's *Caleb Williams,* "that the Muse was not given to add refinement to idleness, but for the highest and most invaluable purposes."[103] Stevenson's worth as a Romantic writer should be judged on the depth of his visions and the techniques he found to communicate his meanings. In the succeeding chapters I shall consider these matters and examine Stevenson's right to a place in the Romantic tradition of English prose fiction.

[103] *Caleb Williams* (New York, 1963), p. 30.

CHAPTER II

A SHEEP IN A TURNIP-FIELD

S T E V E N S O N did not begin his literary career as a writer of romances. First came the essays and the books of travel, which succeeded largely because of their realism. The narrator, an ordinary indoors man on rural tours, who runs from dogs and can't keep his canoe right side up, is appealing because he so resembles his readers. Stevenson's personality pervades these works, and autobiography is the essence of realism. When Stevenson made his first concerted attempt at a long work of fiction, his aim, as we noted in the unpublished preface to *Prince Otto,* was to recreate as much as he could of the real world. The realism does not come off in *Prince Otto,* but according to Stevenson's own definition, he was trying to produce a novel, not a romance. *Treasure Island* and *The Black Arrow* were both begun later than *Prince Otto.* They are children's books, but we must not regard them as the infantile beginnings which their author had to outgrow before he could produce serious works of literature. Instead they represent Stevenson's first tentative steps towards the romance, the genre in which he was ultimately to find his artistic fulfillment.

Nevertheless, the false start in realism had its lasting effect on Stevenson's fiction. Romance was to provide Stevenson with a means for understanding human nature, but the model for human nature, the central character of all his works, derives from the stories, the personal essays, the low-keyed travel adventures, and from *Prince Otto,* the realistic novel begun in the 1870's. Moreover, since it is this central character that distinguishes Stevenson's Romantic vision from the conceptions of the earlier romancers, any study of Stevenson must begin with a consideration of his protagonist.

The first and last thing to note about Stevenson's characters is that they usually fail in life. There is scarcely a full-blooded success in the lot of them. Stevenson puts them to work at a great variety of professions—the military, the law, business, government, medicine, art—but few of them make anything of their lives; certainly none of the central characters ever do. Even the villains, like James Durie of *The Master of Ballantrae* and the pirates of *Treasure Island,* are failures in the last analysis. And very few of the characters, whether good *or* evil, manage even to fail greatly. Perhaps the only unqualified successes to be found in all of Stevenson's fiction are Doctor Desprez of "The Treasure of Franchard" and Will o' the Mill; and these men do well only because their goals have been so modest: they have set out—systematically, one might say— to do absolutely nothing with their lives. Most of the characters, however, especially the protagonists, are like the "shipful of failures" Stevenson was surprised to encounter on the immigrant ship to America. He had expected to meet brave souls, set out on a great adventure, ready for a new world. Instead, he found "quiet, orderly, obedient citizens, family men broken by adversity, elderly youths who had failed to place themselves in life."[1] If Stevenson's fiction is, as we have been so oftentimes told, a fiction of heroism, then the heroism does not reside in the characters.

The hero of romance had of course been somewhat un-exciting from as early as *The Castle of Otronto,* to say nothing of *Sir Charles Grandison,* and William Hazlitt had

[1] *The Amateur Emigrant, Works,* II, 236-237.

written a playful, little essay to explain "Why Heroes of Romance are Insipid." He reasoned that otherwise "they would be no longer those 'faultless monsters' which it is understood that they must be to fill their part in the drama."[2] A more practical explanation is that, in the Gothic romance at least, the hero had to be kept in the background to give the villain his legitimate opportunities to terrorize the heroine. But in Stevenson the unheroic hero is more than a device or an example; he stands for a principal theme.

Stevenson is supposed also to be an optimist, a brave and cheerful invalid, but it is hard to see him in such a role except in contrast to the melodramatic and mawkish extremes of *fin de siècle* pessimism. To a modern reader Stevenson's hopefulness seems sufficiently, if not overly, qualified; for what faith he had in the ultimate decency of things was always spoken in the teeth of a conviction that life and toil are utterly futile. His is a defeated optimism, heavily shadowed with the fears of the skeptics, and he believed that "the whole world" may be "a labyrinth without end or issue,"[3] that "man is indeed marked for failure in his efforts to do right."[4] The essay "Reflections and Remarks on Human Life," for example, contains this sort of cheerless advice to young people:

> You will always do wrong: you must try to get used to that, my son. It is a small matter to make a work about, when all the world is in the same case. I meant when I was a young man to write a great poem; and now I am cobbling little prose articles. . . . Our business in this world is not to succeed, but to continue to fail, in good spirits. (XXVI, 127)

2 *The Complete Works of William Hazlitt*, ed. P. P. Howe, 21 vols. (London, 1933), XVII, 247.
3 "Crabbed Age and Youth," *Works*, II, 82.
4 *"Pulvis et Umbra," Works*, XII, 288.

This disheartened belief in the futility of all action is perhaps best capsulized in the fable "The House of Eld." There Stevenson describes a land in which all men have iron gyves riveted to their right legs. The brave, young hero is told that if he wishes to rid himself and his countrymen of their fetters, he must encounter an evil magician, who will present himself, on successive occasions, as the hero's mother, his father, and his uncle, the catechist; and that though he loves these three, he must kill the enchanter in each of his disguises. The hero proceeds courageously to do what is required of him, and is delighted to see the gyve fall from his own leg. When he returns home, however, he finds that his countrymen, free now of the iron on the one leg, have taken to wearing it on the other. He finds also that his parents and his uncle have indeed been horribly murdered. "The House of Eld" seems to have been written in the 1880's, but the tone of even so early a work as *Virginibus Puerisque* (1874) is distinctly weary.

Hope is the boy, a blind, headlong, pleasant fellow, good to chase swallows with the salt; Faith is the grave, experienced, yet smiling man. Hope lives on ignorance; open-eyed Faith is built upon a knowledge of our life, of the tyranny of circumstance and the frailty of human resolution. Hope looks for unqualified success, but Faith counts certainly on failure, and takes honourable defeat to be a form of victory. (II, 37)

There are characters in Stevenson whose lives are fully based on this negative current of thought. The young man with the cream tarts of "The Suicide Club" wishes to live and die foolishly because of the absurdity of life. The Master of Ballantrae settles all important matters by a toss of the coin so that he may in this way express his contempt for human reason. And Doctor Desprez of "The Treasure of Franchard" tries, at least, to live with an "enthusiasm" for

"Golden mediocrity!" "Fix your mind on my example," Desprez tells his disciple; "despise riches, avoid the debasing influence of cities. Hygiene—hygiene and mediocrity of fortune—these be your watchwords during life!" (XI, 278-280) [5]

Stevenson presented Doctor Desprez as an amiable fool, but there can be no doubt he was highly attracted to such Lotos-Eater points of view.[6] For in a world where logic "is generally wrong" and "reasons are as plentiful as blackberries; and like fisticuffs . . . serve impartially with all sides"[7]—there was an undeniable charm for him in the wisdom of the idler, which at least keeps a man free from intolerance, dogmas, and burning falsehoods. "His way," Stevenson wrote, "takes him along a by-road, not much frequented, but very even and pleasant, which is called Commonplace Lane, and leads to the Belvedere of Commonsense. Thence he shall command an agreeable if no very noble prospect."[8]

But always there is more tension in Stevenson's fiction

[5] The speech just quoted, along with many other things in "The Treasure of Franchard" is strongly reminiscent of St. Leon's praise of poverty in William Godwin's romance.

Oh, Poverty . . . if these are the delights that attend thee, willingly will I resign the pomp of palaces and the splendour of rank to whoever shall deem them worth his acceptance! Henceforth I desire only to dedicate myself to the simplicity of nature and the genuine sentiments of the heart. . . . I will sit in the midst of my children and revel in the luxury of domestic affections; pleasures these that may be encumbered, but cannot be heightened, by all that wealth has in its power to bestow! Wealth serves no other purpose than to deprave the soul, and adulterate the fountains of genuine delight. (I, 270-271)

[6] The Lotos-Eaters was, as a matter of fact, one of the favorite poems of Stevenson's youth. In his last days, it was succeeded in his esteem by The Lake Isle of Innisfree, another poem of retirement. The appreciation for Tennyson's poem is found in a letter to R.A.M. Stevenson in the Widener Collection. The "slavery" to The Lake Isle of Innisfree is confessed in a letter to Yeats, Apr. 14, 1894, Works, XXIII, 371-372.

[7] An Inland Voyage, Works, I, 89-90.

[8] "An Apology for Idlers," Works, II, 92.

than such thoughts would seem to promise. His characters often end up in Lotos-land, but they did not always wish to be there. The most fully realized of Stevenson's idlers, the title character of "Will o' the Mill" (1878), begins with a tremendous hunger to come down from the mountains in which he has been placed by birth and to participate fully in life. At first the world of men seems indescribably beautiful to him.

> Bit by bit, he pieced together broken notions of the world below; of the river, ever moving and growing until it sailed forth into the majestic ocean; of the cities, full of brisk and beautiful people, playing fountains, bands of music and marble palaces, and lighted up at night from end to end with artificial stars of gold; of the great churches, wise universities, brave armies, and untold money lying stored in vaults; of the high-flying vice that moved in the sunshine, and the stealth and swiftness of midnight murder. I have said he was sick as if for home: the figure halts. He was like someone lying in twilit, formless pre-existence, and stretching out his hand lovingly towards many-coloured, many-sounding life. (XI, 94-95)

He can hardly bring himself to wait until he will be old enough to join this beautiful world. Later he falls very much in love and becomes engaged to a suitable and loving girl. Yet he neither enters the world nor makes his marriage. Resisting these and other temptations, he manages to get through all of his days without ever once acting, and when the time comes, he greets Death as a friend, who, very literally, of course, removes for him even the *possibility* of life.

Will holds back from life and from action because of an intellectual conviction of the futility of all effort. He is converted to this belief by a fat young man, a skeptical philosopher, who advises him to regard the size first of the cosmos and then of himself, and makes him see that on earth "we are in a rat-trap." The fat young man asks Will, "Did you ever see a squirrel turning in a cage? and another squirrel sitting philosophically over his nuts? I needn't ask you which of them looked more of a fool" (XI, 101).

The philosophy of the idler probably gets its most favorable presentation in "Will o' the Mill," but this sympathy is rare with Stevenson. More frequently the activist strain in him made him despise such thoughts and both the mind and the age which had produced and encouraged them. "Acts may be forgiven," he wrote; "not even God can forgive the hanger-back,"[9] and he later repudiated the sentiments of "Will o' the Mill" as "cat's meat."[10]

For some time he was very much troubled by the unheroic politics of the 1880's. The desertion of Gordon in the Sudan particularly disturbed him and moved him to write, "in this year of—grace, said I?—of disgrace, who should creep so low as an Englishman."[11] And, as he confides to J. A. Symonds, he despised himself along with his government.

But why should I blame Gladstone, when I too am a Bourgeois? when I have held my peace? Why did I hold my peace? Because I am a sceptic: *i.e.,* a Bourgeois. We believe in nothing, Symonds: you don't, and I don't; and these are two reasons, out of a handful of millions, why England stands before the world dripping with blood and daubed with dishonour.[12]

He longed desperately to do something heroic. The Curtin family was persecuted by Irish nationalists. Stevenson

[9] Quoted in J. C. Furnas, *Voyage to Windward* (New York, 1951), p. 223.
[10] Isobel Strong, "Vailima Table-Talk," *Memories of Vailima* (London, 1903), p. 35.
[11] Letter to Edmund Gosse, Mar. 12, 1885, *Works,* XXI, 338.
[12] Feb. 1885, *Works,* XXI, 335-336.

wanted in the very worst way to buy their farm and live on it so that he might be shot down and thereby serve to publicize the barbarism which he felt was going on in Ireland.[13] And during the civil war in Samoa he wrote, "It is dreadful to think that I must sit apart here and do nothing; I do not know if I can stand it out."[14]

And yet sitting apart seemed always to be Stevenson's fate. Only at the end of his life did he become actively engaged in politics, and the recently published diary of Fanny Stevenson indicates that biographers have overestimated the extent of his involvement even in Samoan affairs. It was Fanny and not Louis who was the great partisan of Mataafa.[15] Sometimes, as we have seen, Stevenson blamed his own temperament for the failures. Sometimes he blamed the pigmy age in which he lived. In the spring of 1884, when he was finally completing *Prince Otto*, he wrote, "I prefer galvinism to acquiescence in the grave. All do not; 'tis an affair of tastes; and mine are young. Those who like death have their innings to-day."[16]

IT IS A COMMONPLACE of Stevenson criticism, handed down from one historian of the novel to the next, that *Prince Otto* was modeled on Meredith's *The Adventures of*

---

[13] Stevenson describes this project in a very Hamlet-like letter to Mrs. Fleeming Jenkin (Apr. 15 or 16, 1887, *Works*, XXI, 458-463). He presents five reasons why he should go to Ireland, and twelve reasons why he should not go. Each reason is matched with a tortuous rebuttal. He wants desperately to do the thing—"we shall have some excitement, and that's a fine thing; and we shall be trying to do the right, and that's not to be despised" (p. 460).

[14] Letter to Colvin, June 24, 1893, *Works*, XXIII, 283.

[15] Obviously Fanny distrusted the strength of Stevenson's commitment to Mataafa. She writes, referring to the chieftain, "And if Louis turns his face from him by the fraction of an inch, I shall wear black in public if they murder him. . . . Louis says this is arrant mad quixotism" (*Our Samoan Adventure*, p. 214).

[16] Letter to Trevor Haddon, Apr. 23, 1884, *Works*, XXI, 268.

Harry Richmond. Actually, although Stevenson was indeed very fond of Meredith, the resemblances between the two works are only superficial—they consist almost entirely of the operetta-like, pocket-sized, German principalities which serve both stories for settings—and much more can be learned about Stevenson's book by contrasting it with Meredith's, than by focusing upon their similarities.

The Adventures of Harry Richmond, like many of Meredith's works, is filled with characters who take themselves with exaggerated seriousness. Prince Ernest of Eppenwelzen-Sarkeld, who would correspond to Otto in the matter of rank, knows that the English laugh at little potentates; nevertheless, within his own sphere he considers himself as important as the Kaiser or the Czar. Otto, on the other hand, is a typical Stevenson failure. He fails as a monarch because he "was ashamed" of his "toy kingdom from the first" (v, 402). The title character of *The Adventures of Harry Richmond* is a likeable Meredithian egoist, undergoing his ordeal. He is learning to restrain his passions. Otto is a self-conscious introvert, trying for the first time in his life to assert himself. Moreover, the books are as dissimilar in plot as they are in characters. Meredith's is the story of how the descendant of an English squire almost wins a kingdom through his father's cynical blackmail; *Prince Otto* tells how a hereditary prince loses a crown by overscrupulous ineptitude. Finally, *Harry Richmond* is a fairly successful psychological romance, while *Prince Otto,* in spite of its exotic locale, is, as we have seen, a botched attempt at a realistic novel.

Nevertheless, Stevenson's book is highly derivative, although not of Meredith or the romance. Aspects of many of the characters and even a good deal of the plot appear to have been lifted from the unlikeliest corner of literature in which an optimistic romancer might be expected to look— from the parliamentary novels of Anthony Trollope. The borrowings come from the second novel of the Plantagenet Palliser series, *The Prime Minister* (1876). Stevenson had been an admirer of Trollope's novels from the late 1870's; that is, from just about the time *Prince Otto* was begun and about the time from which Stevenson dated his own skepticism. The terms of his admiration are especially significant. "A young person," he writes, "would get sickened by the dead level of meanness and cowardliness [in Trollope]; you require to be a little spoiled and cynical before you can enjoy it."[17]

Otto and Trollope's Palliser are each types of the undramatic and unglamorous rulers, who had inherited the nineteenth century. Palliser's is a caretaker ministry with no program beyond the mildest sorts of reform and no aim beyond stability. Otto is the hereditary prince of a joke-kingdom, who devotes his time to society and to hunting. The two leaders are certainly not alike in all respects. Otto has more flash; Palliser, more integrity, more stamina, a greater sense of duty. But in the essentials of their characters they are similar, for they are both filled with self-doubt about their ability to inspire love and loyalty, either of their people or of their wives.

As far as the wives are concerned, moreover, Otto and Palliser face identical problems. For each man learns early in the narrative that his ambitious wife, impatient at and contemptuous of her husband's weakness as a ruler, is meddling dangerously in the politics of the nation.[18]

[17] Letter to Mr. and Mrs. Thomas Stevenson, Feb. 21, 1878, *Works*, XX, 378. The admiration is somewhat qualified when he adds that although Trollope's *Way of the World* is a "real, sound, strong, genuine work; the man who could do that, if he had had courage, might have written a fine book; he has preferred to write many readable ones."

[18] The methods by which the two men learn of their wives' activities is also similar. Palliser hears about his wife from some of his workmen who do not recognize him. Otto, in a disguise, learns about his wife from some peasants.

Palliser's wife, Glencora, who wishes to be remembered as the Great Prime Minister's wife, arranges massive, vulgar entertainments and tries to control a parliamentary election. Otto's Princess Seraphina is the dupe of her Prime Minister, Gondremark, who wishes to foster a republican revolution. Seraphina believes, however, that she and Gondremark are plotting an ambitious and glorious war of aggression, which will restore the grandeur to her name and and nation.

When the two rulers discover their wives' activities, they each resolve painfully to take matters into their own hands and for once in their lives move forcefully.[19] But neither has much of a chance to succeed, for in both cases the wives mistake scrupulosity and tenderness for weakness, and in both cases a good deal of weakness actually exists. As Otto's best friend tells him, "I would rather see a man capably doing evil, than blundering about good" (v, 502). After half-hearted and ineffectual attempts, each man contents himself with impatiently and impotently resenting the attacks of blackguard journalists, with cherishing the innocent friendships of out-of-fashion ladies,[20] and with spinning fond dreams of resignation. Even before he begins his attempt to reform his wife, Otto takes the precaution of buying a small farm over the border. Trollope's hero tells his wife that he is "dreaming always of some day when we may go away together with the children, and rest in some pretty spot, and live as other people live." Glencora speaks for both women when she mutters, "It would be very stupid."[21]

Glencora believes that her husband's ministry failed be-

[19] Palliser decides that "he must henceforth take things more into his own hands, or he would be absurd before the world." *The Prime Minister*, 2 vols. (London, 1952), I, 175.

[20] Note here that even the names are similar: Palliser's friend is Lady Rosina; Otto's is called Madame von Rosen, but Rosina is a common name in romance.

[21] *The Prime Minister*, II, 104.

cause "he had no idea of the personal grandeur of the place. He never understood that to be Prime Minister in England is as much as to be an Emperor in France, and much more than being President in America."[22] We have already seen that Otto was ashamed of his toy kingdom. "I could not tolerate," he says, "that people should fancy I believed in a thing so patently absurd" (v, 402). And when *his* Prime Minister refers to "the whole previous policy of Grünewald," Otto laughs at the pretensions of such a small country to so high sounding a thing as a policy. "One would suppose you had no sense of humour," he says. "Would you fish in a coffee cup?" (v, 466) To the ambitious Seraphina, such an attitude seems, of course, to denote a coward and a weakling. Trollope's Glencora says of her husband, "I hate people to be sensitive. It makes them cowards. A man when he is afraid of being blamed, dares not at last even show himself, and has to be wrapped up in lamb's-wool."[23]

Through the women's meddling and the men's ineptitude, both governments eventually collapse. The marriages are preserved, but through fortuitous circumstances, certainly not as a result of effective personal action. Palliser can manage nothing stronger than a pained look when his wife flagrantly disobeys him, and the hypersensitive Otto is so fearful that his wife will laugh at his attempt at a sentimental reconciliation that he prefaces and thereby dooms his efforts by saying, "I am never ridiculous . . . it is my only merit; and you may be certain this shall be a scene of marriage *à la mode*" (v, 450).

All this is not to say that Prince Otto, borrowed as he is from Trollope, does not also belong properly to Stevenson. Quite the contrary; as early as 1876 Stevenson had written a long essay on Charles of Orleans, who "never succeeded in any single purpose he set before him" (IV, 287) and who

22 *Ibid.*, p. 383.
23 *Ibid.*, p. 100.

suffered from an "incapacity to see things with any great-
ness," an incapacity "characteristic of the man as well as of
the epoch" in which he lived (IV, 288-289). Moreover,
Stevenson modeled Otto also on his conception of his own
character, and the self-portrait seems to have been so accurate that even his wife, Fanny, the chief perpetrator of the
highly profitable heroic-Stevenson myth, was forced to note
that her husband truly did resemble Otto to a degree.[24]
Otto's type recurs again and again in Stevenson's fiction.
What is significant about the borrowing which we have
noted, however, is that Stevenson went for assistance in
creating this character to the cynic Trollope, the realistic
novelist, and not to Meredith or to the other Romantic
writers who maintained a belief in some sort of heroic ideal
of character.

In Plantagenet Palliser and in Septimus Harding of *The
Warden*, Trollope had created the two most agreeable abdi-
cators of the century. Here Stevenson differs from Trollope,
for though a great many of Stevenson's characters tender
their resignations, their author is generally not pleased with
their having done so, nor, for that matter, are they pleased
with themselves. Trollope's general attitude is that while
there is perhaps very little heroism in the world, there is
probably even less necessity for it. A life passed pleasantly
and without disgrace, a ministry ended without famine or
bloody revolution—these things represent to Trollope
the highest tokens of success. But not to Stevenson's characters, who hate themselves for their weaknesses; and not
entirely to Stevenson, who, while he understands and sym-
pathizes with his heroes' failures, cannot help bitterly
regretting them. When Otto is told that he has the character
of a born skeptic, he turns on himself with violence:

[24] "Prefatory Note to the *Strange Case of Dr. Jekyll and Mr. Hyde*,"
Works, VII, 342. In the "Prefatory Note" to *Prince Otto* itself (V, 325),
she denies the resemblance with some vehemence.

"Coward is the word. A springless, putty-hearted, cowering coward" (v, 403). His skepticism, he knows, has robbed him of the power to act. "I could never bear to be bustling about nothing," he says with cold self-contempt. "I would do nothing that cannot be done smiling" (v, 402). One of the other characters in the novel describes him as "the nearly perfect fruit of a decadent age" (v, 411).

Otto is some kind of relative to Prince Florizel of *The New Arabian Nights,* and the two men share a penchant for going about in disguises when they should be at home, ruling their kingdoms. Florizel is presented as an all-powerful, even godlike figure. His favorite pseudonym is Theophylus Godall, and he appears to Mr. Rolls, the divinity student, who should therefore be able to judge, as a "man who seemed, like a god, to know all things and to have suffered nothing" (III, 179). Yet despite this seeming power, Florizel's only solution to the temptation of the world is to throw its symbol, the Rajah's diamond, into the river. Moreover, our final view of him after the revolution in Bohemia, happily established as the proprietor of a London cigar divan, is very much like our last sight of Otto and Seraphina as exiles from their country and writers of "dull and conscientious" French verse (v, 615).

Florizel, having lost the suicide game, feels honor-bound to keep his appointment with the murderer from the Club, but when Colonel Geraldine forcefully prevents him, he is "overjoyed to yield to friendly violence" (III, 54). Similarly, Otto could never bring himself willingly to abdicate his crown, but when the revolution takes place he greets the arresting officer much as Will o' the Mill had greeted death. "I have now come to that happy moment of my life," Otto says, "when I have orders to receive but none to give" (v, 531-532), and "he embraced the notion of imprisonment with something bordering on relief. Here was, at least, a step which he thought blameless; here was a way out of his troubles" (v, 530).

These two solutions to the problem of action—welcome imprisonment and inglorious retirement—are standard in Stevenson. They comprise a major theme, perhaps *the* major theme of all his fiction; they appear even in the two fragments—*St. Ives* and *Weir of Hermiston*—on which Stevenson was working at the time of his death. Yet Stevenson was never satisfied with these answers, either artistically or philosophically. As early as 1880, in the early stages of composing *Prince Otto*, five years before it was completed, he wrote to Henley that "the kind, happy *denouement* is unfortunately absolutely undramatic."[25] And while he could write that philosophically "the romance lies precisely in the freeing of two spirits [Otto and Seraphina] from those court intrigues,"[26] the idea of retirement from life always ran counter to Stevenson's own life hunger. On December 1, 1894, just a few days before his death, he wrote to Edmund Gosse, "It is all very well to talk of renunciation and of course it has to be done. But, for my part, give me a roaring toothache" (xxiii, 461).

Consequently, perhaps, Stevenson finishes *Prince Otto*, not with a final view of the hero, but with the account of a further adventure of the Countess von Rosen, the only character in the novel who acts both strongly and effectively. Gondremark, it turns out, bungles at the last moment and fails to profit from the revolution he had engineered, but the Countess always has things under better control. Stevenson employs her as *dea ex machina*, calling her quite frankly, and on a number of occasions, "Providence von Rosen"; but the point is that she can and she does act. It is the Countess who saves Otto's honor and his marriage; indeed she almost saves him his kingdom, although such

25 Feb. 1880, *Works*, XX, 459.
26 Letter to Henley, autumn 1885, *Works*, XXI, 360.

an action would appear contrary to her own best interests, since she is Gondremark's mistress.

Madame von Rosen acts on all sides of the conspiracy, and out of a multiplicity of reasons. She is jealous of the relationship between Seraphina and her lover; she is fond of, perhaps even in love with Otto; but her chief impulse to action is a simple love of duplicity. It is in this last motive that she most resembles such Stevenson characters as John Silver, Alan Breck Stewart, James Durie, and the entire Dantean circle of Stevenson's lesser villains, the trivial hellhounds we shall encounter in the next chapters. She says of herself, "I have broken all the ten commandments; and if there were more to-morrow I should not sleep till I had broken these." And she complains languidly that "sins are so unromantically easy" (v, 487). In contrast to Otto, who brings about evil with the best intentions in the world, Madame von Rosen does good in a spirit of mischief which almost borders on evil—a fine line throughout Stevenson's work. Sir John Crabtree, an English journalist who happens through the book, describes her in contrast to Otto as "a person frankly bad; she pleased me, in the court of Grünewald, like a piece of nature" (v, 418).

No doubt she pleased Stevenson, as well, for she is an instance of what Leslie Fiedler calls "the glittering rascal"[27] in his fiction, the lovable scoundrel; and the activist in Stevenson always rejoiced in these creations. He could never bring himself, however, *and this is the significant point,* to make such characters central either to this novel or to the succeeding romances. The fiction always concerns itself primarily with men like Otto, who, at least until the writing of *David Balfour,* is Stevenson's most striking embodiment of what he calls the "Faithful

[27] See *"The Master of Ballantrae," Victorian Literature: Modern Essays in Criticism,* ed. Austin Wright (New York, 1961), pp. 284-294.

Failure."[28] Von Rosen serves primarily as a foil for his weakness. We have already seen Otto in his rogue-and-peasant-slave mood; she gives him an opportunity to note how all occasions do inform against him. Yet even she cannot inspire him to action.

In spite of the contempt, however, Stevenson could defend Otto, when the prince was attacked, as eloquently as he might defend himself; for in many ways Otto was himself. Thus in answer to an American correspondent, he writes:

> You are not pleased with Otto; since I judge you do not like weakness; and no more do I. And yet I have more than tolerance for Otto, whose faults are the faults of weakness, but never of ignoble weakness, and who seeks before all to be both kind and just. Seeks, not succeeds. But what is man? So much of cynicism to recognize that nobody does right is the best equipment for those who do not wish to be cynics in good earnest.[29]

And this is the principal note of all Stevenson's comedies, comedies which, as David Daiches says, mask a profound pessimism.[30]

The reference a moment ago to *Hamlet* is quite proper in this discussion, for Stevenson, who quotes frequently from Shakespeare, refers more often to Hamlet than to any other character from the plays.[31] More specifically and to the point, Stevenson compares Charles of Orleans to Hamlet, and Charles, as we have seen, was one of the first models for

[28] This concept is enunciated in the essay "A Christmas Sermon" (1887). "Here lies one who meant well, tried a little, failed much:— surely that may be his epitaph, of which he need not be ashamed. . . . There goes another Faithful Failure!" (*Works*, XII, 399).

[29] Letter to Miss Monroe, May 25, 1886, *Works*, XXI, 413.

[30] "Introduction," *Robert Louis Stevenson* (Laurel Reader edition, New York, 1959), pp. 16-17.

[31] See E. P. Vandiver, Jr., "Stevenson and Shakespeare," *Shakespeare Assoc. Bulletin*, XIV (Oct. 1939), 237.

Prince Otto. Charles, according to Stevenson, was "born a great vassal, and . . . conducted himself like a private gentleman" (IV, 287). He had great things to do—a powerful country to lead and "a murdered father to avenge." "Like Hamlet, this son of a dear father murdered was sincerely grieved at heart." And like Hamlet, Charles was "a lad of inactive disposition born to set these matters right" (IV, 255-256). Like Otto, he was more adept at juggling French rhymes, and like Otto, he found helpless imprisonment "both pleasant and profitable" (IV, 263).

This interpretation of Hamlet, as over-intellectual and therefore inactive, had been conventional since Coleridge. Grillparzer used it in his portrait of Rudolf II in *Ein Bruderzwist in Habsburg*. In Bulwer's novel *Leila*, Boabdil is a kind of Hamlet, who realizes that "the wisdom of the Intellect fills us with precepts which it is the wisdom of Action to despise," a thought "too philosophical for a king whose crown sat so loosely on his brow."[32] To a man who removes himself from the field of action, however, or whom circumstances remove; such precepts are more nearly in order. This had been recognized early in *Prince Otto* when Otto's adviser told him,

> Women take to you; footmen adore you; it is as natural to like you as to pat a dog; and were you a saw-miller you would be the most popular citizen in Grünewald. As a prince—well, you are in the wrong trade. It is perhaps philosophical to recognize it as you do. (V, 397)

Philosophy, of course, specifically skeptical philosophy, has been the difficulty from the very first.

Stevenson worked on *Prince Otto* for six years; but before it was published in 1885 he had begun another book on the same theme, a book which soon developed, as he

---

[32] *Leila: or, the Siege of Granada, Bulwer's Works*, V, 630.

believed, into his "most ambitious design."[33] He was mistaken; *The Great North Road* was soon left a fragment. Enough of it was written, however, to expose its problem, which is once again the problem of *Hamlet* in the nineteenth century.

The story offers two Stevensonian failures: the Byronic-looking Archer and the old man, Jonathan Holdaway. Both are essentially unromantic men who feel that destiny has somehow robbed them. Both thirst for the active life and yet are very fearful of living it. Old Jonathan is probably intended as a parody on Archer:

> I want to live. . . . I want to live and to grow rich. I want to drive my carriage and to dice in hells and see the ring, I do. Is this a life that I lived? I want to be a rake, d'ye understand? I want to know what things are like. I don't want to die like a blind kitten, and me seventy-six. . . . The old man thrust out his jaw . . . with the grimace of an irreverent schoolboy. (XIV, 415)

And he promptly begins his life of crime by giving Archer a counterfeit half-crown. But this same problem is less comic as the hero expresses it. Speaking of himself, Archer says:

> The man I have in view hath two ways open, and no more. One to wait, like a poor mewling baby, till Fate save or ruin him; the other to take his troubles in his hand, and to perish or be saved at once. It is no point of morals; both are wrong. Either way this step-child of Providence must fall; which shall he choose, by doing, or not doing? (XIV, 421)

Holdaway's daughter, Nance, is in an ambiguous position, since both men appeal to her for advice and sympathy.

[33] See Sidney Colvin, "*Note*," *The Great North Road, Works*, XIV, 368.

She does her best to discourage her decrepit father from robbing the mails or becoming a rake, but she loves Archer and would prefer him to be something more of a conventional hero than he appears to be. "It doth sometimes go against my heart," she tells her lover, "to see you live on here like a sheep in a turnip-field! If you were braver—" (XIV, 421). But Archer can only answer this request with a philosophical disquisition into the meaning of bravery:

> But what is courage, then? The constancy to endure oneself or to see others suffer? The itch of ill-advised activity—mere shuttle-wittedness—or to be still and patient? To inquire of the significance of words is to rob ourselves of what we seem to know, and yet, of all things, certainly to stand still is the least heroic. Nance . . . Did you ever hear of *Hamlet*? . . . This while I have been talking Hamlet.

And after Archer has given Nance a summary of Shakespeare's play, she concludes unhappily that its hero must indeed have been "a very poor creature" (XIV, 422).

ANOTHER factor besides self-consciousness and skepticism which keeps Stevenson's characters from successful action is their tendency to get themselves committed to causes which appear positively evil to them. Here we move somewhat closer to the requirements of the romance. Such a commitment is found in "The Pavilion on the Links" (1879), where the two heroes, Cassilis and Northmour, and the woman both men love, are bound to defend the life of Bernard Huddlestone, a "cowardly desperado" (III, 292) who has swindled a group of Italian revolutionaries out of the money they had collected to buy arms. As Cassilis writes, "After all, I thought—and perhaps the thought was laughably vain—we were here three very noble human

beings to perish in defense of a thieving banker" (III, 322).
What makes matters worse is that the revolutionaries who
are seeking to kill Huddlestone are "all gentlemen and
soldiers," who "make honourable war," and in whose cause,
some years later, Northmour is to die. "For the credit of the
thing," Northmour says, "I wish we could change sides . . .
and leave that being on the bed [Huddlestone] to someone
else" (III, 330).

But there is at least some certainty in "The Pavilion on
the Links," however uncomfortable. The problem is simply
that the heroes are committed to fight on the wrong side.
Good-hearted virtue exists with the Italians. In *The Black
Arrow*, however, which is still more of a romance, and where
Stevenson treats the problem of commitment most seriously,
it is impossible to find justice or honor on any side: evil
seems to exist everywhere.

Stevenson never liked *The Black Arrow*. As we have seen,
he called it "tushery,"[34] a contemptuous term of his for im-
probable adventure yarns written in archaic English. "I find
few greater pleasures than reading my own works," he writes,
"but I never, O I never read *The Black Arrow*."[35] Certainly
it is a hodgepodge and a failure as a romance, but we must
not dismiss it, as one critic does, as simply "another of the
stereotyped stories of the day,"[36] for it is perhaps the
strangest and most unlikely adventure yarn ever written. It
breaks all the established rules. J. C. Furnas notes the most
serious of these violations:

> The conventions of the "boys' story" were based on
> Rights and Wrongs. To enlist the hero with the White
> Rose should have made the Red a villainous cause by

[34] Letter to Henley, May 1883, *Works*, XXI, 180.
[35] Letter to William Archer, Mar. 27, 1894, *Works*, XXIII, 365.
[36] Melvin Orth, "Robert Louis Stevenson as a Novelist" (diss. University of Colorado, 1953), p. 66.

definition, the White candid indeed. But Louis drily lighted up the futilities of medieval dynastic wars. . . . The triumph of Right, if it can be considered to occur, is chillingly incidental.[37]

There are many more dismissed conventions in this work. To create a military hero who, when he shoots an arrow at an enemy, feels "a half desire that he might miss" (XIII, 32) ; who generally loses his battles through mismanagement and irresolution; and, when he does win, feels "confounded" with his victory (XIII, 198) —to create such a protagonist is certainly not to serve a stereotype. What has happened, of course, is that Stevenson has carried his Trollopean protagonist into an utterly foreign world, a world requiring everything he is incapable of: firm and unthinking commitments, passionate beliefs, and unscrupulous behavior.

Dick Shelton begins as a conventional enough hero, anxious to be tested in war. "Prithee, Sir Daniel . . . I beseech you let me to the battle. I can strike a stroke, I promise you" (XIII, 49) . Dick's first problem, however, is that he does not know "for whom . . . [he is] to fight" (XIII, 16) . Sir Daniel, his guardian, is "one that goes to bed Lancaster and gets up York." And "every change had brought him some increase of fortune" (XIII, 18) . "I lie in Kettley," Sir Daniel says, "till I have sure tidings of the war, and then ride to join me with the conqueror. Cry not on cowardice; it is but wisdom" (XIII, 49) . Dick is embarrassed by this opportunism and must swallow it as best he can. "They cannot better die than for their natural lord" (XIII, 17) , he tells himself, but the aphorism will no longer serve when he learns that Sir Daniel, his natural lord, is also one of the murderers of his father. Here is the problem of Hamlet again, in its incidents perhaps even more complicated, for Dick has a genuine fondness for Sir Daniel and the other

[37] *Voyage to Windward*, p. 221.

murderers. "Nay, then, what a world is this," he complains, "if all that care for me be blood-guilty of my father's death? Vengeance! Alas! what a sore fate is mine, if I must be avenged upon my friends!" (XIII, 130).

Sir Daniel is indeed a villain, but his accomplices in the murder of Sir Richard Shelton are true friends to Dick, and their loyalties are as hopelessly divided as his own. Sir Oliver, the weak but pious priest, who decides to "do evil for good," swears falsely on a Bible "for the lad's sake. . . . Heaven pardon me" (XIII, 140). And Bennet Hatch, who taught the hero the use of arms, helps him to escape Sir Daniel, although he knows Dick intends revenge on him as well as on his master. Loyalties are mixed on every level of the action.

After his escape, Dick joins with Sir Daniel's enemies, the fellowship of the Black Arrow, a sort of Robin Hood gang. But the Black Arrow is quite as corrupt as the villains who oppress it. The organization was founded by Ellis Duckworth, "a ruined man longing for vengeance and money" (XIII, 201). Rather than robbing the rich to feed the poor, Duckworth, a more realistic outlaw, robs the poor to feed himself. Under threat of violence, he takes double rents from Sir Daniel's tenants, adding cynical insult to injury by giving worthless written receipts.

Ellis Duckworth and Sir Daniel are men of action, but they are both evil men as well, men who feel no need of commitment beyond a dedication to the cause of their own personal gain. They are like Will Lawless, one of Duckworth's men, whose names, both first and last, emphasize his boldness and his lack of scruples. "Tut, brother," Lawless says, "I do naught but for my pleasure. Mind not for me. I am one, by the mass, that mindeth for himself. When that I lack, I have a long tongue, and a voice like the monastery bell—I do ask, my son; and where asking faileth, I do most usually take" (XIII, 238).

But for a conscientious man like Dick, action is nightmare. In standard adventure story fashion, he commandeers a ship to rescue his typical heroine from the conventional fortress of the romantic tale. Here stereotype ends, however, for the rescue is mismanaged, and Dick's followers are slaughtered. In the retreat, to complete the nightmare, the ship is piled up on the rocks. Moreover, the poor sailor Arblaster, from whom the ship was stolen, is not conveniently forgotten as one might expect in an adventure story. When he is swept up in the Battle of Shoreby and condemned to death, Dick magnanimously uses his influence with Richard of Gloucester to free him. " 'Arblaster,' said Dick, 'I have done you ill; but now, by the rood, I think I have cleared the score.' " But it is not nearly so easy:

> "An I had my ship," said Arblaster, "I would 'a' been forth and safe on the high seas—I and my man Tom. But ye took my ship, gossip, and I'm a beggar; and for my man Tom, a knave fellow in russet shot him down. . . . Nay," said he, "let be. Y' have played the devil with me, and let that content you." (XIII, 340-341)

What is a hero to do in a world like this?

Commitment, however, remains the central problem of the book. Furnas notes that Dick chooses sides in the War of the Roses "by accident,"[38] but this phrase expresses only palely the casual way in which Dick finds his loyalty. Three times in the course of the story he is asked to declare himself for Lancaster or for York. The first time he is taken by surprise. "I shame to say it," answered Dick, "I can scarce clearly answer. But so much I think is certain: since I serve with Ellis Duckworth, I serve the house of York. Well, if that be so, I declare for York" (XIII, 224). Five chapters later he is asked again to declare himself. In the meantime nothing has happened to influence him one way or the

[38] *Ibid.*

other, but for consistency's sake, he remains a Yorkist. "My lord," he says, "it was but a little while back that I was asked that question, and knew not how to answer it . . . but having answered once, I will not vary. My lord, I am for York" (XIII, 284). Another two chapters pass, again without relevant incident or thought, and once more the question is put. Now Dick shows no hesitation. "My lord, I make no secret; I am clear for York." This time the answer is crucial, for the questioner, although Dick does not know it, is Richard of Gloucester. And Gloucester's reply—"By the mass . . . it is well for you" (XIII, 309) —makes us understand that loyalty is not such a frivolous matter with all men.

But capricious as it is, Dick finds himself capable of acting on his commitment ot the Yorkist cause. For the first time in the story he fights not only valiantly but capably, and is instrumental in obtaining Gloucester's victory at Shoreby. He gains his knighthood as a result, and again the book begins to read like a typical adventure yarn.

Once more, however, Stevenson pulls Richard and the reader up short. Flushed with victory, Dick hears his actions challenged by the daughter of one of the Lancaster leaders. "What made ye in the battle?" she asks, "Y' are of no party, y' are but a lad—but legs and body, without government of wit or counsel! Wherefore did ye fight? For the love of hurt, pardy! . . . They that have no judgment should not draw the sword. . . . Ye that fight but for a hazard, what are ye but a butcher? War is but noble by the cause, and y' have disgraced it" (XIII, 350). And it is partly because he recognizes the justice of these charges that Dick decides to resign from the active life. "I am unfit for life," he says. "I will, for penance sake and to avoid worse evil, once I have finished this adventure, get me to a cloister" (XIII, 351).

In this resignation we witness another instance of the defeat of action by skepticism. As to war being made noble by the cause, we and Dick have the advantage over Dick's questioner. We have seen that none of the causes, at least in this war, will bear inspection. But there are darker forces even than skepticism working against the hero of *The Black Arrow*, forces which convince him before the end of the romance not only that action is meaningless, "mere shuttle-wittedness," but that it is positively evil. And here again Stevenson is making use of a nineteenth century conception of Hamlet, whom a character from Bulwer's *Eugene Aram* interprets as a man "naturally full of fire and action. One dark discovery quells his spirit, unstrings his heart, and stales to him for ever the uses of the world."[39] The refusal of unclean experience, moreover, had been an important Romantic theme since Blake's *The Book of Thel*.

Dick Shelton's dark discovery concerns himself, but it is made through his observations of another man's nature. This is one of the techniques of the *Doppelgänger*, which we discussed at some length in the previous chapter. With Stevenson, it often works out in this fashion: the protagonist encounters another man whom he recognizes as his spiritual double, a man whose character seems at first antithetical to the hero's own. Actually, as the hero comes to realize, the double does not represent a nature entirely foreign to his own; rather he is the logical extreme of a single element in the hero's character, which the hero, convinced now of his duality, must either accept or reject.

We have already spoken of characters in Stevenson who would seem to represent the reverse of the protagonist's nature. Madame von Rosen is such a character; so is Will Lawless. But these, as we noted, are foils, not *Doppelgänger*. The first authentic spiritual double in Stevenson's fiction is Richard of Gloucester, who appears towards the end of *The Black Arrow*. Gloucester, although certainly not a *lovable* scoundrel, is very much like Lawless and the Countess. He

operates free of scruples and of morality, and, as with von
Rosen, his author enjoyed creating him. He seems, in fact,
to have been the only character in the romance who satisfied
Stevenson. When Marcel Schwob wrote in 1890 for permission to translate the book, Stevenson answered, "you are
hereby authorized; but I warn you, I do not like the work.
. . . I had indeed one moment of pride about my poor *Black
Arrow*: Dickon Crookback I did, and I do, think is a spirited
and possible figure."[40] Seven years earlier he had written of
Richard, "he is a fellow whose hellish energy has always
fixed my attention."[41]

The *Doppelgänger* relationship is established largely
through Gloucester's insistence upon it. Stevenson had
written in "The Philosophy of Nomenclature" that when
"two children find they have the same name . . . they have a
bond of union stronger than the exchange of nuts and
sweetmeats" (xxv, 92). A fondness for people with his own
first name turns out to be Richard of Gloucester's "chief
superstition" (xiii, 341). He calls Dick his "namesake"
(xiii, 323) and is so certain of their relationship that he believes his own success and Dick's to be mutually dependent.
Thus he says before the Battle of Shoreby:

> Either you shall gain your spurs and I begin a life of
> mighty honour and glory in the world's eye, or both of us,
> as I conceive it, shall fall dead and be unheard of. Two
> Richards are we. Well, then, Richard Shelton, they shall
> be heard about, these two! (xiii, 314)

And later he emphasizes their single identity by exclaiming,
"One Richard for another. I tell you, if I rise, ye shall rise
by the same ladder" (xiii, 317).

[40] Aug. 19, 1890, *Works*, XXII, 252-253.
[41] Letter to Colvin, Oct. 1883, *Works*, XXI, 215. Eino Railo, *The
Haunted Castle*, p. 179, notes the resemblance between Richard and Mrs.
Radcliffe's Schedoni, one of the earliest of the Gothic villains.

But while Stevenson may have been pleased by Richard of Gloucester's "hellish energy," Richard Shelton certainly was not. Very early in their acquaintance, "Dick already entertained a great terror and some hatred for the man" (XIII, 310). And Gloucester, once he has discovered the lack of such an energy in Dick, is just as quick to renounce his protégé. "Sir Richard, let me tell you plainly . . . will die Sir Richard" (XIII, 376).

It is not valour of hands, it is a man's mind of iron, that he lacks. He will not rise. . . . 'Tis a fellow that will fight indeed bravely in a mellay, but hath a capon's heart. (XIII, 368)

What ultimately unfits Richard Shelton from action, more surely even than his conviction of life's futility, is his fear that he is responsible for the success of his double. Stevenson ends the heroics of the Battle of Shoreby with this chilling note: "Thus, by Shelton's courage . . . the lad, who was afterwards to be handed down to the execration of posterity under the name of Richard III, had won his first considerable fight" (XIII, 330). And the final reason which Dick gives for his decision to "foreswear . . . the trade of arms" is "alas! I may have set York upon the throne, and that may be the worser cause, and may do hurt to England" (XIII, 351). After this thought, Dick's paralysis is almost complete. He has scarcely the courage now even to marry, and when the opportunity comes to revenge himself on the wicked Sir Daniel, he finds himself powerless to act.

Your life is forfeit—doubly forfeit, for my father's death and your own practices to meward. But I myself have done amiss; I have brought about men's deaths; and upon this glad day [Dick's wedding day] I will be neither judge nor hangman. An ye were the devil, I would not lay a hand on you. (XIII, 371-372)

Thus Hamlet in the 1880's, in the romance as in the novel. But the techniques of the romance have given Stevenson a way into the psychology of his character, a means of understanding his curious behavior. What has happened in *The Black Arrow*, as will perhaps be clearer when we have examined a few similar cases, is that Richard Shelton, terrified by the evil or wildness which he has observed in his namesake, is shocked into rejecting a part of his own nature. Moreover, the resignation from the active life which this rejection occasions in Richard must be understood as a failure in terms of Stevenson's psychology of double identity. We have already seen some of this psychology expressed—playfully, to be sure—in the essay "A Chapter on Dreams." There Stevenson described his fiction as a collaboration between himself and his "little people." This idea of successful collaboration goes far towards summing up the psychology. (Remember that Janet believed insanity was caused by the undoubling of the personality.) Similarly Stevenson believed that a man ought not to live at either extreme of his nature. The "ascetic and the creeping hog," he wrote, "although they are at different poles, have equally failed in life."[42] In "Lay Morals" he explains how psychological success is attained:

Now to me, this seems a type of that rightness which the soul demands. It demands that we shall not live alternately with our opposing tendencies in continual seesaw of passion and disgust, but seek some path on which the tendencies shall no longer oppose, but serve each other to a common end. It demands that we shall not pursue broken ends, but great and comprehensive purposes, in which soul and body may unite like notes in a harmonious chord. (XXIV, 208)

[42] "Lay Morals," *Works*, XXIV, 208.

Such an analysis of the problems of life is certainly a facile one. His essays have perhaps done Stevenson a great deal of harm, for they are largely responsible for his reputation as a shallow optimist. The solution we have just noted is similar to and quite as optimistic as Meredith's, whose Emma Dunstane recommends blithely that passions not be expelled but kept "sober, a trotter in harness."[43] The difference is that in his fiction, Stevenson, unlike Meredith, is unwilling or unable to brazen such a formula out. His characters are somehow incapable of re-uniting their divided souls and living harmoniously with both parts. Men, as Stevenson found them in life, and as he had portrayed them in his early "realistic" works, are bound to "pursue broken ends" in spite of "that rightness which the soul demands." And "great and comprehensive purposes" were not so easy for troubled Victorians to come by. As a result, Stevenson's characters do not usually end as 'whole men, but either as paralytics or as monsters, depending on which side of the disaggregated mind wins the perennial war in the members.

The protagonists, as we have begun to see, end always as paralytics, as men spiritually disqualified from the life of action. These characters come from novels belonging to the realistic tradition—from Thackeray and from Trollope —but they live in surroundings and face problems which are more appropriate to works of the romance tradition. Stevenson's most characteristic technique, after that of the *Doppelgänger*, is to place an essentially unromantic man in an inherently romantic situation. The best of the realistic novels, expecially after *Madame Bovary*, had done precisely the opposite. The great realists believed in man, but not in his possibilities, and their heroes go nobly to defeat. Stevenson always maintained at least a hunger for life, but he

[43] *Diana of the Crossways*, p. 192.

could not bring himself to create characters strong enough to live it; *his* heroes go tamely into retirement.

Even *Treasure Island,* the "elementary novel of adventure," shows some aspects of this same problem. Stevenson wrote that for the sake of "circumstantiation" and because he was himself more or less grown up, he "admitted character, within certain limits, into his design."[44] Morton Zabel reads the book as a *Bildungsroman,*[45] and so to some extent it is; Jim Hawkins must gain his maturity by rejecting Long John Silver in spite of the latter's charm and vitality. His development is like that of the narrator in Conrad's "The Secret Sharer," who must not only accept the violent man as his double, but must let him go when the proper time comes. Maturity, however, is not always presented as a good thing in Stevenson, and the rejection of Silver involves also a rejection of what is young and alive in Jim's own character. Stevenson, of course, is not about to labor such a chilling point in a work of this type, and so Jim's vitality is allowed to pass away with no protest louder than a sigh. The only voice raised against the process is Silver's own. "Ah, you that's young," he says—"you and me might have done a power of good together!" (v, 261), by which, no doubt, he means a power of bad. But Stevenson does not necessarily mean this. For in *his* fictional world there is no Agincourt to follow the banishment of plump Jack Silver; rather, as we have seen, there is only the tortuous futility of the Battle of Shoreby, and Jim Hawkins, content with his treasure, is primed for a life of quiet and inglorious retirement; oxen and wain-ropes, as he concludes, could not drag him away from it.

[44] "A Humble Remonstrance," *Works,* XII, 216.
[45] "Introduction," *Robert Louis Stevenson: The Two Major Novels* (New York, 1960), pp. xvii-xviii.

CHAPTER III

SENTIMENTAL COUNTRYMEN AND

HIGHLANDERS CIVILIZED

DAVID BALFOUR concludes the narration of his adventures[1] with a recognition of their essentially comic nature:

> For the life of man upon this world of ours is a funny business. They talk of the angels weeping; but I think they must more often be holding their sides, as they look on. (x, 427)

Stevenson believed that all art, if it aims at perfection or nobility, should be "mirthfully conceived,"[2] and except for a few of the grimmer pieces of short fiction, all of his works contain at least some touches of comedy. Even *The Master of Ballantrae*, which in its premises and its incidents gives us little enough cause to laugh, is saved from becoming

---

[1] This passage comes from *Catriona* (in American editions, *David Balfour*). Although almost seven years separate its publication and that of *Kidnapped*, I shall treat the two works as parts of a single work. There is ample justification for this procedure. *Kidnapped*, as originally planned, was to conclude with the Appin murder trial, but the trial does not take place until the middle of *Catriona*. *Catriona* is not so much a sequel as it is the second and concluding installment of a serial story. Only one of the three plots of *Kidnapped* is concluded within the first book—David has secured his inheritance. But Alan's escape is not yet accomplished. He waits in the bush for David to arrange his passage to France. Meanwhile, on the other side of Scotland, James of the Glens waits in prison for David to return and testify at his trial.

[2] "Fontainebleau," *Works*, XXIV, 455.

morbid by its two narrators, Mackellar and the Chevalier Burke, the clowns of the story, each something of a caricature of the dour or evil Durie brother whom he follows.

The two Balfour books, however, represent Stevenson the comic writer most fully; for while *Kidnapped* and *Catriona* are both serious works, embracing, as Henry James writes, "every occasion" that they meet "to satisfy the higher criticism,"[3] the comedy in them consists in more than moments of humorous characterization and comic incident. They differ also from such works of almost unalloyed comedy as the stories in *The New Arabian Nights* series. The title character of "The Young Man with the Cream Tarts" is indeed a comic creation; so is his fellow member of the Suicide Club who wishes to be murdered because he has read Darwin and cannot bear to be descended from an ape. But these are disquieting figures, like characters who appear in the modern theatre of the absurd. They are related to Mr. Malthus, the honorary member of the club, who is an old cripple and can realize the fact of his existence only by putting it constantly in jeopardy. The laughter that such characters provoke has a taste of desperation to it. This is not so in *Kidnapped* and *Catriona*, where the comedy is of a more tolerant kind; where human nature is viewed as ridiculous, to be sure, but is nevertheless accepted as, after all, quite worthwhile and perhaps even, when we stretch a point, a little noble.

Stevenson's comic view is especially important to us because the character traits it deals with are essentially the same as those we find in the more solemn works. The problem of action remains a perplexing one, and again largely because of man's dual nature. More important still,

---

[3] "Robert Louis Stevenson," *Henry James and Robert Louis Stevenson*, p. 157.

the technique of doubles with which Stevenson had experimented in *The Black Arrow* is used to much greater effect in the Balfour books, where the two central characters —David Balfour and Alan Breck Stewart—are introduced as opposites and developed into complementary halves of one another, *Doppelgänger* in the sense in which Richter, the coiner of the term, had understood it: as a pair of friends, each only a half-man, dependent upon his *alter ego* for completion.[4]

IN FEBRUARY 1885, just after he finished writing *The Black Arrow* and while still working on *The Great North Road*, Stevenson read Mark Twain's *The Adventures of Huckleberry Finn*. The next month he laid aside the highwaymen book and began writing *Kidnapped*. It is surprising that so little has been written about the influences of Twain and Stevenson on one another, for these men make a very natural comparison. They were certainly the two most colorful literary personalities of their time. In addition, both men were humorists, and each wrote successful travel books and boys' adventure stories. Twain and Stevenson, moreover, were both fascinated by doubles—twins or lookalikes. David Daiches notes that the hero of Stevenson's *The Beach of Falesá* behaves like Huck Finn in passing beyond his own prejudices, but Daiches does not follow up this insight. He treats Mark Twain's hero as an analogue to Stevenson's, certainly not as an influence.[5]

Yet the similarities between *Kidnapped* and *The Adventures of Huckleberry Finn* are far too numerous to be passed over. Here are just a few of the points which the two

[4] See Tymms, pp. 29-35.

[5] "From Scotland to Samoa: Stevenson and 'The Beach of Falesá,' " *White Man in the Tropics: Two Moral Tales* (New York, 1962), p. 127.

books have in common: Both concern newly rich orphans whose lives and fortunes are threatened by greedy men. In each case, the boy's closest living relative kidnaps and attempts to murder him. And in both books, the boy escapes from his imprisonment under circumstances which lead others to presume him dead. He next spends a few lonely days isolated on a near-shore island and then begins a long journey in the company of an older man of a different, supposedly more primitive race, a man who is a fugitive from justice and a suspected murderer. *Kidnapped,* like *Huckleberry Finn,* is the picaresque story of a boy's wanderings through the heart of his native country. Both works are part adventure story, part travel book, part social satire, and part serious psychological romance.

Stevenson wrote *Kidnapped* when he was thirty-four, yet Doris Dalglish, like many other critics, regards it as "merely the experiment of a clever boy still anxious to avoid grappling with adult problems."[6] This is a good example of "incurable romantic" and "eternal boy" talk, and it is well known how much of it Mark Twain criticism had to listen to, and for how many years. Stevenson, however, since he was a writer of romance, was not likely to be put off by the age of Mark Twain's protagonist. He wrote that *Huckleberry Finn* "contains many excellent things; above all, the whole story of a healthy boy's dealings with his conscience, incredibly well done."[7] This was significant praise, because Stevenson was himself already something of an expert on the dealings between boys and their consciences.

The most important similarity between Mark Twain's romance and Stevenson's is that both books depend for suspense and significance on the same thematic question: Can the boy transcend his conscience and bring himself fully to

[6] *Presbyterian Pirate: A Portrait of Stevenson* (London, 1937), p. 74.
[7] Letter to J. A. Symonds, Feb. 1885, *Works,* XXI, 335.

accept his despised companion? Huck, who has been brought up a white man in a slave state, finds himself helping the escape of a Negro. Similarly, David has been brought up a good and loyal Whig in the tense period following the 1745 rebellion. Alan Breck Stewart, whose escape David assists and finances, is a proscribed rebel. The problem as Stevenson states it has, of course, fewer social overtones than it has in Mark Twain's treatment, but perhaps Stevenson brings out the psychological aspects more clearly. Leslie Fiedler has written on both books. He says of *Kidnapped*:

> David must measure the Scoundrel [Alan] against himself, and more unwillingly comes to love that of which he must disapprove. Here good and evil are more subtly defined, more ambiguous [than in *Treasure Island*]: pious Presbyterian and irreverent Catholic, solid defender of the *status quo* and fantastic dreamer of the Restoration; in short, Highlander and Lowlander, Scotland divided against itself. . . . The somber good man and the glittering rascal are both two and one; they war within Stevenson's single country and in his single soul.[8]

From the first, readers have accepted the personal relationship described in *Kidnapped* as a conflict of racial types. "Almost all critics," Stevenson wrote, "recognised in David and Alan a Saxon and a Celt."[9] And though Stevenson complained of this reading, we should not be misled. Stevenson was and remained a very strong believer in racial theory, a good disciple of Herbert Spencer. In *Virginibus Puerisque*, for example, he contrasts "the Latin and the Teuton races" (II, 34). In other works he describes characteristics of the Orientals, the Hebrews, and the Polynesians, and in one of his letters compares the basic natures

---

[8] *"The Master of Ballantrae,"* p. 287.
[9] Letter to J. M. Barrie, Feb. 1892, *Works*, XXIII, 26.

of the English and the French.[10] What Stevenson objected to in the criticism of *Kidnapped* was the mistaken notion that David was a Saxon. He objected to this reading because he saw the English and the Scotch Lowlanders as entirely separate races. "Get the Anglo-Saxon heresy out of your head," he wrote to his cousin Bob; "they superimposed their language, they scarce modified the race. . . . The Scandinavians did much more to Scotland than the Angles. The Saxons didn't come."[11] He sees the Englishman as genial and wholesome, made so by "the typical English Sunday, with the huge midday dinner and the plethoric afternoon." The Lowland Scotch "Sabbath observance," however, builds an entirely different character.

About the very cradle of the Scot goes a hum of metaphysical divinity; and the whole of the two divergent systems is summed up, not merely speciously, in the first two questions of the rival catechisms, the English tritely inquiring, "What is your name?" the Scottish striking at the very roots of life with, "What is the chief end of man?" and answering nobly, if obscurely, "To glorify God and to enjoy Him for ever."[12]

The division of races, however, is even more sharply marked by the Highland line than by the River Tweed. "Galloway and Buchan, Lothian and Lochaber," Stevenson writes, "are like foreign parts."

[10] Stevenson sends the following table of comic comparisons to his friend Simoneau in the summer of 1883:

The English.	The French.
hypocrites	free from hypocrisy
good, stout reliable friends	incapable of friendship
dishonest to the root	fairly honest
fairly decent to women	rather indecent to women

Works, XXI, 197.

[11] Letter to R.A.M. Stevenson, Sept. 1894, *Works*, XXIII, 436.

[12] "The Foreigner at Home," *Works*, XII, 16-17.

A century and a half ago [about the time of *Kidnapped*
and *David Balfour*] the Highlander wore a different
costume, spoke a different language, worshipped in another church, held different morals, and obeyed a different social constitution from his fellow-countrymen either
of the south or north. Even the English, it is recorded, did
not loath the Highlander and the Highland costume
as they were loathed by the remainder of the Scots.[13]

And it is this division, a division characterized not so much
by strangeness but by animosity, that Stevenson sought
to portray in the David Balfour romances.

But Stevenson was not interested in such a conflict merely
for its picturesque or even for its social aspects, as, to some
extent, Scott certainly was. To be sure, Stevenson shared
some Scotch attitudes with Sir Walter. Like Scott he was
at once charmed and repelled by the Highlanders; impatient with, yet grudgingly in favor of their enemies. In
one of his letters Scott writes:

Seriously I am very glad I did not live in 1745 for though
as a lawyer I could not have pleaded Charles's right
and as a clergyman I could not have prayed for him yet
as a soldier I would I am sure against the convictions of
my better reason have fought for him even to the bottom
of the gallows.[14]

Stevenson, who was also exempt from military service for
reasons of poor health, was never sure enough of himself to
have made so brave a statement. But his preference is
clearly the same. In a much lower key than Scott, he writes,
" 'Tis funny to be thus of two civilisations—or, if you like,
of one civilisation and one barbarism. And, as usual, the

13 *Ibid.*, p. 21.
14 Letter to Miss Clephane, 13 July 1813, *Letters of Sir Walter Scott*,
ed. H.J.C. Grierson assisted by Davidson Cook, W. M. Parker, and others,
12 vols. (London, 1932), III, 302.

barbarism is the more engaging."[15] But here the similarity ends, for in his major Highland novels—*Waverley, Rob Roy,* and *Redgauntlet*—Scott's protagonist is an Englishman; Stevenson's, as we have seen him insist, is very definitely, almost blatantly, a Scotch Lowlander. Scott, as David Daiches writes, typically "introduces a polished and elegant representative of eighteenth-century British civilization, [and] brings him for a brief period into sympathetic contact with a representative of the older, heroic tradition."[16] Stevenson's hero, on the other hand, is neither polished nor elegant, and he is not altogether charmed by the glittering Highlander, at least not at first sight. He has been much more carefully trained to recognize and to turn aside from the devil.

The differences are even greater when we compare Stevenson with such Scott followers as William Black, Fiona Macleod, and Robert William Buchanan. These men dealt largely with the mystical side of the Gaelic temperament and with the Highlander as nature's nobleman.[17] There is no Celtic mist in Stevenson.[18] In the novels of these other Scotch writers and indeed in much of Scott himself, the Lowlander or Englishman is used primarily as a foil to heighten the Highlander's shine. In Stevenson, on the other hand, the Lowlander is quite clearly the central character. Moreover, his attitude to the savage world he views is not useful merely as a guide to the author's opinion on Scotch–English problems; David Balfour's reaction, and the forming of it, is the very theme of *Kidnapped*. Consequently, perhaps, his is quite a different reaction. Steven-

---

[15] Letter to Colvin, Nov. 1893, *Works,* XXIII, 322.

[16] "Introduction," *The Heart of Midlothian* (New York, 1963), pp. vi-vii.

[17] See Alma Emmons, "The Highlander in Scottish Prose Fiction" (diss. Cornell University, 1941).

[18] For a full discussion see David Morris, *Robert Louis Stevenson and the Scottish Highlanders* (Stirling, Scotland, 1929).

son's Lowlander, unlike those in the other tradition, does not tremble before the Highlander as though in the presence of his better. He is, as Lettice Cooper writes, "A block of integrity. One of the most self-respecting heroes of fiction. . . . He is not aggressive, but he does not allow himself to be put upon."[19] Where Scott romanticizes Rob Roy, David Balfour elaborately and mockingly compliments Rob's son "in case he was proud of having an outlaw to his father" (IX, 280). David knows his life is in danger, but he is quite calm in his self-righteousness when he tells the warlike card-player, the clan chief Cluny Macpherson, that "gambling is a very poor employ for gentlefolk" (IX, 259). And when Alan Breck, angry, his sword practically drawn, trumpets the boast that he is a Stewart, David answers, "I ken ye bear a king's name. But you are to remember, since I have been in the Highlands, I have seen a good many of those that bear it; and the best I can say of them is this, that they would be none the worse of washing" (IX, 272). He is clearly not to be either intimidated or seduced.

The differences exist largely because Stevenson's purpose in using his Highlander and Lowlander was different from the purposes of Scott and his followers. Stevenson was not writing local color, as, at their worst, Scott and the others were doing. And he was not writing sentimental realism or social commentary, as they were doing at their best. He was writing psychological romance. Scott's Englishman is urged to give up his infatuation with the Highlands for the sake of the Empire. As Daiches writes, Scott's hero "retires at the end to the 'refined' modern society from which he came, enchanted with his adventure, yet sobered by it into a realization that Highland chiefs are after all little better than freebooters and that the tradition they represent has no place in the modern world."[20] In the 1880's, Stevenson was

19 *Robert Louis Stevenson* (Denver, 1948), p. 58.
20 "Introduction," *The Heart of Midlothian*, p. vii.

no longer concerned for the unity of Great Britain. His hero is asked to accept the Highlander not for the health of his country, but for the good of his psyche.

Daiches has written elsewhere that "the two poles of modern Scottish sentiment are the Covenanting tradition and the Jacobite tradition."[21] David and Alan represent these extremes, which are poles of the mind as much as they are poles of nationality. These two characters together, moreover, form the classic embodiment of Stevenson's theory of duality.

David Balfour, the Lowlander, is characterized by conscience and scrupulosity, so much so as to make him absolutely incapable of action. By himself he cannot win his rightful inheritance, he cannot appear to give testimony in a murder trial, and he cannot bring himself to woo the girl he loves. All the problems we have seen in the last chapter belong also to David, only much more so. Like Richard Shelton, David seeks desperately for some commitment to spur him to action. "I had no thought but to be done with the next stage," he writes, "and have myself fully committed; to a person circumstanced as I was, the appearance of closing a door on hesitation and temptation was itself extremely tempting" (x, 50). And like Prince Otto he abandons political life because he sees it as sordid, and because he regards his own actions in it as futile.

I had had my view of that detestable business they call politics—I had seen it from behind, when it is all bones and blackness; and I was cured for life of any temptations to take part in it again. A plain, quiet, private path was that which I was ambitious to walk in, when I might keep my head out of the way of dangers and my conscience out of the road of temptation. For, upon a retrospect, it appeared I had not done so grandly, after all; but

21 *Robert Louis Stevenson* (Norfolk, Conn., 1947), p. 52.

with the greatest possible amount of big speech and preparation, had accomplished nothing. (x, 279)

There is still another important way in which David resembles Prince Otto. In *Catriona* he is kidnapped and confined on the Bass Rock near Edinburgh to prevent his giving testimony in the Appin murder trial, testimony which he is afraid but determined to give. In this situation, David, like Otto, positively welcomes his imprisonment.

I should trifle with my conscience if I pretended my stay upon the Bass was wholly disagreeable. It seemed to me a safe place, as though I was escaped there out of my troubles. No harm was to be offered me; a material impossibility, rock and the deep sea, prevented me from fresh attempts [to testify]; I felt I had my life safe and my honour safe, and there were times when I allowed myself to gloat on them like stolen waters. (x, 185)

For the sake of his conscience, David tries to secure an escape by bribery, but his attempts are so feeble and half-hearted that they fail, and when he is finally released, his friendly jailor tells him, "Ye see, I was never entirely sure . . . which way of it ye really wantit" (x, 213). Neither, in fact, was David.

The source for this set of incidents is *Les Misérables,* where Jean Valjean, on his way to the trial at Arras in which he must denounce himself to save an innocent man, is overjoyed to discover that the damaged wheel on his Tilbury cannot be repaired in time and that no other vehicle seems available. "He had nothing to reproach himself with. If he did not go further, it did not concern him; it was not his fault, it was not the doing of his conscience, but of Providence."[22] The difference is that Valjean persists

22 *The Novels of Victor Hugo,* trans. Laccelles Wraxall, 5 vols. (New York: P. F. Collier), II, 116.

in his determination and ultimately procures a rattletrap which enables him to continue his hard journey. And, of course, Valjean's appearance at the trial dramatically decides the outcome, while David, as we have seen, accomplishes nothing.

But David Balfour's inaction is not the result of cowardice. He is not, like Scott's passive heroes, afflicted with weak nerves.[23] Far from it; as everyone recognizes, he is the bravest character in the two books. Catriona calls him a hero (x, 102); and the opposing factors in the Appin murder trial, Charles Stewart and Prestongrange, though they are always uncertain of David's motives, never doubt his courage. Even Alan Breck Stewart, who is the model for reckless bravery in the work, realizes that his own courage is a poor thing in comparison with David's. "What makes the differ with me," Alan tells David, "is just my great penetration and knowledge of affairs. But for auld, cauld, dour, deidly courage, I am not fit to hold a candle to yourself" (x, 169).

David's inaction is the product of his integrity and his conscientiousness; and it is a Lowland trait. Yet as we progress through the romances we shall find Lowlanders who are the last thing from ineffectual, who are, indeed, the strongest actors in all of Stevenson's fiction. Captain Smollett of *Treasure Island* is a Lowlander; so are the fierce Covenanters of the fragment *Heathercat*. Some of the Lowlanders are even villains. What distinguishes such characters from the Highlander and what relates them to the almost paralytic David Balfour, however, is that they are all committed to some ideal of personal duty. Thus, though the Lowlander's villainy can never be very grand, he need not be at all honest, for he may be committed to no more noble an ideal than that of respectability or, as in the case of David's

23 See Alexander Welsh, *The Hero of the Waverley Novels* (New Haven, 1963), pp. 159-166.

Uncle Ebenezer, of parsimony. The apothecary of the poem
Robin and Ben is an excellent example of the conscientious
Lowland thief. Note that he needs a "theory of theft," an
italicized creed, to back up his dubious morality.

> The smiling chemist tapped his brow.
> 'Rob,' he replied, 'this throbbing brain
> Still worked and hankered after gain.
> By day and night, to work my will,
> It pounded like a powder mill;
> And marking how the world went round
> A theory of theft it found.
> Here is the key to right and wrong:
> *Steal little, but steal all day long*;
> And this invaluable plan
> Marks what is called the Honest Man.'[24]

The Lowlander is always conscientious, especially in his
vices. Captain Hoseason takes money to kidnap David
Balfour; yet he is a "true-blue Protestant" and his ship is
named *The Covenant*. He will make any kind of evil agree-
ment, but he can be absolutely trusted to deal justly within
the terms of it (x, 37). Ebenezer Balfour is too stingy to draw
a separate cup of beer for his nephew, but he pours him
an "accurate half" from his own cup. As David writes,
"There was a kind of nobleness in this that took my breath
away; if my uncle was certainly a miser, he was one of that
thorough breed that goes near to make the vice respectable"
(IX, 36).

David Balfour is related to these strong actors and petty
thieves in that he is their logical extension. They are all
men of principle, members of the bourgeoisie, products of
civilization, although not entirely civilized. Each has settled
on a principle which, while it may not bear very careful

<hr>

[24] *Robert Louis Stevenson: Collected Poems*, ed. Janet Adam Smith
(London, 1950), p. 441.

scrutiny, serves at least to give his life direction, and, far from rendering him inactive, it permits him to perform the bloodiest deeds in an odor of piety. "A dog," Stevenson writes in *Travels with a Donkey*, is "an animal I fear more than any wolf. A dog is vastly braver, and is besides supported by the sense of duty. . . . He represents the sedentary and respectable world in its most hostile form. There is something of the clergyman or the lawyer about this engaging animal" (I, 339-340). But David Balfour is too conscientious to settle for any commitment which will not stand even the last philosophical test. An appeal to his patriotism, for example, fails utterly to bind him. David is, as he says, a very good Whig; is fully convinced that his testimony at the Appin murder trial, which cannot alter the verdict, will seriously harm his country and his king and even the Protestant religion in Scotland. Nevertheless it remains that the accused James of the Glens is innocent, and David must speak for him. His sweetheart Catriona calls David "too nice" (X, 101), and Henry James pronounces him "a good boy but an exasperating."[25]

We have already seen that Stevenson equated the bourgeois with the skeptic and the skeptic with the coward. In *"Aes Triplex"* he had written that "to be over-wise is to ossify; and the scruple-monger ends by standing stockstill" (II, 128). Well, David Balfour is the ultimate bourgeois, the perfectly civilized man. Moreover, Stevenson must have seen David's retirement from active life as quite consistent with the principles of that first, though indirect, creator of Lowland Scotch civilization and of the Covenanting tradition—John Calvin himself. For he writes that Calvin represents

> that passive obedience, that toleration of injustice and absurdity, that holding back of the hand from political

[25] "Robert Louis Stevenson," p. 141.

affairs as from something unclean, which lost France, if we are to believe M. Michelet, for the Reformation; a spirit necessarily fatal in the long run to the existence of any sect that may profess it; a suicidal doctrine that survives among us to this day in narrow views of personal duty, and the low political morality of many virtuous men.[26]

The other tradition, the Jacobite, as it is embodied by the Highlander Alan Breck Stewart, is not nearly so delicate. Alan's most obvious difference from David is established immediately after their first joint action, the battle in the roundhouse of the brig *Covenant*. David, like Richard Shelton, is confounded by his victory—"the thought of the two men I had shot sat upon me like a nightmare" (IX, 112). Meanwhile, Alan, without conscience,

> turned to the four enemies, passed his sword clean through each of them, tumbled them out of doors one after the other. As he did so, he kept humming and singing and whistling to himself, like a man trying to recall an air; only what *he* was trying was to make one. All the while, the flush was in his face, and his eyes were as bright as a five-year-old child's with a new toy. (IX, 110-111)

The two heroes contrast with one another in almost every respect. Where David is precociously mature and responsible, Alan, a man in his middle thirties, is childish and undependable. Where David is self-deprecatory, Alan is incredibly vain and boastful. He brushes his coat "with such care and labour as I supposed to have been only usual with women" (IX, 115). He "had a great taste for courage in other men, yet he admired it most in Alan Breck" (IX, 133).

Alan seems at times to espouse a moral system for which "he was ready to give his life," but Stevenson was a poor

26 "John Knox and His Relations to Women," *Works*, IV, 345.

relativist and like David saw primitive morality as "all tail-first" (IX, 194) —really no morality at all, but a formalized expression of savage instincts. Alan hates all Campbells because his clan and the Campbells are feuding. This hatred is the first article of his faith. Beyond this, he has a thirst for vengeance which he believes Christianity encourages, and if he believed otherwise, he says, he "would be nae Christian" (IX, 130). Alan fights bravely, but, like so many of Stevenson's Highlanders and kindred figures, he cannot be trusted in his loyalty. In the '45 he is "beaten on both sides" (IX, 271). Later he serves the King of France. His morals are essentially those of the barbarian; he does not reflect on them; and he can defend them only with a blow of his fist on the top of a table, or of his sword on the head of a man. He certainly does not let them bother him when he wishes to act.

The Highlander is so different from the Lowlander as to make him what Stevenson calls a foreigner at home, and yet Scotland, for reasons which Stevenson cannot fully understand, is one nation and not two.

> Is it common education, common morals, a common language or a common faith, that join men into nations? There were practically none of these in the case we are considering. The fact remains: in spite of the differences of blood and language, the Lowlander feels himself the sentimental countryman of the Highlander.[27]

In the same way, and for as little good reason, David Balfour and Alan Breck Stewart are sentimental countrymen of one another, so much so that the two men nearly merge into a single identity.

Nevertheless, as with Richard Shelton and Richard of Gloucester in the latter part of *The Black Arrow,* neither

27 "The Foreigner at Home," *Works,* XII, 22.

David nor Alan is very anxious to acknowledge the bond between them. "Your ways are not mine," David says, "and they're not God's: and the short and the long of it is just that we must twine" (IX, 191). Alan has "often observed," as he says, "that you Low-country bodies have no clear idea of what's right and wrong" (IX, 196). Their ethics, Alma Emmons points out, are "irreconcilable."[28] Moreover, on a much more practical level, David is convinced that Alan's companionship during the escape is both a burden and a danger to him. This is especially evident after Alan has irresponsibly gambled away all of their money and begins borrowing from the supply which David was humiliatingly driven to beg back. But even before these incidents, David thinks to himself, "O, man, if you would only take one point of the compass and let me take any other, it would be the best for both of us" (IX, 237). We are not permitted into Alan's point-of-view, but surely he must be able to imagine an easier escape than one shared with a green Lowlander who divides his time between moralizing from a tender conscience and fainting from tender feet.

Nevertheless, they remain together, largely, we are led to believe, because each is convinced that his companion needs him. But they never understand either one another or the reasons behind their friendship; and the celebrated quarrel scene in *Kidnapped* shows not only the strength of the bond between them, but also the tremendous distance which that bond must gap. The closest they ever come to a reconciliation is when David admits, "We're neither one of us to mend the other—that's the truth! We must just bear and forbear, man Alan" (IX, 275).

The belief of David and Alan in their mutual dependence is much more than a humorous plot element; it is a literal fact, for one thing, and it is, moreover, a principal theme of the two works in which these characters appear. Alan, the

[28] Page 106.

"Homeric Highlander," as Henry James calls him,[29] would starve in the civilized world of money and bargains were it not for David's shrewdness. He counts on his friend for the less romantic necessities of their adventure, for their food, for instance; and it is David who must finance and arrange Alan's escape to France. Nor is this dependence caused by circumstances alone; at Cluny Macpherson's card table Alan shows himself constitutionally incapable of keeping his money. At the end of their adventures, David saves his friend again by discovering James More Macgregor's scheme to sell Alan to the English.

On the other side, David needs Alan to act for him. We have already seen that David will not succeed in the great world of politics, but even the "plain, quiet, private path" he is "ambitious to walk in" cannot be won without a certain amount of action. David's goals in both *Kidnapped* and *Catriona* are modest enough and, it would seem, very easily attainable. In *Kidnapped* he sets out to gain his inheritance. In *Catriona* his aim is to win the heroine. The inheritance is his by solid, legal right. Catriona seems an even easier prize. Since she is the pauper daughter of a double traitor, David is her only suitor; and her rascal father, once he discovers that the young man will be wealthy, is much more than anxious to assist his plans. Moreover, Catriona has obviously been in love with David since their first meeting. Circumstances may be said to favor the match. But by his own efforts David is incapable of winning either the inheritance or the girl. At the end of each book, Alan must be called in to cut through the Gordian Knot of David's scrupulosity and ratiocination. Both times, the ease with which Alan succeeds is dramatically anticlimactic, but anticlimax is, after all, the essence of cutting Gordian Knots; Alan's ease shows how little action was required of

[29] "Robert Louis Stevenson," p. 159.

David, and how incapable David has been of performing even that.

Once, in an attempt to build up David in Catriona's eyes, Alan describes himself as "a kind of henchman to Davie here; I'm like a tyke at his heels" (x, 399). Of course, Alan's pride would never permit him to believe such a description, but it is apt, nevertheless. Theirs is a relationship between two half-creatures—one perfectly moral, but civilized out of the possibility of action; the other so uncivilized, so savage, that his powerful actions are immoral, wasteful, and directionless. Daiches writes that Alan illustrates "the pathetic if not tragic waste and frustration involved when gesture takes the place of moral purpose."[30]

But *Kidnapped* and *Catriona* are not tragic works. The angels, as we have been told, are not weeping; they are holding their sides. What makes the romances comic is simply that the two heroes do not utterly reject their attraction for one another. They bear and forbear, and they are mutually beneficial. Without Alan, David would be a mind without a body. And if Alan is no worse than a "tyke," then it is largely because of David's training and direction. Without David, Alan would be a wolf, torn to pieces by fierce, half-civilized Lowland dogs. The two together make a tolerable man; separate, however, they come to very little —Alan in his silly uniform and David on his plain, quiet path.

CATRIONA is the female counterpart of Alan, and during those portions of the story when Alan is out of the action, she performs as his substitute in the relationship. She too is a Highlander, and she operates on the same principles, or rather instincts, which actuate Alan. Stevenson always felt constrained when writing about women, especially passion-

[30] *Robert Louis Stevenson*, p. 62.

ate women, because he feared "grossness,"[31] but in all matters, almost including sex, Catriona is subject to very powerful emotions.

At the beginning her story, Catriona's clan loyalty and her loyalty to her father are very high. She is ambitious even to die for her king (x, 131), and she effects her father's escape from prison by taking his place in the jail cell, an act of reckless Highland heroism. Later, however, when she sees how far her father has disgraced himself, she rejects him entirely, with a violence, hatred, and scorn which surprises poor David, whose emotions are always "under more control" (x, 131). Up to a point in the romance she will not suffer a word in her father's dispraise; following that point, she will not hear anything in his favor.

Alan's financial and moral dependence on David, which we traced in *Kidnapped*, is repeated and expanded in the second work when David must care for Catriona. Indeed, he lends her sixpence at their very first meeting. Later because she is too proud to tell her Scottish benefactors about her father's poverty, she arrives in Holland with no money; and when the irresponsible James More Macgregor fails even to meet her at the dock, David must undertake her physical support and the care of her reputation. In David's view, Catriona's honor is in at least as great danger as her life. During the time in Leyden when they share the same quarters, virtuously, as brother and sister, he operates under the assumption that if he does not behave towards her with studied coldness, they will immediately fall into one another's beds. "The conscience," as Stevenson writes in the "Epilogue" to *An Inland Voyage*, "is no gentleman, he is

[31] Letter to Colvin, May 1892, *Works*, XXIII, 73. "With all my romance," he writes, "I am a realist and a prosaist, and a most fanatical lover of plain physical sensations plainly and expressly rendered; hence my perils. To do love in the same spirit as I did (for instance) D. Balfour's fatigue in the heather; my dear sir, there were grossness—ready made!"

a rabbinical fellow" (I, 162). When David oversteps the bounds one night, admitting his love for Catriona, he is in torment. "The milk was spilt now," he writes, "the word was out and the truth told. I had crept like an untrusty man into the poor maid's affections; she was in my hand like any frail, innocent thing to make or mar" (x, 343). To be sure, David distrusts himself as well as Catriona in this tight situation, but it never seems to enter his mind that she might resist the sexual advances he fears he will make. As in his relationship with Alan, David conceives of himself as the only responsible and moral agent.

Many of the incidents of *Kidnapped* repeat themselves in more extended and more highly comic forms in *Catriona*. Thus David and Alan's flight through the heather is repeated in David and Catriona's penniless trudge from Rotterdam to Leyden. And the quarrel in *Kidnapped* is played over again in the cold war which David and his "sister" wage through several chapters of *Catriona*. There is very little occasion for Catriona to play Alan's part in acting for David, but the one time such an opportunity occurs, she embraces it readily. When James More Macgregor descends upon the couple in Leyden, at first sponging off David and later threatening to blackmail him for living with his daughter, the Lowlander paralysis manifests itself once more. Again it is not the lack of courage that causes David's inaction; although he knows himself to be perfectly innocent, he is simply not certain that the scoundrel does not have some claim to his blackmail. After all, the world might misunderstand. But Catriona will not sit idly by while David is done out of his rights, and once again, the Lowlander waits ingloriously in the street, as he waited in the darkness at the end of *Kidnapped*, while the Highlander beards her father and sends him on his unscrupulous way.

This substitution of doubles, from Alan to Catriona, makes possible the conventional marriage conclusion of

comedy. Leslie Fiedler has written that the relationship between David and Alan is "almost a full-fledged love affair,
a presexual romance."[32] If this is so, then, as David grows
older, the substitution was certainly called for. As brother
and sister, David and Catriona "made a most uneven pair"
(x, 327). They will continue uneven as man and wife, for
they have antithetical personalities. The marriage is a hopeful one, however; for their natures, again like David's and
Alan's, are also complementary. And perhaps better yet,
for the author's purposes, David and Catriona will begin a
Balfour line which a hundred years later will produce the
mixed and therefore interesting soul of Robert Lewis Balfour Stevenson.[33] The final sentence in the first draft of
Catriona, scratched out but still legible in the manuscript at
the Widener Library, makes this point strongly. There
David, addressing the story to his two children, ends with
this sentiment: "If your father was something of a simpleton, and your grandfather not better than a rogue no harm
that you should know it."

STEVENSON employed the device of a substitution of
doubles in one other work, *The Wrecker*,[34] which in many

---

[32] Page 287.

[33] Stevenson, who was descended from Lowland stock on both his
father's and his mother's side, was always anxious to provide himself
with a romantically mixed ancestry. For some time he tried to prove
that the name Stevenson was an alias taken by the proscribed of the
clan Macgregor. Failing in fact, he seems to have turned to fiction. His
mother's name was Balfour. And in a letter to Alison Cunningham,
July 1886 (*Works*, XXI, 418), he jokingly claims David Balfour as "no
doubt some kind of relative of mine."

[34] Stevenson wrote *The Wrecker*, like *The Ebb-Tide*, in collaboration
with his step-son, Lloyd Osbourne. As opposed to their other collaboration, *The Wrong Box*, these two works can be regarded as almost
entirely Stevenson's own. Both writers say as much. Osbourne admits
that in the writing of *The Wrecker*, Stevenson was the "man of
genius. I managed the petty makeshifts and inventions which were con-

respects is the book most like *Kidnapped* and *Catriona*. It was written from 1889-1891, just midway between the two Balfour romances, and through the great majority of its pages it describes a relationship very similar to the friendship of David and Alan.

The complementary half-men in *The Wrecker* are Loudon Dodd and Jim Pinkerton. Temperamentally Pinkerton is the Highlander and Dodd the Lowlander, although both of them are Americans, Scotch only in their ancestry. Dodd's Edinburgh relatives are respectable builders of solid and unimaginative houses. Jim Pinkerton, on the other hand, is an orphan, who spent his boyhood kicking around America as the assistant to a not very savory traveling photographer. The two men meet as art students in Paris and begin a lifelong friendship of mutual dependence, a dependence which, as we might expect, is always somewhat galling to the self-righteous Lowlander, Loudon Dodd.

Pinkerton, like Alan Breck Stewart, is amazingly vain. One of the "vainest men of my acquaintance," Dodd calls him (xvii, 264). Also like Alan, he is blatantly patriotic, furiously American in the most romantic and vulgar ways. He believes that the "whole duty of the born American" is "to be pure-minded, to be patriotic, to get culture and money with both hands and with the same irrational fervour"

---

stantly necessary; I was the practical man, so to speak, the one who paced the distances, and used the weights and measures." (Quoted in Graham Balfour, *The Life of Robert Louis Stevenson*, 2 vols. [New York, 1906], II, 41-42.) Stevenson gives Osbourne more credit than this, but he concludes that their manner of collaboration was such that one person was entirely responsible and gave "the *coup de pouce* to every part of the work" (Letter to R.A.M. Stevenson, Sept. 1894, *Works*, XXIII, 437.) I have treated *The Wrecker* and *The Ebb-Tide* as works of Stevenson, without reference to the influence of his collaborator, which is anyway, except in the passage quoted on pp. 108-109, almost impossible to perceive. *The Wrong Box*, on the other hand, is so clearly Osbourne's novel that I have thought it best to leave it entirely out of the analyses.

(XVII, 80). He has chucked his business to study art in Paris because be believes America needs "more culture and more art" (XVII, 81).

As we have seen with Alan Breck Stewart, who composed music to commemorate his acts of bloodshed, the Highlander or savage personality is closely related to the artistic temperament. For Stevenson, who got the best part of his early artistic education in French Bohemian circles, and some of his racial education from Matthew Arnold, such an association was natural. It occurs as early in his writing as *An Inland Voyage* where the artist is presented as the direct antithesis of the calf-like "fat burgess" (I, 152).

In the fiction, the outstanding example of the outlaw-artist is the down-at-the-heels painter of "The Story of a Lie." Van Tromp, who styles himself the Admiral and pretends to his daughter that he possesses remarkable talent, actually lives a parasitic and a shifting existence in the artist quarter of Paris. He has not painted for some years. It is easy to recognize this windy derelict as a first draft attempt at Rob Roy's son, James More Macgregor, whom we have just met in *Catriona*. Once Van Tromp's fraud is discovered, moreover, his daughter will reject him as irrevocably and as vehemently as Catriona rejected her scoundrel father. Nevertheless, the Admiral comes off pretty well in "The Story of a Lie," rather like Meredith's Richmond Roy. Everyone feels it is too bad Van Tromp tells falsehoods and lives dishonestly, but after all he is an artist, and, as Doctor Desprez of "The Treasure of Franchard" reasons, "a man of imagination is never moral; he outsoars literal demarcations and reviews life under too many shifting lights to rest content with the invidious distinctions of the law!" (XI, 308).

But Jim Pinkerton of *The Wrecker* is not an outlaw or a Highlander by virtue of his brief career as an art student. What marks the wildness in him are his encounters in the

business world after his return to America. The art idea
was anyway just another venture, which Jim can calmly
shrug off as a bad investment when Dodd, with conscientious
honesty, assures him that he has no talent. But his more
conventional business activities are quite another matter.
Lettice Cooper analyzes him as "a man to whom money-
making is all that art was not to Loudon Dodd—a passion,
a preoccupation, a binding claim. Pinkerton in his own line
is the real artist, the game matters to him more than the
rewards, he lives and sleeps speculation."[35] Jim's San
Francisco business office handles all kinds of enterprises—
from bad brandy and worse art to shipwrecks, from real
estate to picnics. He does not mean to be immoral in his
business dealings, but, as with Alan, the moral sense is
simply absent in him. He swindles people and smuggles
opium with the very best will in the world. Business is
high adventure to him.

> Reality was his romance; he gloried to be thus engaged;
> he wallowed in his business. Suppose a man to dig up a
> galleon on the Coromandel coast, his rakish schooner
> keeping the while an offing under easy sail, and he, by
> the blaze of a great fire of wreckwood, to measure ingots
> by the bucketful on the uproarious beach: such an one
> might realise a greater material spoil; he should have no
> more profit of romance than Pinkerton when he cast up
> his weekly balance-sheet in a bald office. (XVII, 155-156)

Loudon Dodd is not nearly so engaging a Lowlander as
David Balfour, but he has most of the markings of the
breed. His "two chief qualities of . . . character" are, as he
admits, "helplessness and . . . instinctive love of procrasti-
nation" (XVII, 432) . Stevenson describes him as "a fizzle and
and a stick, he knew it, he knew nothing else, and there is

---

[35] *Robert Louis Stevenson*, pp. 84-85.

an undercurrent of bitterness in him."[36] Dodd is a failure as a sculptor, a speculator, a smuggler, and a blackmailer. He is the perfectly dull man, and, as one might expect of a self-conscious Stevenson hero, he has constructed a theory of dullness:

> The dull man is made, not by the nature, but by the degree of his immersion in a single business. And all the more if that be sedentary, uneventful, and ingloriously safe. More than one-half of him will then remain un-exercised and undeveloped; the rest will be distended and deformed by over-nutrition, over-cerebration, and the heat of rooms. (XVII, 338-339)

This analysis expresses the usual duality, but it does not in the least explain Dodd's own case. He is dull because he never immerses himself in any business. The businesses with which he toys are the most romantic imaginable. Yet he manages somehow to make them "sedentary, uneventful, and ingloriously safe." If Jim Pinkerton illustrates the romance of reality; then Loudon Dodd illustrates the grinding realism possible even in high romance.

Dodd is perhaps the extreme example in Stevenson of the essentially unromantic man placed in the inherently romantic situation. But life is far too much for him, even in its simplest demands. Like many of Stevenson's Lowlanders, he handles money responsibly, but he is incapable of making any. Eventually, like David with Alan, Dodd must support Pinkerton, but he does it on inherited, not earned money. During most of the story, however, it is Jim who must keep Loudon afloat, both financially and spiritually.

Loudon's principal contribution to the partnership that exists between the two friends is a moral one. He is the Shorter Catechist of the pair, a sort of spiritual wet blanket to Jim's amoral exuberance. When Loudon objects to one

[36] Letter to W. H. Low, Jan. 15, 1894, *Works*, XXIII, 356.

of Jim's business schemes by asking coldly, "do you think it's honest?" Jim gives in at once. "Almost at a word, my point was carried. But the trouble was that such differences continued to recur, until we began to regard each other with alarm" (xvii, 165). So far does Dodd succeed in becoming Pinkerton's conscience that after the bankruptcy of the firm, which was primarily Dodd's fault, Pinkerton writes:

I am haunted by the thought that you may blame me; I know how I despised your remonstrances. O, Loudon, don't be hard on your miserable partner. . . . I fear your stern rectitude of mind like the eye of God. (xvii, 363)

But "stern rectitude of mind" is a typical Pinkertonian overstatement. The best that can be said about poor Dodd is that he has a squeamish conscience. He enjoys a relationship with his friend very much like David Balfour's relationship with Alan Breck, but he is not the pure type that David is. David is so thoroughgoing a Lowlander that his moral scruples raise him above meanness. He becomes almost a disembodied conscience. He never dirties himself. Dodd, on the other hand, has just enough conscience to make him ashamed of Jim, but never enough to allow him to stop taking Jim's money. In Paris, he is not sufficiently Bohemian to approve of the amoral lives which French artists lead, but he borrows money from his house-porter with no expectation of being able to repay. In San Francisco he moralizes at tedious length that "smuggling is one of the meanest of crimes, for by that we rob a whole country *pro rata*, and are therefore certain to impoverish the poor: to smuggle opium is an offence particularly dark, since it stands related not so much to murder, as to massacre" (xvii, 257). But, when put to it, he sets out to become an opium smuggler, nevertheless.

These disparities between Dodd's scruples and his actions

come about because Dodd is not quite a legitimate half-man. There is a little bit of the Highlander in him, although it is "unexercised and undeveloped," as he would say. His father was an American speculator called Big Head Dodd, whose career in the story parallels Pinkerton's to a large extent. Like Pinkerton, Big Head Dodd supports Loudon's art studies in Paris as a business venture. He is, moreover, the same kind of wild gambler Pinkerton is, and both men collapse physically when their fortunes tumble. Loudon is as anxious to deny his father's blood as he is to deny Pinkerton's influence (xvii, 103). Nevertheless, a savage, imaginative side exists in him whether he likes it or not, and Pinkerton is being more accurate than he knows when he bills his friend to lecture in San Francisco as "Americo-Parisienne" and calls his description "rather a good phrase; gives the two sides at a glance" (xvii, 149).

Big Head Dodd and Jim Pinkerton spend much of their lives trying to bring out the undeveloped half of Loudon Dodd, trying to drag him into life, so to speak, to uncivilize him. Big Head Dodd dies before he can accomplish much, but Pinkerton almost succeeds. Loudon notes with horror the change Pinkerton is bringing about in his character —"I saw the stream widen that divided me from all I loved" (xvii, 161) —but in Stevenson's terms such an alteration is certainly for the better. Pinkerton forces the dilettante sculptor to become an art dealer, which is one step up, and he converts the stuffed-shirt aesthete into the most popular man in San Francisco, the master of ceremonies of Pinkerton's Dromedary Picnics. Eventually Pinkerton even instills in Dodd something of his own love for speculation. Together they strain the firm's credit to buy a wreck which they hope contains opium. Dodd is put in charge of the salvaging operation and, for a few pages at least, he behaves as a pure Highlander. When he imagines that a rival crew is racing him to the wreck, he positively looks forward to a fight:

> "Let them get there first!" I thought. "Let them! We can't be long behind." And from that moment, I date myself a man of a rounded experience: nothing had lacked but this, that I should entertain and welcome the grim thought of bloodshed. (xvii, 277)

Perhaps Dodd could have proved himself if it had come to murder, but what he finds at the wreck is less colorful— only a great deal of hard work and a very small quantity of opium, not nearly enough to restore Jim's credit. Dodd had been ready to perform glittering wickedness, to cut throats, but life does not offer him so romantic a way of doing evil. Pinkerton has become bankrupt, and now he begs Dodd to defraud the creditors by claiming that he found no opium at all aboard the wreck. Dodd is convinced that his friend's life is dependent upon his ability to perform this piece of sordid immorality, but he stands helpless while the Lowlander paralysis asserts itself again. He castigates himself bitterly. "Alas," he writes, "I had but the one feeling: that I had sacrificed my sick friend to the fear of prison-cells and stupid starers. And no moralist has yet advanced so far as to number cowardice amongst the things that are their own reward" (xvii, 373) . Here is the rogue-and-peasant-slave sentiment again, and again it does not lead to any action.

S T E V E N S O N saw the portion of *The Wrecker* that we have been discussing as "a novel of manners," intended to show "the tone of the age, its movement, the mingling of races and classes in the dollar hunt, the fiery and not quite un-romantic struggle for existence with its changing trades and scenery." This was the "woof" of the story, but there was also to be a "warp" (XVII, 598), "a violent, dark yarn with interesting, plain turns of human nature."[37] This more sinister part becomes the overt plot of the total work only in the last four chapters, but it has been running beneath the surface for many pages before. Stevenson calls it "a good yarn—but pretty horrible."[38] Elsewhere he writes with some justice that it contains "one of the most genuine butcheries in literature."[39]

The two parts of *The Wrecker* are as different in genre as it is possible for stories to be: one is a novel of manners, the other an adventure tale. They are acted out, moreover, by entirely separate sets of characters. Nevertheless, both the themes and the characters are related to one another. Stevenson writes that *The Wrecker* aims at the "sense of energy and violence in the men."[40] The energy is displayed largely in the novel of manners; the violence in the adventure story. We have already seen how closely energy and violence are tied up in several of Stevenson's works.

The characters of the adventure yarn correspond to the heroes of the novel of manners. The principals of the former are Tommy Haddon and Norris Carthew, who set up a sea-going partnership much like Pinkerton and Dodd. Haddon is "a kind of Pinkerton in play," Dodd writes. "I have called Jim's the romance of business; this was its Arabian tale" (XVII, 493). Carthew and Dodd have had almost identical careers. Both of them went to college, putting off artistic ambitions in order to please their fathers. Carthew speaks for both of them when he says: "It didn't really matter, don't you know? . . . And it seemed an awful shame

---

37 Letter to Colvin, Dec. 25, 1891, *Works*, XXII, 455.
38 Letter to Colvin, Feb. 1, 1892, *Works*, XXIII, 22.
39 Letter to Henry James, Oct. 1891, *Henry James and Robert Louis Stevenson*, p. 206.
40 *Ibid.*, p. 207.

to vex the old boy" (xvii, 475). Like Dodd in Paris, Carthew has been reduced to beggary—a shilling a day advance on his remittance—and he is rescued by Tommy Haddon in nearly the same way Loudon was rescued by Jim.

Carthew seems to differ from Dodd mostly in that the savage side of his personality appears somewhat more pronounced. In the eyes of his ultrarespectable parents and neighbors, he led a wild youth with low companions—"before he was out of long clothes," they say of him, "the cloven hoof began to show" (xvii, 456). But it is, at best, an indolent kind of deviltry he displays, quite closely related to the dilettantism of Dodd. At Oxford Carthew "set a fashion in his clique; envious undergraduates sought to parody his unaffected lack of zeal and fear; it was a kind of new Byronism more composed and dignified. 'Nothing really mattered'" (xvii, 476). Other Stevenson characters who are described as Byronic are Archer of *The Great North Road*, that "sheep in a turnip-field," and the shiveringly delicate Archie Weir of *Weir of Hermiston*.

Nevertheless, the violence in Carthew is destined to show itself, and in such a way as Pinkerton and Big Head Dodd could hardly have hoped for in *their* protégé. Yet it takes a great deal to let it out, for the violence is buried deep. Here is the situation: Haddon, Carthew, and the crew of their schooner are shipwrecked on Midway with a considerable amount of money, their entire bankroll. They are found by a Lowland villain, Captain Trent, a cautious, wizened old man, formerly a pawnbroker, who offers to take them to the mainland if they will give him all their fortune.

But even in such a situation Haddon and Carthew are as little likely to show violence as Pinkerton and Dodd would be. It takes the conjunction of two almost disinterested characters to begin the butchery. One of these, Goddedaal, is Captain Trent's mate. He is described as a friendly, sentimental, concert-going, Shakespeare-loving Viking, very much ashamed of his captain's rapacity. The other, Mac, is one of the sailors on Haddon and Carthew's schooner, *The Currency Lass*. His character is a mixture of generosity, sentimentality, and violence—" 'I'm rather a violent man,' he would say, not without pride" (xvii, 523). Earlier, on the island, he angrily threw a banjo into the campfire and then mawkishly begged its owner's pardon. Stevenson uses this incident to foreshadow the violence which is to come.

So this scene of barbarity and sentimentalism passed off, leaving behind strange and incongruous impressions. . . . But the discordant note had been struck, and its harmonics tingled in the brain. In that savage, houseless isle, the passions of man had sounded, if only for the moment, and all men trembled at the possibilities of horror. (xvii, 534)

Mac is the only one of the Haddon–Carthew company who will not suffer from Captain Trent's thievery. He was not an original member of the crew, and so he has no share in their money. Trent has undertaken to land him in San Francisco passage free. Nevertheless, it is Mac who is the most outraged at Trent. Impulsively he stabs the captain, thus beginning a chain reaction which will make Carthew a murderer. But first the violence is loosed in Goddedaal, Mac's counterpart:

Goddedaal had leaped to his feet, caught up the stool on which he had been sitting, and swung it high in air, a man transfigured, roaring (as he stood) so that men's ears were stunned with it. *There was no thought of battle in the Currency Lasses*; none drew his weapon; all huddled helplessly from before the face of the baresark Scandinavian. His first blow sent Mac to ground with a broken arm. His second dashed out the brains of Hemstead. He turned from one to another, menacing and trumpeting like a wounded elephant, exulting in his rage. But there was no council, no light of reason, in that ecstasy of battle; and he shied from the pursuit of victory to hail fresh blows upon the supine Hemstead, so that the stool was shattered and the cabin rang with their violence. The sight of that post-mortem cruelty *recalled Carthew to the life of instinct,* and his revolver was in hand and he had aimed and fired before he knew. (xvii, 554, my italics)

The violence in Carthew had been slow to rouse itself, but once awake, it is more terrible even than Mac's or Goddedaal's. One thinks of Conrad's Kurtz, who was also recalled to a life of instinct, for now Carthew turns monstrous, dragging out and murdering each of the innocent members of Trent's crew so that there will be nobody alive to give testimony against him. Meanwhile, Mac, the instigator of the violence, is left forgotten to nurse his broken arm in the captain's cabin. As Carthew later explains, "reason had now fled from that silent ship" (xvii, 560) .

What ties the two stories of *The Wrecker* most securely together is that Loudon Dodd recognizes himself in Norris Carthew. Determined to be a criminal, Dodd comes to Midway in search of a fortune in opium. Instead, he finds evidence leading to the discovery of a horrible and irrational slaughter, at which most men would prefer to turn their backs. As we have seen, Dodd is incapable of acting out his determination as regards the opium, but he reacts quite differently to the murder. Although he has not yet heard the story of *The Currency Lass,* but only guesses that Carthew is involved in some sort of dark scandal, Dodd crosses the Atlantic to protect his double from the lawyer Bellairs, who means to blackmail or expose him. And after Dodd has heard the story, he does not reject Carthew, as even Carthew's mother had done, but remains by him as a protector.

"I rather think," Dodd says, "he is my long-lost brother" (XVII, 467). In this respect, Dodd comes off better even than Carthew, who after viewing his own inner violence, withdraws so far from life that it requires considerable detective work on Dodd's part to discover him. But Dodd does find out his double, acknowledges him, and then is enabled to act as his agent in the world of men.

Thus even the novel of manners, when Stevenson writes it, is given a dark undercurrent, and the world of comedy is very closely related to the world of tragedy. The same is true in the David Balfour romances, where the comic figures—David and Alan and Catriona—play out their sport against the background of the murder of Red Colin and the unjust hanging of James of the Glens, both of whom die because of irrational and primitive passions for revenge. Red Colin is shot because of clan hatred between the Stewarts and the Campbells; James of the Glens is hanged because a Campbell is dead and a Stewart therefore must pay for it. Prestongrange, who prosecutes James, explains it to David in this way:

> The Duke [of Argyle] and I are Highlanders. But we are Highlanders civilised, and it is not so with the great mass of our clans and families. They have still savage virtues and defects. They are still barbarians, like these Stewarts; only the Campbells were barbarians on the right side [of the 1745 rebellion], and the Stewarts were barbarians on the wrong. (x, 62-63)

It becomes therefore "a political necessity" (x, 61) that the government satisfy the barbaric instincts of the Campbells with the hanging of an innocent man.

Alma Emmons writes that *Catriona* seems to be a book about Highlanders "in the process of becoming 'civilised.' "[41] In a less literal sense, all of Stevenson's works deal

[41] "The Highlander in Scottish Prose Fiction," p. 120.

with this problem, for the phrase, a somewhat civilized barbarian, will pass pretty well as Stevenson's definition of man in general. There is always an ancestor, probably arboreal, lurking in the nature of each full man. To deny this ancestor is deforming and sometimes fatal, but to recognize him is far from comforting.

In *The Black Arrow* a young man was frightened out of life by his glimpse of the savage man of pure evil. But in the Balfour romances and in *The Wrecker*, which show a little more hope, the heroes make uneasy peace with these half-men. Such figures, it appears, *will* come to terms, although one must have some courage and perhaps a strong stomach to sit down with them. But always the more terrifying figure in a Stevenson romance is the complete man, the Highlander civilized. Even in *Treasure Island*, the wildest of the pirates can be trampled to death by horses or shot down by a boy. They are malignant and wild, but they are blind or self-destructive, and they end by killing one another or by marooning themselves. John Silver, on the other hand, who "is a man of substance," a respectable sea cook with "a banker's account, which has never been overdrawn" (v, 70), performs much more effective evil. Because he keeps "a foot in either camp" (v, 284), he survives all his old shipmates, Flint, England, Pew, and the pirates aboard the *Hispaniola*. He survives because he believes, along with Captain Smollett, his chief opponent, that "dooty is dooty" (v, 253).

David Balfour can make a sort of peace with the unalloyed primitiveness of Alan Breck Stewart, but what drives him out of life, as surely as his recognition of the ineffectuality of his own actions, is quite another recognition: that "the villains of that horrid plot [the hanging of James] were decent, kind, respectable fathers of families, who went to kirk and took the sacrament" (x, 278-279). He is thinking most specifically of Prestongrange; the father of three very beautiful and highly civilized daughters; Prestongrange, who, in the business of unjustly trying and hanging James of the Glens, looks for no reward beyond the conscience of his duties done (x, 62).

George Bernard Shaw claims to have learned from the tales of Stevenson that the romantic hero is mocked by reality.[42] Unfortunately, this is a lesson Stevenson never taught. But what Shaw may actually have derived from Stevenson is this concept of the "Highlander civilised," for as Shaw writes in "The Revolutionist's Handbook":

> No indictment is here laid against the world on the score of what its criminals and monsters do. The fires of Smithfield and of the Inquisition were lighted by earnestly pious people, who were kind and good as kindness and goodness go. And when a negro is dipped in kerosene and set on fire in America at the present time, he is not a good man lynched by ruffians: he is a criminal lynched by crowds of respectable, charitable, virtuously indignant, high-minded citizens. . . . The things our moral monsters do may be left out of account. . . . Judge us by the admitted and respected practice of our most reputable circles.[43]

And it is just such a judgment as this that David Balfour makes before resigning from the active life.

Since Aeschylus, the court of law and the legal system have served in literature as the primary symbols of civilization. Nineteenth century English writers, as a rule, shared an ambivalent attitude of dissatisfaction with and yet reliance upon both this symbol and the society it represented. Scott certainly did not approve the charge of artificial murder on which Effie Deans was tried, but he never-

[42] "Preface to Major Barbara: First Aid to Critics," *The Works of Bernard Shaw*, 33 vols. (London, 1930), XI, 208.
[43] *The Works of Bernard Shaw*, X, 207.

theless respected Jeanie's firm decision to uphold this unjust law. Moreover, the judge in Effie's case goes so far in
his humanity almost to beg the jury to acquit her "if they,
having God and a good conscience, the sanctity of their
oath, and the regard due to the law of the country, before
their eyes, could come to a conclusion favourable to this
unhappy prisoner."[44] No English writer has attacked the
law so furiously as Dickens. Nevertheless, he saw the Anglo-
Saxon court as an essentially rational institution, civilized
often to the point of absurdity, sophisticated and complicated to the extent that its logic turned in and fed upon itself and those it was created to serve and protect. But the
contrast between the two trials of Charles Evremonde in
A Tale of Two Cities—the English trial and the French
trial—show that basically Dickens, too, placed his trust in
the logic of civilization. Even in *Great Expectations*, where
the prison is equated with the slaughterhouse, the lawyer
Jaggers would rather tame than kill his savage prey.
George Meredith was another reformer, but he says, along
with Lady Dunstane, that "the rules of Christian society are
a blessed Government for . . . women. We owe it so much
that there is not a brick of the fabric we should not prop."[45]

Stevenson was himself a lawyer of sorts, but he could not
bring himself into accord with such an attitude. He does
not fail to note the painstaking and oftentimes amusing
logic of the Anglo-Saxon court.

We have a solemn enjoyable way of lingering on a case.
We treat law as a fine art, and relish and digest a good
distinction. There is no hurry: point after point must
be rightly examined and reduced to principle; judge after
judge must utter forth his *obiter dicta* to delighted
brethren.[46]

44 *The Heart of Midlothian*, p. 253.
45 *Diana of the Crossways*, p. 313.
46 *Edinburgh: Picturesque Notes, Works*, I, 395.

Nevertheless, Stevenson saw below this surface of civilization to a residue of ineradicable, basic savagery. There are only three court scenes in Stevenson's fiction. In the first, which occurs in the play *The Hanging Judge*, Justice Harlowe, to save his wife, unjustly condemns a man to death. "I will defend my wife," Harlowe rationalizes, "she is ill, her days are threatened; I will defend her. What do I care for laws? I love my wife! A beast—a senseless beast—would do as I do; shall a man do less? Oh, this talk of crime and sin, right and wrong, what dross it is, what dust to any creature that loves!" (VI, 401). In another of Stevenson's court scenes, Adam Weir, in contrast to Effie Dean's humane judge, gleefully and sadistically tears the last shred of human dignity from the miserable condemned prisoner. And in *Catriona*, the Duke of Argyle sentences James Stewart to death because, as he patiently, almost innocently, explains in open court, if the Jacobites had prevailed in the recent war, a Stewart would now be condemning a Campbell (X, 239).

In this rejection of civilization, Stevenson is again closer to American than to English tradition. More specifically, the Balfour romances resemble here, as in so many other places, *The Adventures of Huckleberry Finn*; and "the territory" which Huck lights out for in preference to being "sivilized" is roughly analogous to David's plain, quiet path. Twain was also capable of probing the thin layer of gentility on his Colonel Sherburns and the stickier sentimentality on his Colonel Grangerfords to the essential, blood-thirsty aboriginal below.

But Stevenson cannot go so far as Twain in approving the uncivilized. Ultimately Huck's acceptance of Jim is a complete one. "I knowed he was white inside," Huck says in final judgment.[47] David, on the other hand, cannot bring

[47] *The Complete Works of Mark Twain*, 24 vols. (New York, 1918), IX, 381.

himself beyond toleration and forbearance of *his* primitive, Alan Breck Stewart. His success is so qualified because Stevenson does not, like Twain, see the savage as one whom society has not yet spoiled and who is therefore less evil. He sees him merely as one whom society has not yet armed, and who is consequently less dangerous. In addition, Stevenson's boy has more conscience and has been more carefully educated in religious matters; indeed, he cannot bring *himself* to pray anything less than the entire Westminster Confession.

CHAPTER IV

THE HOUSE OF GOD

JOSEPH WARREN BEACH writes that "Good and evil
are always conceived by Stevenson in the simple legendary
way."[1] Romance, of course, is closely allied to legend, and
should be, but Beach's statement is intended as a criticism;
indeed, Stevenson's alleged attitude toward good and evil,
perhaps more than anything else, has marked him as merely
a maker of children's books. Thus John Galsworthy writes,
"He had but one main theme, the essential theme of romance, struggle between the good and the bad, of hero
against villain, and often with the heroine absent, or merely
looking over the wall. For there was an eternal boy in
Stevenson, and he wrote 'Virginibus Puerisque.' "[2]

We have looked at enough Stevenson now to be able to
say that he did not conceive of good in the simple legendary
way. David Balfour is a good Presbyterian, but he is not Sir
Galahad; his virtue does not lead to action, for the path of
duty, in Stevenson's works, clearly is not the road to glory.
Neither are Hamlet and Christ very easily reconciled, although we shall see in this chapter that two of Stevenson's
characters attempt to make just such a reconciliation. The
rest of Beach's statement has an element of truth in it, for
while Stevenson shared the Victorian novelists' typical dis-
trust of the hero, he rejected their disbelief in pure vil-

[1] *English Literature of the Nineteenth and the Early Twentieth Centuries, 1798 to the First World War* (New York, 1962), p. 231.
[2] "Four Novelists in Profile," *The English Review*, LV (Nov. 1932),
493.

lainy. Thackeray had given his opinion that "we are no heroes nor angels; neither are we fiends from abodes unmentionable, black assassins, treacherous Iagos, familiar with stabbing and poison—murder our amusement, daggers our playthings, arsenic our daily bread, lies our conversation, and forgery our common handwriting."[3] Stevenson, on the other hand, recounts how he once tried to convince his friend and former teacher, Fleeming Jenkin, of the existence of perfectly evil men. And in one of his short essays, "A Character," he goes even so far as to provide us with a physical description of this type of moral monster, whose years "have not yet quenched his thirst for evil," and whose "eyes still delight themselves in wickedness" (xxiv, 24).

Certainly, evil so described is legendary enough, if by legendary we mean Christian, but Stevenson was sufficiently aware that his belief in pure wickedness was dangerous to his art. Jenkin confessed himself finally convinced by Stevenson's arguments, but at the same time he warned his friend that "this badness is such an easy, lazy explanation. Won't you be tempted to use it instead of trying to understand people?"[4] Here was an admonition directed to the writer rather than the moralist, and, as a writer, Stevenson took it to heart. For no matter how high he permitted the hellish energy to run in his villains, he was always careful to provide them with powerful and understandable motivations for their wicked actions. John Silver feeds his bank accounts, and Richard of Gloucester, his ambition. Even Mr. Hyde, as we shall see, has his reasons. Nevertheless, the essential motivation which spurs each of the villains to action is his innate blackness. And since a belief in the existence of evil was an important part of Stevenson's vision, he would have been wrong to suppress it.

[3] *Lovel the Widower, Thackeray's Works,* III, 230.
[4] *Memoir of Fleeming Jenkin, Works,* XI, 525.

If such a belief happens not to be a part of our own vision, however, there is still a great deal in Stevenson's works to interest us, for the evil is never at the center of the story, nor does the author concern himself very much with defining it. The savages, once again, are never the protagonists. When he wrote *The Black Arrow*, Stevenson enjoyed creating Richard of Gloucester, but he was compelled to write about Richard Shelton, and this compulsion rendered Gloucester's depravity much less significant to the total vision of *The Black Arrow* than it would otherwise have been. The essential point of the story became Shelton's reaction to Gloucester's wickedness, not the fact of this wickedness or the author's belief in it. And when, after *The Black Arrow*, Stevenson largely abandoned the omniscient author mode of storytelling in favor of his narrator–heroes, his own beliefs became invisible. From this point we have nothing to watch except what Stevenson would have us watch: *the protagonist's act of judging the villain, and the effect which that judgment has upon the protagonist's character.*

But whether the story is told in the first person or the third person, the villain's part, as an object to be judged by the hero, is always the same, and the apparency of his evil does not alter this fact. Thus in *The Ebb-Tide*, which Stevenson once jokingly called *"A Tract,"*[5] Huish, who slithers like a recognizable snake in a certain garden, pronounces himself the direct enemy of God:

> He must play his part to exaggeration, he must out-Herod Herod, insult all that was respectable, and brave all that was formidable, in a kind of desperate wager with himself. . . . "Well, Gawd!" said he, apostrophising the meridian, "you're goin' to see a rum start presently, I promise you that!" (XVIII, 194-195)

5 Letter to Charles Baxter, March 1893, *RLS: Stevenson's Letters to Charles Baxter*, p. 325.

Huish is the one character whom Stevenson, in his own person as author,[6] execrates as "wholly vile." He describes him as "a vulgar and bad-hearted cockney clerk . . . [with] no redeeming grace" (XVIII, 12). Yet in spite of his diabolism, Huish's evil does not alter circumstances of the plot, except, as with the villains of the other books, where it serves as a horrifying example, distasteful and frightening enough to bring the central characters of the story literally to their knees in an abject and degrading repentance. These central characters are degenerate, embittered derelicts; and perhaps Stevenson believed he would need the devil himself to bring about such difficult conversions.[7]

Israel Hands of *Treasure Island* is also presented as an anti-Christ. The problem in this book is that young Jim Hawkins, both charmed and repelled by the ambiguous John Silver, is unable to find any firm commitment and is thus incapable of effective action. Hands' character, unlike Silver's, is not at all a mixed one; Hands is purely evil. The sailor he has murdered lies "with his arms stretched out like those of a crucifix" (V, 220). And while Hands, like Cap'n Silver, is willing enough to argue about morality and the value of prayer, his cynical conclusions have a far

[6] One is tempted to blame this departure from general practice on Stevenson's collaborator, but even though he was the boy for whom *Treasure Island* was written, no man ever believed less in heroical good or bad than Lloyd Osbourne.

[7] Stevenson seems to have considered the idea of establishing a full-fledged *Doppelgänger* relationship between Herrick, one of the heroes, and Huish; in the early chapters they both assume the identical false name, Hay. The idea must have been dropped, however, for there is no further mention of it. *The Ebb-Tide* is not the only one of Stevenson's works to so experiment with *Doppelgänger*. In the fragment, *The Castaways of Soledad*, Stevenson tries on doubles, so to speak, until he finds the proper set. First he attempts to fit the narrator with a fellow passenger, George Ramsey, but when nothing interesting develops here, he pairs Ramsey with the second mate, Kinnismont. Here Stevenson finds a much better contrast. Ramsey describes himself as "the penny fiddler" and Kinnismont as "the mute at a funeral" (Buffalo, 1928), p. 21.

different effect on Jim than had the seemingly respectable evil Silver practiced and preached.

> "For thirty years," he said, "I've sailed the seas, and seen good and bad, better and worse, fair weather and foul, provisions running out, knives going, and what not. Well, now I tell you, I never seen good come o' goodness yet. Him as strikes first is my fancy; dead men don't bite; them's my views—amen, so be it." (v, 231-232)

And it is only after Hands has thus exposed himself, and in a prayer, no less, that Jim finds the moral strength to shoot him down. Afterwards, we should note, he has no difficulty in joining full-heartedly with Captain Smollett's party and rejecting Cap'n Silver together with all the pirates.

We have seen that the results of these rejections are sometimes deforming; sometimes they are beneficial. In the play, *Admiral Guinea*, Blind Pew serves to frighten the savagery out of the young hero and make him over into an acceptably tame husband. Similarly, David Balfour's Catriona loses some of her Highland wildness once she has objectively viewed her rascal father. When she casts out James More Macgregor, she rejects some of the outlaw in herself and becomes more tractable, better suited for her final retirement with David.

But there is a class of characters in Stevenson who find reformation or quiet retirement impossible to achieve because the bad example from which they shrink is literally a part of themselves. These are the classic *Doppelgänger* of Stevenson's fiction, divided men who live two separate lives with their alternate identities, or who have, at least, what they believe to be two separate and distinct natures. Such characters, as we shall see, end always as suicides.

Stevenson had a personal taste for divided personalities: for the clergyman who dreams of winning battles or the banker who imagines himself as an artist.[8] He admired "thieves in the shape of tonsured clerks, or even priests and monks,"[9] and was fascinated by "devils . . . with a dash of the angelic," like François Villon.[10] But, as usual, something is lost or gained in the translation from the essays to the fiction, and the characters, when they appear in the stories or romances, do not share their author's relish for their own double existences. No doubt they should share it, for to do so would be to live harmoniously with both body and soul, but as Stevenson recognized, "All allegories have a tendency to escape from the purpose of their creators."[11] The escaped allegory, in this case, produced some of his most significant visions.

The first double personality to interest Stevenson was William Brodie, a real figure from the eighteenth century, who had been the deacon or president of the Edinburgh wrights during working hours, and a thief and murderer after dark. Stevenson was writing a story about him as early as 1866, but this attempt failed and was destroyed.[12] Later, in an essay of 1878, he describes Brodie as one of the principal legends of Edinburgh:

A great man in his day was the Deacon; well seen in good society, crafty with his hands as a cabinet-maker, and one who could sing a song with taste. Many a citizen was proud to welcome the Deacon to supper, and dismissed him with regret at a timeous hour, who would have been vastly disconcerted had he known how soon, and in what guise, his visitor returned. . . . Still, by the mind's eye, he may be seen, a man harassed below a mountain of duplicity, slinking from a magistrate's supper-room to a

8 See "The Lantern Bearers," *Works*, XII, 264.
9 "François Villon, Student, Poet and Housebreaker," *Works*, IV, 220.
10 "Memoirs of Himself," *Works*, XXVI, 223.
11 "Bagster's *Pilgrim's Progress*," *Works*, XXIV, 72.
12 Graham Balfour, *The Life of Robert Louis Stevenson*, I, 79-80.

thieves' ken, and pickeering among the closes by the flicker of a dark lamp.[13]

And in the same year, 1878, Stevenson and W. E. Henley wrote the play, *Deacon Brodie, or the Double Life,* which was produced and published, and then in 1884, completely revised by both of its authors. Stevenson never cared greatly for any of the works in which Brodie figured, but Brodie himself, quite obviously, continued to fascinate him. Jerome H. Buckley sees the Deacon as a conscientious rebel against Edinburgh society and equates him to one of the earliest of the German *Doppelgänger,* Karl Moor of Schiller's highly influential work, *Die Räuber.* Buckley writes that "Brodie turns to crime through none of the stock villain's innate rottenness; his sin is a deliberate protest against a Philistine environment."[14] Certainly this is close to the view Brodie takes of his own evil. He is convinced that respectability is nothing but a suit of clothes with which all men cover their evil "naked selves." "Shall a man not have HALF a life of his own?" he insists.[15] Brodie believes, like Byron's Conrad, that the nature of man is essentially evil, and that he, the housebreaker, differs from so-called honest men only by virtue of his greater courage and his freedom from self-deluding hypocrisy. Yet he is filled with Satanic pride and hatred when he says:

I felt it great to be a bolder, craftier rogue than the drowsy citizen that called himself my fellow-man. It was meat and drink to know him in the hollow of my hand,

13 *Edinburgh: Picturesque Notes, Works,* I, 399-400.
14 *William Ernest Henley,* p. 102.
15 *The Works of Robert Louis Stevenson: Monterey Edition,* eds. Charles Curtis Bigelow and Temple Scott, 10 vols. (New York, 1906), VIII, 264. Since our interest at the moment is on Brodie as the first of Stevenson's *Doppelgänger,* we shall follow the original version of the play, reprinted in the edition cited above. Later, we shall have occasion to make reference to the revised version, reprinted in the *Vailima Edition* of Stevenson's works.

hoarding that I and mine might squander, pinching that might wax fat. It was in the laughter of my heart that I tip-toed into his greasy privacy. I forced the strong-box at his ear while he sprawled beside his wife. He was my butt, my ape, my jumping-jack.[16]

Brodie's contempt for middle class society extends even to his own family, which is indeed one of the most respectable in Edinburgh. When he discovers that his uncle, the Procurator-Fiscal, buys smuggled brandy, Brodie glories in having discovered this evidence of what he believes to be his uncle's evil nature. He exalts in proclaiming that he, Brodie, who has stolen his sister's dowry, and the respectable old man are equally villainous. "Rogues all! Rogues all, Procurator! 'Tis the last word of my philosophy, and it will soon be yours."[17] Brodie denies, moreover, that there is any distinction to be made between his own criminality and the everyday sharp business practices of his Scotch neighbors. "Every man for himself, and the devil for all," he says. "They call that cynicism in France, but here we call it business instinct."[18]

The Deacon's view, that the essential man is evil and that his respectable or honest actions are nothing but a disguise, is set directly against the more Presbyterian philosophy of his uncle, who believes simply that "an honest man's an honest man, and a randy thief a randy thief, and neither mair nor less."[19] The audience, however, is not asked to choose between the two conceptions; neither provides for man's double nature, and so the play rejects them both. Lawson turns out to be an honest man, whatever his methods for getting brandy. Brodie's own life, moreover, gives the lie both to himself and to his uncle, for in spite of his denials in the early parts of the play, the civilized side of Brodie's personality is at least as real as the savage.

[16] Page 279.   [17] Page 277.   [18] Page 293.   [19] Page 259.

He carries a great deal more of his daylight character than his carpentry skills into his second existence. Indeed, the chief motives for his thefts are almost laudable: he wishes to win back the stolen dowry so that his sister may marry the man she loves, and he wants to escape into respectability with his own faithful mistress and his loving children. In this second motivation he is very much like John Silver, who says of his pirate loot, "I puts it all away, some here, some there, and none too much anywhere, by reason of suspicion. I'm fifty, mark you; once back from this cruise, I set up gentleman in earnest" (v, 100). Silver intends to buy a coach and stand for "Parlyment" (v, 105). Brodie is also like the villain of another Stevenson and Henley play, *Macaire*, who steals for "a palace, a barouche, a pair of luminous footmen, plate, wine, respect, and to be honest!" (vi, 285).

Nevertheless, when Brodie, in Jonas Chuzzlewit style, leaves his respectable identity behind him in the locked bedroom, we expect to see him next as a dangerously evil man, ruthless, savage, divorced from all tender and decent emotions. "Lie there, Deacon! sleep, and be well to-morrow," Brodie says. "As for me, I'm a man once more till morning!"[20] What we see instead is a simpleton, easily gulled of his money by his more seriously wicked confederates, and a citizen, who spends a perfectly domestic evening with his mistress and his child. The boy would do credit to the most solid of Edinburghers, as he glowingly sings, "My faither's a Deacon, a Deacon, a Deacon." Already Brodie is sick of his double life—"Sick of wearing two faces and living two lives! Sick of the evening's riot and the morning's shame!"[21] Indeed, the reviewer for *The Critic*, who must have preferred his evil legendary, was disappointed in Brodie as a villain. He noted that "there is a touch of weakness and vacillation about him which is not in harmony

[20] Page 265.   [21] Pages 289-290.

with the hardihood of habitual criminality. Compunctions of conscience are unknown to the professional outlaw, and when the deacon becomes sentimental he is unnatural and therefore uninteresting."[22] Perhaps so, but these vacillations point to the central meaning of the work.

As the play progresses, Brodie comes to realize that his original "rogues-all" philosophy was too simple to explain even his own psyche. At length, when he is apprehended by his friend Leslie, he is ready to plead for the reality of both sides of his and indeed of everyone's nature—not only for the civilized, as we might expect under the circumstances, but for the savage as well.

> You found something to love, something to honour in me. O that was a part of me! It was not a lie; it was a part of me you loved. Have you not ill thoughts yourself? It must be; we have all our secret evil. Only mine has broken loose; it is my maniac brother who has slipped his chain; it does not change the part of me you loved.[23]

But of course the maniac brother does change Brodie in the eyes of his friend, for Leslie is a dull and orderly Edinburgher, who believes as firmly in appearances as Brodie had previously believed in essences. And perhaps it is because he gets no corroborative opinion from Leslie that Brodie is not long able to maintain his new tolerance for both halves of his nature. What is remarkable in Stevenson, however, is that he should have achieved such a tolerance even for a moment; that he should have been able to recognize the respectable carpenter as a part of himself, and at the same time acknowledge the maniac as his brother. Once he loses this tolerance, as indeed he must, he will again select a part of his nature as the only real one and try to live entirely with it. This is the way to his destruction. He

---

22 "Stevenson's Deacon Brodie," *The Critic* (New York), X (May 14, 1887), 244.
23 Page 306.

is lost no matter which part he chooses, for choice itself is the error, albeit an inevitable one. There are two versions of *Deacon Brodie*, and in each the hero determines differently; yet neither draft is much more optimistic than the other. Both lead towards his death.

The idea we have just been considering, the theme of the disguised significant self, occurs elsewhere in Stevenson. There is, in fact, a regular disguise *motif* running through much of the early fiction, appearing in *Prince Otto*, in *The Black Arrow*, and in several of the stories from *The New Arabian Nights*. But it is not at all necessary in such works for the hero to begin, as Brodie does, with a belief in his essential depravity. Indeed, the title character of the story "Markheim" starts by denying that there is any evil at all in his real nature. Such a conviction is equally wrong, and certainly it is equally dangerous, for it, too, must lead inevitably to a rejection of self and to suicide.

Markheim has just committed a murder, but he is certain that God understands and forgives him. "His act," Markheim admits, "was doubtless exceptional, but so were his excuses, which God knew; it was there, and not among men, that he felt sure of justice" (XI, 143). Like Hogg's justified sinner, and like Bulwer's Eugene Aram, Markheim believes that evil actions need not stain the character of the good man. Thus he says:

> I have lived to belie my nature. All men do; all men are better than this disguise that grows about and stifles them. You see each dragged away by life, like one whom bravos have seized and muffled in a cloak. . . . I was born and I have lived in a land of giants; giants have dragged me by the wrists since I was born out of my mother— the giants of circumstance. And you would judge me by my acts! But can you not look within? Can you not understand that evil is hateful to me? (XI, 147-148)

This comfortable explanation is, of course, exactly contrary to Deacon Brodie's. Here it is the good self which is essential, and the evil acts which form the misleading disguise. Nevertheless, Markheim is as little able as Brodie to maintain his theory. He doubts it even as he speaks, for his troubled conscience has projected an imaginary double, a diabolic lookalike, to debate the matter with him. Pressed by the arguments of his double, which are, of course, his own arguments, Markheim must recognize the duality of his nature. He must admit that he has "in some degree complied with evil." Yet he is not about to make peace with this wickedness. Instead, he defies it.

Shall one part of me, and that the worst, continue until the end to over-ride the better? Evil and good run strong in me, haling me both ways. I do not love the one thing, I love all. I can conceive great deeds, renunciations, martyrdoms; and though I be fallen to such a crime as murder, pity is no stranger to my thoughts. . . . And are my vices only to direct my life, and my virtues to lie without effect, like some passive lumber of the mind? Not so; good, also, is a spring of acts. (XI, 152)

Of course, everything we have seen in Stevenson tells against such a hope. The only action that can come from good seems to be the act of resignation from life, and Markheim, forced to the wall by the renewed arguments of his imaginary double, finally realizes this fact; and, as we might expect, he embraces it as a solution. "If I be condemned to evil acts," he reasons, "there is still one door of freedom open—I can cease from action. If my life be an ill thing, I can lay it down" (XI, 154).

Markheim's double, as we have noted, has been presented as a devil-figure. Up to the very last moment he has been encouraging the hero to "act," urging him to kill the murdered pawnbroker's maid, who threatens to return and discover the crime. Action, as usual in Stevenson, runs on hellish energy. However, after Markheim's conscience asserts itself and he decides to put into effect "what remains for me by way of duty" (XI, 153), that is, to give himself up to the police, "the features of the visitor began to undergo a wonderful and lovely change: they brightened and softened with a tender triumph" (XI, 155). This is by far the highest token of praise accorded to one of Stevenson's resigning heroes. The act of life-desertion seems almost to be presented here as the will of heaven. The story takes place on Christmas Day, and the hero's choice might be interpreted as an example of Christ-like renunciation. So it is evident that we must have to do in this chapter not only with legendary evil, but with legendary good as well.

Edgar Knowlton has shown through close textual similarities that "Markheim" owes a great deal to *Crime and Punishment*,[24] which Stevenson had read with great pleasure in its first French translation.[25] This influence would seem to make the case for "Markheim" as a Christian allegory even stronger. But probably Knowlton goes beyond his evidence when he calls Stevenson's story "a cameo version," simply a retelling of Dostoyevsky's.[26] Certainly the plots, as well as the styles, afford similarities. In both works the murder victim is a rapacious and colorless old pawnbroker whom the hero believes he is privileged to kill without moral harm. And each hero believes he has two identities. We have already heard Markheim on his theory of disguises; Raskolnikov claims it was the devil and not he who killed the old woman. In both stories, moreover, the hero finally surrenders himself to the authorities. But,

---

[24] "A Russian Influence on Stevenson," *MP*, XIV (Dec. 1916), 449-454.

[25] Stevenson called it "easily the greatest book I have read in ten years. . . . Henry James could not finish it: all I can say is, it nearly finished me. It was like having an illness." Letter to Symonds, Spring 1886, *Works*, XXI, 398.

[26] Knowlton, p. 449.

as we have seen, Stevenson never merely retells the stories from which he borrows. Always he touches them with his own particular problems and conflicts, which are related to, but are certainly not identical with those he finds in the parent story. The conclusion of "Markheim," for example, is not nearly so optimistic as the ending of Dostoyevsky's romance.

At the start of his story, Stevenson's hero, although he expresses his life-hunger in a Dostoyevskyan metaphor, has probably a greater love for life than Raskolnikov ever has. Markheim says:

> Life is so short and insecure that I would not hurry away from any pleasure. . . . We should rather cling, cling to what little we can get, like a man at a cliff's edge. Every second is a cliff if you think upon it—a cliff a mile high —high enough, if we fall, to dash us out of every feature of humanity. (XI, 133)

Raskolnikov, who has been only half alive through most of *Crime and Punishment*, never feels life so immediately as this, but it is the purpose of his final surrender to bring him into life. "Go at once," Sonia tells him, "this very minute, stand at the cross-roads, bow down, first kiss the earth which you have defiled and then bow down to all the world and say to all men aloud, 'I am a murderer!' *Then God will send you life again.*"[27] And when he tells his sister that he has chosen not to commit suicide but to give himself up, Dounia exclaims, "Then you still have faith in life? Thank God, thank God!"[28]

But the punishment for murderers was more severe in England than in Russia. Raskolnikov had to fear fifteen to twenty years of penal servitude, years which, as the author believed, would fit him once again for living. Markheim

---

[27] Fyodor Dostoyevsky, *Crime and Punishment*, trans. Constance Garnett (New York, 1950), p. 407.
[28] *Ibid.*, p. 501.

will be hanged. He is not choosing between suicide and surrender as Raskolnikov is, because for Markheim, surrender can only mean a kind of suicide. Moreover, like so many of Stevenson's life deserters, he embraces his death almost gleefully. "Life, as he thus reviewed it, tempted him no longer; but on the further side he perceived a quiet haven for his bark" (XI, 155).

Dostoyevsky writes about men like Ivan Karamazov, who try unsuccessfully to renounce life. And Christianity is one of the strongest forces preventing their self-destruction. Stevenson's characters, on the other hand, are originally full of a desire to live, but it is an appetite which they are unable to maintain. Christianity for them is a negative force, one which seems to justify inaction and to encourage suicide. Thus Markheim imagines he pleases heaven when he withdraws from action, and he gives himself up "with something like a smile" (XI, 155).

Deacon Brodie seemed to be headed in the very same direction as Markheim, that is, towards some sort of virtuous resignation from life. At one point in the action, he refrains from committing a murder because he hears a psalm being sung, and he firmly refuses the escape which his friends and family offer him, because, as he says, he is "waiting for the rope." But in the original version of the play, his savage or active nature reasserts itself at the last moment. He betrays and denounces his family and his mistress as "Rogues, rogues; accessories after the fact, officer, all accessories after the fact." As for himself:

> I've lived a man, and I'll die as I've lived. I had but one pleasure in life; it was to fool and juggle and jockey you one and all. I've done it always, damn you; and damn you, I'll do it once more!

In his attempt now to escape, he receives his death wound, and he dies convinced again of his original belief in man's

essential evil. For his last words are the defiant and significant tag line from the beginning of the play, "Rogues all!
—rogues—rogues."[29]

This ending, however, is from the 1878 draft of the play,
and it sounds anyway more like Henley, the author of
Invictus, than Stevenson. In the revision, the mistake was
rectified, and the one Stevenson hero who had been allowed to die defiantly, like a legendary villain, is brought
ingloriously to his knees and made to pray with his sister.
He had vilely denounced her in the earlier version, but
now he takes a loving farewell of her and of all his friends
and assures the arresting officer that "there is but one man
guilty; and that man is I." Moreover, one feels that his
death in this version is not brought about by any desire to
escape and to experience more life, but rather to save his
family the disgrace of a trial and a public hanging. And his
last words in this draft are not "Rogues all!—rogues—
rogues," but "The new life ... the new life!" (VI, 115).
Thus the energetic part of Stevenson's divided man, even
at its most hellish, is not very likely to win the war in the
members.

"Markheim" and the revision of *Deacon Brodie* are
works of the middle 1880's; there is a temptation to account for the emphasis on Christianity one finds in them
with the fact that about this time Stevenson was regaining
some of his own lost faith. Indeed, we shall later on look at
still a third work of this period, "Olalla," which shows a
very similar emphasis. After his youth, Stevenson was never
formally a Christian. Lloyd Osbourne writes that "in the
accepted religious meaning," his step-father "was wholly
an unbeliever." Moreover, the faith Stevenson found in his
middle thirties was not the mysticism of Dostoyevsky, much
less that of John Knox; it was the new ethical Christianity
which Tolstoy was preaching. Osbourne writes:

[29] Pages 321-322.

Tolstoy had a profound influence over him and did much to formulate his vague and sometimes contradictory views. Tolstoy virtually rediscovered Christianity as a stupendous force in the world, not the Christianity of dogma, supernaturalism, hell, and heaven, but as a sublime ethical formula that alone could redeem society. Stevenson in this sense was an ardent Christian.[30]

It was in response to this faith that Stevenson, as we noted earlier, considered martyring himself in Ireland over the Curtin affair. But certainly there are significant differences which Stevenson must have seen, between his own contemplated sacrifice and the renunciations Markheim and Brodie make. For one thing, Stevenson felt that his death would benefit society in a positive way; Brodie and Markheim wish only to remove themselves from further temptation to do evil. Stevenson saw his own martyrdom, moreover, not as a cessation from endeavor, as his two heroes did, but indeed as a strong piece of action, and one requiring a good deal of initiative and courage. He was itching for action; the very last thing he sought was a quiet haven for his bark.

The solutions of Markheim and Brodie were never Tolstoy's. Yet there is some similarity between their problems and those Tolstoy tried to answer. Tolstoy felt that man's belief in his duality stemmed from an interior debate between his personality and his reason:

> One self, his personality, bids him live. But another self, his reason, says: "You cannot live." The man feels that he is divided. And this division torments and rends his soul.[31]

This is very similar to what we have seen in Stevenson, but while Tolstoy understood and noted that the agony oc-

---

[30] "Introduction," *Works*, I, xix-xx.
[31] "On Life," *On Life and Essays on Religion*, trans. Aylmer Maude (London, 1950), p. 37.

casioned by this recognition often leads men to suicide and to philosophies of suicide, he certainly never endorsed such solutions or called them Christian. Indeed, he himself struggled against suicidal tendencies. And Tolstoy's non-resistance philosophy, like Stevenson's, was a positive force, certainly not a justification for inaction: What is demanded, Tolstoy wrote, is not a "renunciation of the personality," but "its submission to the law of reason."[32]

The truth is that Stevenson's personal religious beliefs, even those derived from Tolstoy, found no more expression in his fiction than did his socialism. He became interested in Tolstoy's Christianity because it was very compatible with beliefs and attitudes he already held. But after the influence of Tolstoy, as before it, the theology in Stevenson's stories belongs entirely to the characters, not to the author. If we want further proof, we need only note that Christian thought, rather like that which informs "Markheim" and *Deacon Brodie*, appears in stories which were written long before Stevenson's conversion to Tolstoy, indeed, in the period of his greatest disbelief. The best of these is "The Merry Men" (1881), which is a Hawthorn-esque tale of a fanatically pious Presbyterian of Lowland stock, who finds himself gleefully participating in what he believes to be the world's basic evil. Theology, of course, figures strongly in such a story, and in such a way as to cast light on Stevenson's use of religion both in the "Christian" works of the mid-decade and in the tragedies which follow after them.

Gordon Darnaway, the protagonist of the story, has carefully cultivated the Lowland side of his character. The narrator describes him as "a sour, small, bilious man, with a long face and very dark eyes; fifty-six years old. . . . He never laughed, that I heard; read long at the Bible; prayed much, like the Cameronians he had been brought up

[32] *Ibid.*, p. 85.

among; and indeed, in many ways, used to remind me of one of the hill-preachers in the killing times before the Revolution" (xi, 24). He farms a small island called *Aros Jay*, which means *The House of God*. We have seen from other works that such a distorted character can expect psychological trouble, if not theological. In Gordon's case, the two troubles come together in a way that sets a pattern for Stevenson's tragic stories and romances.

The Merry Men of the story are a group of dangerous breakers near the island. To the characters, at least, they seem to represent all the savagery of the universe in its most barbaric form. Like the pirates in *The Master of Ballantrae* or *Treasure Island* (one is named George Merry), the rocks are wild, irrational, gleeful, and destructive. Elsewhere Stevenson uses the term, merry men, to describe practical jokers of his Edinburgh college days,[33] and certainly the Merry Men of *Aros Jay* are not without their madcap nature. In a storm they send spray a hundred feet high, so that they seem to "dance together—the dance of death, it may be called. . . . Whether they got the name from their movements, which are swift and antic," the narrator speculates, "or from the shouting they make about the turn of the tide . . . is more than I can tell" (xi, 16).

The Merry Men are strongly personified throughout the story. The narrator endows them with the power to revolve mischief and to give warning of coming storms. He shows them drawing a helpless ship into their midst so that they may gleefully tear it to pieces. And at the height of the storm, he reports that "the noise of them seemed almost mirthful, as it out-topped the other noises of the night; or if not mirthful, yet instinct with a portentous joviality. Nay, and it seemed even human. As when savage men have drunk away their reason, and, discarding speech, bawl together in their madness by the hour" (xi, 63-64).

[33] "The Modern Student Considered Generally," *Works*, XXV, 70.

Stevenson himself had always been greatly affected by
such spectacles. In 1890 he wrote that he had "always
feared the sound of wind beyond everything. In my hell it
would always blow a gale."[34] And in *Storm* one of the
poems of the 1870's, Stevenson celebrated his delight in
this kind of wildness:

> Ei! merry companions,
> Your madness infects me.
> My whole soul rises and falls and leaps and
>   tumbles with you!
> I shout aloud and incite you, O white-headed
>   merry companions.
> The sight of you alone is better than drinking.
> The brazen band is loosened from off my forehead;
> My breast and my brain are moistened and cool;
> And still I yell in answer
> To your hoarse inarticulate voices,
> O big, strong, bullying, boisterous waves,
> That are of all things in nature the nearest
>   thoughts to human,
> Because you are wicked and foolish,
> Mad and destructive.[35]

Gordon Darnaway, with his morbid Cameronian temperament, is not so easily infected by wild nature as Stevenson was. Gordon believes that the sea is a place of horrors—
"if it wasna prentit in the Bible, I wad whiles be temp'it
to think it wasna the Lord, but the muckle, black deil that
made the sea" (XI, 28). He shrinks back and wishes to shut
out the sea's "wickedness" which he describes in terms of
" 'a' that's in it by the Lord's permission: labsters an'
partans, an' sic like, howking in the deid; muckle, gutsy,
blawing whales; an' fish—the hale clan o' them—cauld-

[34] Letter to Colvin, Dec. 1890, *Works*, XXII, 316.
[35] *Collected Poems*, p. 85.

wamed, blind-eed uncanny ferlies. O, sirs,' he cried, 'the horror—the horror o' the sea!' " (XI, 30) .[36]

Gordon's religious mania makes him regard the Merry Men as a special example of the world's wickedness. Therefore he despises them. Yet he is also fascinated, finding them irresistible and their dance "bonny" (XI, 56) . "Whenever the Merry Men were dancing, he would lie out for hours . . . watching the tumult of the sea, and sweeping the horizon for a sail" (XI, 60) . Once before, as Gordon watched a shipwreck, the Merry Men drove him to drunken madness and perhaps to the frenzied murder of the wreck's one survivor. Darnaway's home is now furnished with the salvage. During the action of the story, moreover, we see him watching another storm, at first contemplating the possibility of a wreck with "a timid joy in his eyes" (XI, 56-57) , and later, when the wreck is a certainty, poring and gloating over it "like a connoisseur. . . . He seemed rejuvenated, mind and body" (XI, 58) . And at the height of the storm, the narrator hears Gordon's shrill and thrilling voice accompanying the shouts of the Merry Men.[37]

[36] It is possible that when Stevenson wrote this passage he had in mind the following from *Moby Dick* (Chap. LVIII):

> Consider the subtleness of the sea; how its most dreaded creatures glide under water, unapparent for the most part, and treacherously hidden beneath the loveliest tints of azure. Consider also the devilish brilliance and beauty of many of its most remorseless tribes, as the dainty embellished shape of many species of sharks. Consider, once more, the universal cannibalism of the sea; all whose creatures prey upon each other, carrying on eternal war since the world began.
>
> Consider all this; and then turn to this green, gentle, and most docile earth; consider them both, the sea and the land; and do you not find a strange analogy to something in yourself? For as this appalling ocean surrounds the verdant land, so in the soul of man there lies one insular Tahiti, full of peace and joy, but encompassed by all the horrors of the half known life. God keep thee! Push not off from that isle, thou canst never return.

[37] The source for this conception may be *Melmoth the Wanderer* (Edinburgh, 1820), where John Melmoth, watching a wreck, "for a moment . . . echoed the storm with yells of actual insanity" (I, 159). Else-

The two sides of Gordon Darnaway's character, the developed and the potential, are given symbolically at the beginning of the story when the narrator says he had "an air somewhat between that of a shepherd and that of a man following the sea" (XI, 24). But Gordon's religious training has hardly taught him to live with his whole nature, anymore than it has prepared him to see the wildness in nature and in himself as merely primitive ecstasy. "See to them dancin', man!" he says to his nephew. "Is that no' wicked?" (XI, 66). Yet he cannot deny that he is attracted. His conclusion therefore is that he is himself one of the damned. He rejects his duality and regards himself as wholly evil. "I'm a deil, I ken't," he says. "I'm wi' the sea, I'm just like ane o' her ain Merry Men" (XI, 72).

Not for a moment does Darnaway compromise in his religious convictions. His Cameronian morality remains unshaken, and he is perfectly clear as to the implications of his defection. "If it wasnae sin," he says, "I dinna ken that I would care for't. Ye see, man, it's defiance" (XI, 72). Indeed, on the very verge of madness, he can discuss this one matter quite rationally:

> At the hinder end, the Lord will triumph; I dinna misdoobt that. But here on earth, even silly men-folk daur Him to His face. It is no' wise; I am no' sayin' that it's wise; but it's the pride of the eye, and it's the lust o' life, an' it's the wale o' pleesures. (XI, 73)

Gordon Darnaway fully expects damnation; it is consequently not surprising when he loses his mind at the sight of the Negro sailor, the survivor of the second wreck. He takes the black man for the devil come to carry him away, runs from him, and is finally drowned along with the Negro, who chases him into the sea.

---

where in the same romance, Maturin writes that "it is actually possible to become *amateurs in suffering*" (II, 218).

This sort of simultaneous death is almost a regular feature of Stevenson's tragic doubles stories; we shall see it
again both in *Jekyll and Hyde* and in *The Master of Ballantrae*. The pattern of events leading up to the deaths is
also similar in the three stories. What happens is that the
predominantly Lowland hero recognizes an irrational element in his nature which he has hitherto repressed. At the
same time, he encounters some object or person that seems
purely evil to him, and equates this with his own irration-
ality, regarding it as a projection or double of himself. As
the hero comes to despise the double and his fascination
for it, he grows more and more like it, until, in terror and
madness, both he and it are destroyed. Christianity in
many of these stories has two functions; it helps the hero
to equate the unrestrained with the unholy and thereby
to shore up his distaste for action, and, as we have seen, it
can be bent into a specious rationale for life desertion or
even for suicide.

But there is another element of "The Merry Men"
which we have not yet brought into the analysis, a sub-plot
John Robert Moore has traced to a little-known story of
William Aytoun's, "The Santa Trinidada." Aytoun's
story concerns a man who, like a number of figures in the
Doppelgänger tradition, is tempted to evil by the Devil,
appearing to him in the guise of a stranger. This stranger
leads Malcome McLean to participate in a midnight ceremony of black magic and to dive into the sea for gold from
the Spanish Armada. Parts of this plot are indeed performed in "The Merry Men" by the narrator, Gordon's
nephew, Charles Darnaway.

Moore believes that Stevenson did not successfully in-
tegrate Aytoun's tale with his own, and that the story of
Gordon Darnaway's insanity would have been better told
without it, would have been more solid in structure and

clearer in purpose.[38] Certainly the plot connection between the two tales is slight. The crew of the ship whose destruction Gordon Darnaway watches was also searching for the gold, but Gordon does not know this. Indeed, he has not even heard of the gold. Moreover, Charles Darnaway, the nephew, does not discover the treasure he looks for. Like all the resigning heroes in Stevenson he begins with firm enough purpose, but when he touches a human bone on his second dive, he feels "the full horror of the charnel ocean," and he gives up. He prays "long and passionately" and makes a "deep determination to meddle no more with the spoils of wrecked vessels or the treasures of the dead" (xi, 49). The hero of Aytoun's story persevered and was drowned in his search for the gold.

Nevertheless, there is a thematic connection between the two plots which is perhaps already apparent. Both men, Gordon and his nephew, regard the sea as a place of horrors; Gordon allows himself to be sucked into it, whereas Charles, a more typical Stevenson hero, draws back at the last moment. Moreover, Charles, as the narrator in Stevenson's tale, performs as his uncle's judge and is perhaps partly responsible for the latter's death. If this is so, then the incidents of the sub-plot, since they define Charles Darnaway's character, are crucial to an understanding of the story.

Charles, the university student, considers himself more modern and less superstitious than his uncle. Actually the two men are much alike. Charles' religion is just as dour as Gordon's, as both uncle and nephew muse ponderously on the Christian names of the wrecks which their bay contains, the *Espirito Santo* and the *Christ-Anna*. On the other side, Charles is also fascinated by the Merry Men. Struggling at the height of the storm to maintain his

[38] "Stevenson's Source for 'The Merry Men,'" *PQ*, XXIII (Apr. 1944), 140.

sobriety, he admits that "thought was beaten down by the confounding uproar; a gleeful vacancy possessed the brains of men, a state akin to madness; and I found myself at times following the dance of the Merry Men as it were a tune upon a jigging instrument" (xi, 65). Moreover, Charles regards what happens to Gordon not as a lamentable case of madness, as the free-thinker Stevenson certainly did, but as "a strange judgment of God's" (xi, 19).

Stevenson seems to be using his narrator as a second or externalized conscience for his protagonist. As Charles rejects his uncle as evil—"I lost toleration for the man" (xi, 54) —so does Gordon Darnaway reject himself. Charles, like his uncle, interprets the latter's wild actions as "sin"; it may be that he imagines more evil deeds than have actually been performed. Earlier we said that Gordon had perhaps committed a murder. There is no evidence for this belief except a long narrow mound of earth which Charles discovers and takes for a grave. No one has told or indeed subsequently does tell Charles about a dead man, but he immediately suspects that the mound contains the corpse of a survivor of last February's wreck, a survivor whom he is certain his uncle must have murdered. Again no one confirms this suspicion, but by the end of the story Charles has built it into a firm conviction and indeed into something of a romance. He takes his weakened uncle to the mound of earth, uncovers his own head to the rain, and sermonizes:

A man . . . was in God's providence suffered to escape from mortal dangers, he was poor, he was naked, he was wet, he was weary, he was a stranger; he had every claim upon the bowels of your compassion; it may be that he was the salt of the earth, holy, helpful, and kind; it may be he was a man laden with iniquities to whom death was the beginning of torment. I ask you in the sight of

Heaven: Gordon Darnaway, where is the man for whom Christ died? (XI, 74)

Whether or not there was a murder, such a performance seems almost calculated to drive the nearly distracted old man into full insanity and towards death. If it does not, then Charles' next actions certainly do. For now the black man suddenly appears, and while Gordon, fallen on his knees, prays wildly for protection from this seeming devil, Charles admires the Negro's pulpit manner (XI, 77). He drags his uncle to his feet and literally pushes him in the direction of his worst fear. "Forward and embrace it; welcome like a father yon creature who comes trembling to your mercy" (XI, 76). Now, indeed, Gordon goes totally mad.

Charles is also a cause of his uncle's death the next day, although again he acts as he believes for the best. Gordon's hired man, Rorie, and the Negro have gone out by themselves to bring the lunatic home. Gordon has fled to the top of the island and refuses to come down. Using the sea for a barrier on one side, the men attempt to drive Gordon in the direction of his house. Now, however, Charles interferes on the fourth side, "cutting off the madman's last escape" and forcing him towards the sea.

My uncle Gordon saw in what direction, horrible to him, the chase was driving him. He doubled, darting to the right and left, but high as the fever ran in his veins, the black was still the swifter. Turn where he would, he was still forestalled, still driven towards the scene of his crime. Suddenly he began to shriek aloud, so that the coast re-echoed; and now both I and Rorie were calling on the black to stop. But all was vain, for it was written otherwise. The pursuer still ran, the chase still sped before him screaming; they avoided the grave and skimmed close past the timbers of the wreck; in a breath they had cleared the sand, and still my kinsman did not pause, but dashed straight into the surf; and the black, now almost within reach, still followed swiftly. . . . Rorie and I both stopped, for the thing was now beyond the hands of men, and these were the decrees of God that came to pass before our eyes. (XI, 86-87)

Thus the Lowland forces within Gordon's psyche, and some of those outside it, forces represented by the narrator, drive Gordon to a screaming death. Again, the fierce dog tears the wolf to pieces, though he tears himself in the process. But the civilizing principle that has given strength to the dog this time has been Christianity, especially the negative Christianity the author remembered from his youth.

That Stevenson, who was a free-thinker in 1881, could have regarded Gordon Darnaway's death as, in any way, a judgment of God is certainly not to be thought of. "The Merry Men" and the other works of this chapter do not view reality in a Christian context. Stevenson is not busy separating the sheep from the goats. Instead, he observes how Christians may regard the world, and how their creed sometimes makes them unable to accept nature, either human or external, incapable of living with their own passions or with the passions of the physical universe. At certain stages of his life, Stevenson himself may or may not have believed in legendary evil or in Christian good, but the author's beliefs are hardly an issue in such a story as "The Merry Men," anymore than they are an issue in *Moby Dick* or "Heart of Darkness." For romance in the nineteenth century does not oftentimes concern itself with the author's definitions of evil, legendary or otherwise. Rather it is interested in the mythic confrontation of man with his own conception of the powers of blackness.

CHAPTER V

THE WAR IN THE MEMBERS

I SEND YOU herewith a Gothic gnome . . . but the gnome is interesting, I think, and he came out of a deep mine, where he guards the fountain of tears. It is not always the time to rejoice. . . . The gnome's name is *Jekyll & Hyde*; I believe you will find he is likewise quite willing to answer to the name of Low or Stevenson.[1]

THE PART we have just seen Charles Darnaway play in "The Merry Men" was largely thematic. Everything he thought of Gordon, Gordon thought first of himself. And if Charles helped to drive his uncle towards madness and death, certainly his uncle's own conscience was leading in the same directions. Technically, Charles must be regarded not as the central character, but as a detached narrator, as an onlooker point of view, the first of several to appear in Stevenson's fiction.

We should pause to consider this device, for the use of uninvolved or seemingly uninvolved narrators is one of the most striking features of works in the romance tradition. Stevenson's name has been especially associated with this method of narration,[2] but we should remember that it was a technique in quite frequent use throughout the century. Parts of *Frankenstein,* for instance, are told by a romantic

[1] Letter to W. H. Low (Jan. 2, 1886), *Works*, XXI, 381-382.
[2] Lionel Stevenson, for instance, calls the use of Marlow, in Conrad's *Lord Jim,* "the Stevensonian onlooker point of view," *The English Novel: A Panorama* (Boston, 1960), p. 439.

sea captain who, in both his attitudes and his responses, looks very much forward to Conrad's Marlow. Indeed, the major work of the tradition in England, *Wuthering Heights*, uses no less than four points of view, all of them from minor characters. And Browning, of course, had employed both minor and major, detached and very much involved characters as his narrators in *The Ring and the Book*. It is interesting to consider this widespread usage in light of the critics who regret Doctor Livesay's narrative in *Treasure Island* and the Chevalier de Burke's memoirs in *The Master of Ballantrae*. No doubt, it gives more interesting shape to the history of the novel to think so, but Stevenson was not racing with Henry James to see who could write the first single point of view novel. Both writers were, however, interested in the detached narrator, like Charles Darnaway, who gives an oblique and often distorted view of the protagonist, and who is, moreover, not always so uninvolved as he may at first appear.

Stevenson's *Strange Case of Dr. Jekyll and Mr. Hyde* is written from more points of view than any other of his works. It contains two first person narratives, a chapter written in the impersonal style of a newspaper report, and the account of a seemingly uninvolved third person point of view character, Mr. Gabriel Utterson, who sometimes observes Jekyll and Hyde directly and sometimes listens to the stories told by still other characters who have observed them. What the reader who has not looked at the story for some time tends to think of as *Dr. Jekyll and Mr. Hyde* is only the last quarter of it, the part which Jekyll himself recounts.

No doubt this oblique approach to narration added to the suspense and mystery for the work's initial audience. The reader who comes to the story fresh (it is almost impossible to find such a one nowadays) does not know that Jekyll and Hyde are one man until the work is almost three-quarters over, and for this reader the shock is still a potent one. But Stevenson has another and a more serious reason for using all these points of view. The most important focus in the story, as we might expect, will be on Jekyll's attitudes towards his double. Before we come to these reactions, however, Stevenson feels it necessary to present us with a number of other opinions of Hyde, attitudes which should prepare us for Jekyll's and which might furthermore serve us as a standard of comparison.

The first response to Hyde comes from Mr. Richard Enfield, "the well-known man about town" (VII, 348), who describes the incident in which Hyde knocks down and tramples the little girl. Enfield takes a loathing to Hyde at first sight (VII, 351). He prides himself as a connoisseur of beauty, and so he finds Hyde's unspecifiable deformity distasteful to the point of nausea. "There is something wrong with his appearance; something displeasing, something downright detestable. I never saw a man I so disliked, and yet I scarce know why" (VII, 355). Enfield also provides us with a number of other reactions. He tells, for instance, about the women whom the sight of Hyde turned "as wild as harpies" (VII, 352), and about the colorless, "cut-and-dry" Edinburgh apothecary, "about as emotional as a bagpipe," who turned "sick and white with the desire to kill him" (VII, 351). Like the doctor, Enfield would have also liked to murder Hyde; but he is a thoroughly civilized man, and he has contented himself with blackmail.

G. J. Utterson of Gaunt Street, to whom Enfield tells this story, is himself something like the unemotional Edinburgh apothecary, and his association with Enfield is really the first *Doppelgänger* relationship the story presents. The two men are distant kinsmen. Nevertheless, they seem to have little in common, for Utterson is "austere with himself" and drinks gin when he is alone "to mortify a taste for vintages" (VII, 347). To strengthen his moral fiber, he has for twenty years denied himself the pleasure of going to the theater. Yet Utterson and the *bon vivant* Enfield are fast friends.

It was a nut to crack for many, what these two could see in each other, or what subject they could find in common. It was reported by those who encountered them in their Sunday walks, that they said nothing, looked singularly dull, and would hail with obvious relief the appearance of a friend. For all that, the two men put the greatest store by these excursions, counted them the chief jewel of each week, and not only set aside occasions of pleasure, but even resisted the calls of business that they might enjoy them uninterrupted. (VII, 348-349)

But while the ascetic Utterson has generally a toleration for "down-going men" like Enfield (VII, 348), he has no sympathy for Hyde, whom he regards with suspicion even before their first encounter. When they do meet, Utterson feels a "hitherto unknown disgust, loathing, and fear." He says to himself, "God bless me, the man seems hardly human!" (VII, 365-366). And it is not only a disgust at *Hyde* which this meeting inspires in him, but "a nausea and a distaste for life" itself (VII, 367). Utterson, who is an attorney, believes that Hyde has some kind of legal hold on Jekyll and is victimizing him. Nevertheless, he regards his friend Jekyll's misfortune in much the same way Charles Darnaway had considered his uncle's madness. Utterson remembers that Jekyll "was wild when he was young; a long while ago to be sure; but in the law of God, there is no statute of limitations" (VII, 368).

The third important, uninvolved narrator reaction comes from Hastie Lanyon, who is a Scottish doctor, like Jekyll himself. Lanyon is a bold and boisterous scientist of the soundest modern principles. He drinks wine when he is alone, instead of gin, but he lacks Utterson's toler-

ance, and has allowed his friendship with Henry Jekyll to
lapse because of the latter's "fanciful" medical theories.
" 'Such unscientific balderdash,' added the doctor, flushing
suddenly purple, 'would have estranged Damon and
Pythias' " (vii, 359-360). Edward Hyde fills this scientist
with "a disgustful curiosity" (vii, 422), and once Lanyon
has learned the Jekyll-and-Hyde secret, he rejects Jekyll
entirely. "I wish to see or hear no more of Dr. Jekyll. . . . I
am quite done with that person; and I beg that you will
spare me any allusion to one whom I regard as dead"
(vii, 390). But his reaction goes much farther. The insight
into life that Lanyon receives when he watches Hyde's
transformation into Jekyll is so potent as to shock this
seemingly robust person literally to death. His soul sickens
and his "life is shaken to its roots." The vision he has been
vouchsafed of man's duality proves too much for him, and
he writes:

> sleep has left me; the deadliest terror sits by me at all
> hours of the day and night; I feel that my days are num-
> bered, and that I must die; and yet I shall die incredu-
> lous. As for the moral turpitude that man unveiled to me,
> even with tears of penitence, I cannot, even in memory,
> dwell on it without a start of horror. (vii, 426-427) [3]

These then are the principal reactions which prepare
us for the encounters of Jekyll and Hyde with one another
—loathing, disgust, fear, and shocked horror. We may
leave them for a space now while we discuss other prelimi-

[3] In a previous version in manuscript at Yale University Library,
Stevenson ended the Lanyon section as follows:

As for the moral turpitude that man unveiled to me, it is a matter
that I disdain to handle. He found me an elderly, a useful and a happy man; that he has blighted and shortened what remains to me of
life, is but a small addendum to the monster's tale of his misdeeds.

This and other extracts from the same manuscript are printed here with
the kind permission of the Graduate Department at Yale.

nary matters, but we must return to them, for it is especially important that we understand and evaluate these attitudes before we come to Jekyll's own reactions. Otherwise it will be almost impossible for us to enter into the heart of the story with anything like a fresh mind. *Jekyll and Hyde* has developed into a popular myth, one of the very few to come out of the Victorian period, and its meanings have consequently become blurred. The story was vulgarized within a year of its publication by T. R. Sullivan's popular and sensationalistic stage interpretation, featuring Richard Mansfield. And so powerful was the influence of this play that we generally use Mansfield's, and not Stevenson's pronunciation of Jekyll's name.[4] After Sullivan's play, there were three successful movie versions, starring, respectively, John Barrymore, Frederic March, Spencer Tracy; each one did its bit to coarsen Stevenson's ideas.[5] In quite another way, the story was allegorized almost out of existence by the sermons and leading articles in religious newspapers of the late 1880's. The result is that the term Jekyll-and-Hyde, even as used by psychologists, has little reference to Stevenson's work. Most nonexperts, as a matter of my own observation, are rather surprised to learn that the story has a known author, or if they associate Stevenson's name with it, they often assume he took the plot from some well-worn folk legend. We all have our

[4] For Stevenson's pronunciation—Jeekyl—see Richard Aldington, *Portrait of a Rebel* (London, 1957), p. 183.

[5] Early critics of the stage versions were quick to catch the distortions, although powerless to discourage them. William H. Rideing, reviewing the play for *The Critic* (May 14, 1887), writes that Mansfield interpreted the respectable, middle-aged doctor as "a lachrymal, long-visaged, strutting young gentleman, apparently not more than twenty-five, clean shaven, raven-haired, sombre as Hamlet—a cross between Eugene Aram and Edgar Allan Poe—who dresses in black diagonals, loops his arms in front of him and moves by a series of Irvingesque dislocations: a colporteur, a college tutor, an elocutionist, a tragedian out of employment —anything but the substantial, prosperous Dr. Jekyll we were first acquainted with" (244).

preconceived ideas of Jekyll and Hyde, and it is consequently difficult for us to avoid reading our own notions
into Stevenson's story.

If we have seen the movies, we tend perhaps to regard
Jekyll as an essentially good man who looks upon his dangerous experiment as a noble service to mankind. He is a
sort of Tennysonian hero, like King Arthur, who strives
to free man from the evil in his nature. In the Spencer
Tracy version, for instance, Jekyll is the only man in London tolerant and honest enough even to admit that man is
not entirely good. But if the movie Jekyll has a tincture of
evil in his nature, certainly the evil does not manifest itself
in any of his actions—least of all, in the swallowing of the
elixir. When the experiment backfires, releasing evil rather
than good, the Jekyll we have imagined continues with the
powders partly because of morbid fascination and partly
in the interests of objective science. Finally, Hyde domi-
nates him entirely, driving him to death.

This has, indeed, proved to be a very saleable version of
the story, but it is hardly fair to saddle Stevenson with it.
And it is especially unfair to complain afterwards, as
critics oftentimes do, of the story's "slightly too obvious
meaning." One such critic, smarting over the insult to his
intelligence, explains the moral of *Dr. Jekyll and Mr. Hyde*
in the following sarcastic language:

> If you weren't careful, the evil in you would swallow up
> the good, as the wicked Hyde does Dr. Jekyll. And you'd
> be lost. So be careful! Nearly as crude as that.[6]

Now there is no suggestion in Stevenson's version of the
Strange Case of Dr. Jekyll and Mr. Hyde that carelessness
was Henry Jekyll's chief fault. On the contrary, according
to one of Stevenson's letters, the "harm" was in Jekyll pre-

[6] C. Keith, "Stevenson To-day," *Queen's Quarterly* (Winter 1950-
1951), 456.

cisely because he was *too* careful, "because he was a hypocrite. . . . The Hypocrite let out the beast of Hyde." And the beast of Hyde, while he *is* indeed evil, is not wicked in the way most stage and screen presentations have shown him. In the same letter Stevenson writes that Hyde was "not, Great Gods! a mere voluptuary. There is no harm in voluptuaries; and . . . none—no harm whatever in what prurient fools call 'immorality.'. . . [Hyde] is the essence of cruelty and malice and selfishness and cowardice, and these are the diabolic in man—not this poor wish to love a woman, that they make such a cry about."[7] It is perhaps unfortunate in this respect that all four of the important stage and screen productions of *Jekyll and Hyde* were made in America, where the popular mind is especially apt to regard sex and evil as synonymous terms.

Once again, however, Stevenson's moral views are not the major issue; his heroes, as we have seen, are usually not so broad-minded as he is. Gordon Darnaway's sins, even if he really did commit the murder, are largely voluptuary and Bacchic according to the author's lights. But Gordon certainly does not regard them with any tolerance. Similarly Deacon Brodie is led into a life of crime and to his "rogues all" philosophy by his recognition of his sensual nature—by the pleasure he takes in drinking and in loving his mistress. And, as we shall see, very much the same thing happens with Henry Jekyll.

The published version of the *Strange Case of Dr. Jekyll and Mr. Hyde* is not the original. The first draft was destroyed by Stevenson because his wife found it not meaningful enough. But from the accounts we have of it, this original version seems to have been very much like *Deacon Brodie*. The physical change the chemicals wrought in Jekyll was intended simply as a disguise. There was no at-

[7] Letter to John Paul Bocock, 1887, quoted in George S. Hellman, *The True Stevenson: A Study in Clarification* (Boston, 1925), pp. 129-130.

tendant moral or temperamental transformation. With his altered face and stature, the respectable Dr. Jekyll was enabled merely to indulge his customary nighttime passions without fear of discovery or embarrassment.

But even the more allegorized published version has many points in common with *Deacon Brodie, or the Double Life,* which was, of course, already something of an allegory. The most important similarity is that Jekyll, like Brodie, has led two lives for many years past. Long before the physical appearance of Hyde, Jekyll admits, "I concealed my pleasures; and . . . when I reached years of reflection, and began to look round me and take stock of my progress and position in the world, I stood already committed to a profound duplicity of life" (VII, 428). Moreover, the disguise *motif* is not altogether dropped in the final version. After the experiment, the respectable doctor "would still be merrily disposed at times" (VII, 435). As Jekyll writes:

I began to profit by the strange immunities of my position. Men have before hired bravos to transact their crimes, while their own person and reputation sat under shelter. I was the first that ever did so for his pleasures. I was the first that could thus plod in the public eye with a load of genial respectability, and in a moment, like a schoolboy, strip off these lendings and spring headlong into the sea of liberty. But for me, in my impenetrable mantle, the safety was complete. Think of it—I did not even exist! (VII, 436) [8]

[8] In William Godwin's Gothic romance, *The Travels of St. Leon* (London, 1799), the hero, fleeing the Inquisition, drinks the *elixir vitae* and is changed from a wrinkled, white-haired, exhausted old man to a vigorous and handsome youth. As he explains, "One of the advantages of the metamorphosis I had sustained, consisted in its tendency, in the eyes of all that saw me, to cut off every species of connection between my present and former self (III, 278). And later, speaking again of his altered appearance, St. Leon comments, "I now carried a disguise perpetually about with me" (IV, 1).

Thus the adventures of Hyde are, at least in their voluptuary aspects, merely a continuation of the nighttime life of Dr. Jekyll.

Jekyll, in direct contrast to Stevenson's statement about him, asserts that he "was in no sense a hypocrite," but he means something special by this, something which requires explanation. He means, as he says, that both sides of him "were in dead earnest" (VII, 429), that he was not a bad man posing during the day as a good one. He does not mean that he took Sunday afternoon strolls with his *alter ego*, as Utterson and Enfield do. As a matter of fact, he specifically declines an invitation from this engaging pair, who recommend that he take a "quick turn" with them to whip up his "circulation" (VII, 395). His one self is deathly ashamed of the other, and the doctor believes, moreover, that this mortification does him a world of credit.

> Many a man would have even blazened such irregularities as I was guilty of; but from the high views that I had set before me, I regarded and hid them with an almost morbid sense of shame. It was thus rather the exacting nature of my aspirations, than any particular degradation in my faults, that made me what I was. (VII, 428-429)

This passage might have been spoken fifteen years later by Shaw's Roebuck Ramsden, who, if we can believe the devil, Mendoza, also leads something of a double life, and no doubt Jekyll would be as surprised as Ramsden at having his sincerity called into question. For Jekyll believes he is telling the truth when he says, "I was no more myself when I laid aside restraint and plunged in shame, than when I laboured in the eye of day, at the furtherance of knowledge or the relief of sorrow and suffering" (VII, 429).

As for Jekyll's goodness, we have very little evidence for it besides the doctor's own word. There is a period just after Hyde's murder of Sir Danvers when Jekyll goes about actively striving to do good, but this activity is presented almost as though it were contrary to his more general habits. As to his actions prior to this stage, no one in the story will go beyond the author's statement that "he had always been known for his charities" (VII, 389). The public nature of his good actions is, in fact, heavily stressed. Enfield calls him "the very pink of the proprieties. . . . One of your fellows who do what they call good" (VII, 353). And when Utterson finds a book of Jekyll's which Hyde has disfigured with blasphemies, he describes it as "a pious work for which Jekyll had several times expressed a great esteem" (VII, 412). Yet Utterson does not discover any reverent marginalia in *Jekyll's* hands. Neither do we witness Jekyll actually doing any of the good he boasts of and is known for. In a previous draft of the story, obviously intermediate between the destroyed first manuscript and the published version, Stevenson was somewhat more specific in detailing Jekyll's virtues. There Jekyll calls himself "a man of distinction, immersed in toils, open to generous sympathies, never slow to befriend struggling virtue."[9] But even these generalities were not permitted to stand.

Perhaps the problem is simply that Stevenson, here as elsewhere, cannot sufficiently bring himself to believe in positive acts of virtue. The only goodness Stevenson seems capable of rendering in his fiction is the act of renunciation, and sacrifice seems hardly to be Henry Jekyll's strong point. In the John Barrymore motion picture version, the doctor nobly kills himself in order to save his threatened fiancée from the menace of Hyde. In Stevenson's story, on the other hand, Jekyll disappears for the last time, absolutely careless as to what wickedness Hyde may perform with his body. The benevolence in Jekyll seems to stem not from any innate springs of virtue, but, as he admits, from

[9] Stevenson refers to this intermediate draft in an unpublished letter to F. W. H. Myers, Mar. 1, 1886. See note 3 above.

an "imperious desire to carry my head high, and wear a more than commonly grave countenance before the public" (VII, 428). As with so many of Stevenson's Lowlanders, the ideal to which Henry Jekyll is committed is not goodness, but mere respectability.

But we should also note that Jekyll is the type of hypocrite who deludes himself along with the world. No doubt he believes that his day-life of negative virtues represents real good, just as he believes that his night-life of sensuous indulgence represents real evil. And these convictions, though Stevenson would have rejected them both, are what lead Henry Jekyll to the recognition of his double nature.

> Even a deeper trench than in the majority of men, severed in me those provinces of good and ill which divide and compound man's dual nature. . . . And it chanced that the direction of my scientific studies, which led wholly towards the mystic and the transcendental, re-acted and shed a strong light on this consciousness of the perennial war among my members. With every day, and from both sides of my intelligence, the moral and the intellectual, I thus drew steadily nearer to that truth . . . : that man is not truly one, but truly two. (VII, 429)

This diagnosis, no matter how mistakenly arrived at, is again a healthy one. It is indeed a truth according to Stevenson's most consistent thought, and it is a truth a man always does well to face. What is unhealthy is the treatment the good doctor prescribes. Jekyll was wrong in attempting to segregate the two sides of his life, and he was even more wrong in glorifying the one side while alternately condemning and indulging the other. His chemical experiment is simply a logical extension of this treatment. It is by no means a new departure. The Spencer Tracy movie, as we have said, makes a great deal of Jekyll's noble attempt to eradicate the evil in man's nature, but Stevenson's

Jekyll is at least as much interested in freeing his evil nature from restraint as he is in giving scope to the good in him. Indeed, one critic, Alfred Michel, believes he is more interested in the former proposition.[10] According to Jekyll, though, each of the two natures is dear to him, and he sees himself as "radically both." He believes, however, "It was the curse of mankind that these incongruous fagots were thus bound together—that in the agonised womb of consciousness, these polar twins should be continuously struggling." And he sees his experiment as the final cure for this condition.

> If each, I told myself, could but be housed in separate identities, life would be relieved of all that was unbearable; the unjust might go his way, delivered from the aspirations and remorse of his more upright twin; and the just could walk steadfastly and securely on his upward path, doing the good things in which he found his pleasure, and no longer exposed to disgrace and penitence by the hands of this extraneous evil. (VII, 430)

Thus Jekyll, far from wishing to end his double nature, is attempting to make it permanent. He does not mean, at the beginning at least, to reject either of his identities. And when Hyde, the evil nature, appears for the first time, the experiment may be thought of as incomplete, but it should certainly not be considered a failure.

Now that Hyde is out in the open, Jekyll must react to him, and since Jekyll's nature is more distorted by Lowland morality than any of the other narrators'—he lacks the tolerance of Utterson and Enfield and the robustness of Lanyon—we may expect his attitudes to be even more extreme than theirs. Like Gordon Darnaway's, Jekyll's reactions are confused and mixed. On the one hand, Jekyll

10 *Robert Louis Stevenson: Sein Verhältnis zum Bösen* (Bern, 1949), p. 100.

was "conscious of no repugnance, rather a leap of welcome" at the appearance of Hyde. "This, too, was myself. It seemed natural and human" (VII, 434). As the relationship develops, moreover, he begins to regard Hyde as his own child. Their ages are right for this: Jekyll is fifty, Hyde is in his twenties. And Hyde is the smaller of the two. Like an indulgent father of a scapegrace son, Jekyll writes a check to keep Hyde out of trouble. Later, he even makes Hyde the beneficiary of his will. But while Jekyll is quick enough at first to accept his secret kinship with Hyde and very naturally refers to the latter as "me," he is just as quick to recognize Hyde as wicked, "tenfold more wicked" than himself (VII, 432). "Edward Hyde, alone in the ranks of mankind," he says, "was pure evil" (VII, 434).

Certainly Hyde does not merit the indulgence Jekyll allows him. One wonders also whether at his very first appearance he quite deserves so full a condemnation. I suggest this because it is clear from the incidents which follow that Hyde grows more wicked as the story progresses, and if this is so, he can hardly have been "pure evil" at the beginning. It is true that by the end of the story Hyde "is the essence of cruelty and malice and selfishness and cowardice," as we have heard Stevenson say, but at the start he seems perhaps to be something less than this.

No doubt, although the story does not present it, Hyde continues with, and indeed improves upon, Jekyll's voluptuary adventures; but this sort of behavior is pure evil only in the minds of Jekyll and other products of the negative morality from which Stevenson had himself rebelled. And if there is a possibility that Jekyll judges his *alter ego* unjustly, let us re-examine some of the earlier condemnations of Hyde to see whether they too are not excessive in view of the facts.

Hyde's first narrated adventure, as we recall, is described

by Richard Enfield. Enfield tells how he saw Hyde and a little girl approaching one another at a street intersection.

> Well, sir, the two ran into one another naturally enough at the corner; and then came the horrible part of the thing; for the man trampled calmly over the child's body and left her screaming on the ground. It sounds nothing to hear; but it was hellish to see. It wasn't like a man; it was like some damned Juggernaut. (vii, 350-351)

This incident shows Hyde as a creature without compassion, but it does not show him as either malicious or cruel. He takes no pleasure, as far as we know, in hurting the child. He tramples "calmly," and the Juggernaut simile underscores the impersonality of his action. Hyde is simply indifferent to the girl's pain. He is, as we might expect after the chemical amputation, a man without a conscience, completely uncivilized.

But Enfield and the other bystanders, as we have seen, react to Hyde as though his wickedness were of a more positive nature. Here is the full text, parts of which we have seen before.

> I had taken a loathing to my gentleman at first sight. So had the child's family, which was only natural. But the doctor's case was what struck me. He was the usual cut-and-dry apothecary, of no particular age and colour, with a strong Edinburgh accent, and about as emotional as a bagpipe. Well, sir, he was like the rest of us; every time he looked at my prisoner, I saw that Sawbones turn sick and white with the desire to kill him. . . . Killing being out of the question, we did the next best. We told the man we could and would make such a scandal out of this, as should make his name stink from one end of London to the other. If he had any friends or any credit, we undertook that he should lose them. And all the time, as

we were pitching it in red hot, we were keeping the women off him as best we could, for they were as wild as harpies. I never saw a circle of such hateful faces. (VII, 351-352)

Hyde does not appear purely evil in this adventure, but he does seem to bring out all the cruelty and malice in those who judge him. This is consistent with what we have seen in other of Stevenson's stories. Enfield, the bystanders, and the other narrators are rejecting a part of themselves when they reject Hyde, and the more strenuously they excise him, the more thoroughly they come to resemble their notion of him, and the more profoundly they are affected by the encounter. The sight of the monster merely provides an anecdote for Enfield, the man about town—he thinks no more about it; but it seriously disturbs the life of the tolerant, ascetic Utterson; and it kills Lanyon, who had previously refused altogether to believe in man's duality.

Hyde, of course, is a part of Jekyll, and the harm caused by Jekyll's rejection of him is mirrored in Hyde's own changing nature. At the beginning of their relationship, Hyde was indifferent to Jekyll. "Jekyll had more than a father's interest; Hyde had more than a son's indifference" (VII, 441-442). But Hyde, if he does not react to interest, certainly responds to hatred. Enfield describes him standing in the middle of that circle of hateful faces "with a kind of black, sneering coldness—frightened too, I could see that—but carrying it off, sir, really like Satan" (VII, 352). Similarly, we are told that by the end of the story Hyde's indifference to Jekyll has turned into active hatred because "he resented the dislike with which he was himself regarded" (VII, 452).

The change in Hyde is a slow one and it must be observed through several of the points of view, but it is, nevertheless, very perceptible and quite extreme. Hyde progresses from conscienceless and impersonal indifference to malicious hatred, from a Juggernaut to a devil. And if he appears sufficiently evil to us at his first appearance in the story, we should remember that Jekyll has been pushing him away from his conscience for more than twenty years. In the Yale manuscript Jekyll writes of his youth as a time when "I became in secret the slave of disgraceful pleasures: my life was double."[11] Moreover, the rest of society, as represented by the bystanders and the narrators, with their strong morals or their weak stomachs, have been assisting and encouraging Jekyll in the destructive polarization of his nature. The experiment in the laboratory is only a step in this separation—albeit the most dramatic. There were steps before it, and, tragically, there are steps to follow it.

As the poles widen, Hyde becomes more and more evil. Yet Jekyll continues his dissociation. He decides that Hyde alone is guilty of the nighttime activities, and simultaneously Hyde's crimes "began to turn toward the monstrous" (VII, 437). Jekyll approves of the behavior of the bystanders, describing it as a "too just resentment" (VII, 438). Soon afterwards, he considers the possibility of doing away with Hyde altogether, and for a while, choosing, as he says, "the better part" (VII, 442), he denies Hyde any license for two full months. The result is that when Jekyll releases Hyde again, he comes out "roaring" (VII, 443). Hyde displays much more than indifference and lack of conscience in his senseless and brutal murder of Sir Danvers Carew. "Instantly," Jekyll writes, "the spirit of hell awoke in me and raged. With a transport of glee, I mauled the unresisting body, tasting delight from every blow" (VII, 444).

Nor does the rejection end even here. Indeed, the purpose of Jekyll's next move, his increased performance of benevolent actions and church duties, is to make himself over as much as he can into the direct antithesis of Hyde.

[11] These last four very significant words are crossed out in the manuscript.

The result is what we might expect. Hyde comes for the first time without the help of chemicals while Jekyll sits in Regents Park, reflecting complacently that "after all . . . I was like my neighbours; and then I smiled, comparing myself with other men, comparing my active goodwill with the lazy cruelty of their neglect" (VII, 447).

The *Strange Case of Dr. Jekyll and Mr. Hyde* is not an allegory of the evil in man swallowing up the helpless good; rather it is a story of a whole man driving one part of his nature to depravity until the entire ego is destroyed. G. K. Chesterton has written:

> The real stab of the story is not in the discovery that the one man is two men; but in the discovery that the two men are one man. After all the diverse wandering and warring of those two incompatible beings, there was still one man born and only one man buried. . . . The point of the story is not that a man *can* cut himself off from his conscience, but that he cannot. The surgical operation is fatal in the story. It is an amputation of which both the parts die.[12]

But this is a point Jekyll never understands. After the murder of Carew, Jekyll announces that he is "quite done with" Hyde (VII, 383), and whereas at the beginning of the relationship he had referred to his *alter ego* in both the first and third person indiscriminately, towards the end of the story he denies Hyde's humanity altogether and cannot bring himself to speak of him as I. "He, I say—I cannot say I. That child of Hell had nothing human" (VII, 449). And Jekyll's last reference to Hyde is to speak of him as "another than myself" (VII, 454).

Hyde responds to such treatment with hatred of Jekyll and with increased evil. Near the end he fiendishly destroys Jekyll's papers, and, like the devil in a saint's life, he

---

[12] *Robert Louis Stevenson* (New York, 1928), p. 54.

writes blasphemies in Jekyll's sacred books. We have noted that Deacon Brodie was a kind of Jonas Chuzzlewit. Hyde, in his final manifestation, makes a much better one, and like Jonas kills himself with a bottle of poison. But even when Hyde is most wicked, Jekyll cannot be regarded as a victim. The doctor feels he is the tormented one, because he has a conscience, but it is Hyde, after all, who is driven finally to commit suicide out of sheer terror. It is still another case of dog against wolf, and as usual in Stevenson, the dog is by far the more formidable. Early in the story, Jekyll pleads with his lawyer for Hyde's rights. He does not demand that Utterson befriend Hyde; this, he knows, would be asking too much. "I only ask," he says, "for justice; I only ask you to help him for my sake, when I am no longer here" (VII, 373). Utterson promises that he will deal justly with Hyde, yet immediately after Jekyll's "death" he refuses even to hear another such plea—not for justice this time, but for mercy.

"Utterson," said the voice, "for God's sake, have mercy!"

"Ah, that's not Jekyll's voice—it's Hyde's!" cried Utterson. "Down with the door!" (VII, 409)

In writing such a story of a creature turned diabolic in response to the hatred and rejection afforded him by society and by the man to whom he owes his life, Stevenson must have been aware of similarities to the first important monster story of the century, Mary Shelley's *Frankenstein*. There are several points of strong comparison, the most basic of which is that both works employ *Doppelgänger* to emphasize the duality of human nature. Eino Railo writes that *Frankenstein* "is not without a flavour of the double-existence idea."[13] Muriel Spark goes much further. She writes:

13 *The Haunted Castle*, p. 311.

There are two central figures—or rather two in one, for
Frankenstein and his significantly unnamed Monster
are bound together by the nature of their relationship.
Frankenstein's plight resides in the Monster, and the
Monster's in Frankenstein. That this fact has received
wide, if unwitting, recognition is apparent from the
common mistake of naming the Monster "Frankenstein."
. . . The several implicit themes I propose to examine,
show these characters as complementary beings and as
antithetical ones.[14]

For our purposes, the most important of the themes Miss
Spark examines is the one she calls "the pattern of pursuit,"
for she believes it is "an anticipation of the Jekyll-and-
Hyde theme."[15] This is a *motif*, of course, which both writers
could have gotten from still another writer in the tradition, Mrs. Shelley's father, who had already presented it
in *Caleb Williams*. But wherever it appears in the works of
the romance tradition, this theme of pursuit is characterized by two major features. In the first place, the pursuer's
attitude towards his quarry is always a mixture of love and
hate. And secondly, the reader is never allowed to be quite
certain whether the pursuer is not in fact being hunted
himself. Falkland persecutes Caleb, for instance, because
he fears him; and Frankenstein's Monster leaves obvious
signs of his passage so that Victor will not give up his
search in despair. Both Caleb and the Monster, moreover,
bitterly lament the treason they have done their enemy-
masters.

Another similarity between *Frankenstein* and Stevenson's story is that in both works the hero is excessively self-
righteous. We have seen that this was also a part of the inter-
vening tradition as practiced by Hogg, Bulwer, and Dostoyevsky. It figures also in such works as *Les Misérables*, in

[14] *Child of Light*, p. 134.
[15] *Ibid.*, p. 137.

The Scarlet Letter, and in what is perhaps the greatest of
the pursuit stories of the century, *Moby Dick.* In *Frankenstein,* as in several of Stevenson's works, the greatest
harm comes from two things within the hero's own nature
—a delicate sensibility which cannot bear to look at the
Monster's ugliness, and an overdeveloped moral conscience
which shrinks from the Monster's deeds; in other words,
from Enfield and from Utterson. Frankenstein's Monster is
turned into a premeditating murderer only when Victor,
for the sake of the human race, destroys the half-finished
female he had been creating. The Monster becomes "a
malignant devil"[16] only after Frankenstein begins to conceive of himself as an agent of God. "I pursued my path
towards the destruction of the daemon," Frankenstein tells
Walton, "more as a task enjoined by heaven, as the me-
chanical impulse of some power of which I was unconscious, than as the ardent desire of my soul."[17] As a
Promethean rebel against God, Victor Frankenstein created his Monster, but it is as God's servant that he undertakes to kill it. Moreover, he believes his commission from
heaven entitles him to sacrifice not only his own life to the
cause of killing the Monster, but also the lives of Walton
and the members of Walton's crew. Surely Frankenstein is
one of the earliest and one of the most terrible of the
century's justified sinners.

The emotion in the reader which these works of rejection, pursuit, and mutual destruction aim at is pathos. We
are meant to mourn the noble intention and the frantic
energy wasted by these rejections of self or of nature. We
are probably meant to believe the words of Frankenstein's
Monster when he says that his "thoughts were once filled
with sublime and transcendent visions of the beauty and
the majesty of goodness." And certainly we are meant to

16 *Frankenstein* (Garden City, N. Y., n.d.), p. 198.
17 *Frankenstein,* p. 183.

conclude that the Monster is sinned against by Victor and by "all human kind," and that it is in this way that "the fallen angel becomes the malignant devil."[18]

Edward Hyde lacked the Monster's literary education; he had neglected his Milton. He was anyway never an angel. According to Stevenson's theory of duality, though, he was originally not a devil either, but a necessary part of Henry Jekyll's and of every man's character. And he could have been a useful part, as well—not when we first meet him; it was already too late by this time; but years earlier, in the days before Jekyll began to live his double life, channeling all his energy into voluptuary pleasures and all his aspirations into a creed of negative virtues.

For Galsworthy was right, as it turns out: Stevenson's *is* the essential theme of romance. But since his allegiance was to the other tradition, perhaps Galsworthy was not the proper man to define this theme, which is not "struggle between the good and the bad, of hero against villain,"[19] but of man and nature and of hero against self. Like *Frankenstein* and the other romances of pursuit, the *Strange Case of Dr. Jekyll and Mr. Hyde* is a story of pathetic waste. It is also the story of a weak man—but not weak because he dabbles irresponsibly with evil, as the American play and the American movies would have it. Henry Jekyll's weakness is like that of every other Stevensonian protagonist we have discussed; it resides entirely in his tragic inability to accept his own nature.

18 *Frankenstein*, p. 198.
19 Romance is concerned with such struggles only in the metaphoric way implied by Northrop Frye. See Chapter I, page 20.

CHAPTER VI

THE DEVIL AND ALL

WHEREVER we look in narrative literature, close relatives with antithetical personalities, particularly pairs of brothers or sisters, have been used as a powerful device for characterization. Indeed, this technique may be said to be the prevailing one in *Genesis,* and it is found in countless legends and fairy tales. Shakespeare's reliance on sibling warfare, in *The Tempest, Hamlet,* and *King Lear,* is so marked as to lead an imaginative critic like Joyce's Stephen Dedalus to speculate upon the playwright's dealings with his own brothers. And such eighteenth century works as *Tom Jones* and *A School for Scandal* give ample evidence that the device has no necessary connection with dualistic psychology or with romantic thought. Indeed, the novels of sentiment especially liked to use one brother or sister as the scientific control, so to speak, against which the other's education or development might be gauged.

As we might expect, such a technique appears almost everywhere in the nineteenth century. Scott, for instance, casts his light and dark heroines as sisters in what is perhaps his major work, *The Heart of Midlothian.* And at the very center of realism, George Eliot, whose favorite device for characterization is a contrasted pair of characters, uses brothers and sisters for this purpose in *Silas Marner,* in *Middlemarch,* and, of course, in *The Mill on the Floss.* Even so confirmed a realist as Arnold Bennet structures his most famous novel, *Old Wives' Tale,* around a contrasted pair of sisters.

The existence of so widespread a practice should make us cautious about hastily regarding pairs of brothers as sets of doubles. On the other hand, the danger is not too great, and a critic with his wits about him will be able to distinguish without much difficulty between the brothers Forsyte and Karamazov. Moreover, it was only natural that writers of the romance tradition should find in this conventional device of warring brothers a ready-made vehicle to express their theories of dualism. Thus one of the earliest works in the tradition, Schiller's play, *Die Räuber,* employs brothers as what Ralph Tymms calls doubles-by-division. And it is quite fitting, though perhaps not quite accurate, that Fyodor Karamazov should see a resemblance between himself and Karl, the more terrible and heroic of the brothers from Schiller's play. Brother or sister doubles were used throughout the century for various purposes: comic effects, as in Twain's *Pudd'nhead Wilson*; political motive, as in Grillparzer's *Ein Bruderzwist in Habsburg*; and for sensational thrills, as in Dumas' *Les Frères Corses.* But more usually they were employed to express the author's psychological vision, as in Melville's *Pierre* and as in the first draft of Shelley's *The Revolt of Islam.*[1]

Stevenson was himself an only child, and perhaps as a consequence of this, very few of his characters have brothers or sisters. We have spoken of Deacon Brodie's sister, but not a single one of those characters we have considered up to this point has a brother. Usually the heroes are without relatives of any sort, for Stevenson, believing as he did that fiction should present a significant simplification of some side or point of life,[2] was careful not to present superfluous characters merely for the sake of

[1] Shelley's first plan, quashed by his fearful publisher, was to make the lovers Laon and Cythia brother and sister.

[2] "A Humble Remonstrance," *Works*, XII, 221.

realism. Consequently, when a Stevenson hero is endowed
with a relative, we do well to take note of the fact.

Often the relatives are rivals. In the fragment *The Owl*,
for instance, the Count des Escherolles and his mysterious
cousin Alain, like the rivals in Hoffmann's story, "The
Doubles," are in love with the same girl. The tale breaks
off soon after the two men confront one another at night in
the home of their beloved, where des Escherolles is a guest
and Alain, the Owl, is a mysterious prowler. The latter
remarks that he and his less terrible cousin are lookalikes,
and he warns him imperiously to flee the house at once.
Yet the relationship is not a simple one of hatred, for in
the next scene, the last in the fragment, the Owl shows regard and concern for his rival's safety.

In the unfinished adventure story *St. Ives,* two cousins
are rivals for an inheritance. This fragment is probably
Stevenson's least distinguished long work, and comes closer
to the worst sort of Alexandre Dumas potboiler than anything previously discussed. Nevertheless, the doubles who
appear in it, Anne and Alain St. Ives, have some points of
interest. These cousins are lookalikes in both face and
stature. Anne can wear clothes tailored exactly from
Alain's measurements. As Anne's valet tells him, "Indeed,
Mr. Anne, you two be very much of a shape" (XIX, 247).
Moreover, they are both spies for Napoleon; although,
curiously, Stevenson presents such an activity as perfectly
respectable and rather noble for Anne, the hero, and yet
absolutely despicable and cowardly for Alain, who is the
villain.

Anne is somewhat more heroic than the other protagonists
we have looked at—perhaps this is why he failed to keep his
author's attention, since the book was left a fragment—but
he does have at least two of the characteristics we have
come to associate with Stevenson's overly self-conscious
heroes. He has a very serious problem of commitment. He

is a French soldier in 1813, despite the fact that he is an aristocrat whose parents and subsequent foster parents, a long series of them, were executed in the Terror. Moreover, while he is a political and military enemy to England, he stands to inherit a very large English estate. And again, Anne has the typical protagonist's fondness for confinement. When we first meet him he is a prisoner of war in Edinburgh. There he leads a rather pleasant life, carving wood figures and giving French lessons to his jailor. As he admits, "I am scarcely drawing the portrait of a very melancholy man. It is not indeed my character; and I had, in a comparison with my comrades, many reasons for content" (xix, 26-27). He breaks prison finally, not to rejoin Napoleon, but to pay a dutiful visit to the sickbed of his dying English uncle.

Alain, on the other hand, is a clear type of the Stevenson villain. Probably he is influenced somewhat by the author's reading of Jules Barbey d'Aurévilly and his philosophy of dandyism,[3] although it is possible that Stevenson simply recalled Richardson's Lovelace or Etherege's Dorimant. Alan Breck Stewart, we recall, was also something of a dandy, for the artist and the savage and the criminal are always close together in Stevenson's fiction. With Alain St. Ives, however, who is "perhaps the biggest rogue now extant" (xix, 75), real evil and dandyism are much more clearly connected:

> Somehow, he commands an atmosphere; he has a spacious manner; and he has kept up, all through life, such a volume of racket about his personality, with his chaises and his racers and his dicings, and I know not what—that somehow he imposes! It seems, when the farce is done, and he locked in the Fleet prison—and nobody

[3] Stevenson proclaimed himself "a Barbey d'Aurévillyan" in 1893, while he was writing St. Ives. Letter to Sidney Colvin, June 6, 1893, Works, XXIII, 250.

left but Buonaparte and Lord Wellington and the Het-
man Platoff to make a work about—the world will be in
a comparison quite tranquil. (XIX, 269)

The chapter in which Alain first appears is called "The
Devil and All at Amersham Place."

Again, the most interesting features of the romance are
the attitudes the doubles take to one another. Alain's
feelings about Anne are simple and straightforward—"I
warn you that the day when I set my foot on your neck, the
spine shall break" (XIX, 281-282). But Anne's reactions are
more complicated. He would like, first of all, to deny the
association with Alain entirely. His cousin's appearance
upsets him. "He was lividly pale, and his lip was caught up
in a smile that could almost be called a snarl, of a sheer,
arid malignity that appalled me." And, like the Count des
Escherolles in *The Owl*, Anne is, at first, reluctant to admit
his cousin's physical resemblance to himself. Thus he
writes, "It is out of the question that I should deny the resemblance altogether, since it has been remarked by so
many different persons whom I cannot reasonably accuse
of a conspiracy. As a matter of fact, I saw little of it and confessed to nothing" (XIX, 276). Yet when Anne sees his cousin
humiliated and disinherited (in Anne's own favor, it
should be stated), his identification with Alain is immediate. "I confess," he writes, "my heart was already almost
altogether on the side of my insulted and unhappy
cousin. . . . At that moment I loathed both my uncle and
the lawyer for their cold-blooded cruelty" (XIX, 288-289).

Alain chases his double throughout the chapters of the
fragment in typical pursuit story fashion, and the notes for
the conclusion called for a final confrontation between the
pair. It is foolish to wish that Stevenson had finished so
bad a story as *St. Ives*; he did much better to drop it and
work instead on *Weir of Hermiston*. Nevertheless, if the

book had been finished, we might know a little more about Stevenson's use of the double. As it is, however, the scene mentioned in Stevenson's outline appears in the workman-like ending that Sir Arthur Quiller-Couch supplied, but, unfortunately, Anne and Alain do not appear there as doubles; they are simply conventional hero and villain.

Kidnapped also contains such a rivalry. There the two brothers, Alexander and Ebenezer Balfour, David's father and uncle, are contestants for both a woman *and* an estate. Ebenezer was the wilder and more romantic of the two. As a youth he had "a fine gallant air; people stood in their doors to look after him, as he went by on a mettle horse. . . . Nor was that all, but he had a spirit of his own that seemed to promise great things in the future. In 1715, what must he do but run away to join the rebels" (IX, 316) . Yet in spite of his gallant spirit, Ebenezer Balfour comes to terms. He allows the rivalry to be ended by taking the estate for himself and thereby resigning to his brother all interest in the woman they have both loved.

This little background plot in the adventures of David Balfour shows an influence from the most skillfully de-veloped of all the double stories, *Wuthering Heights,* which makes perhaps better use and keeps more careful track of blood lines than any other work of the century. Ebenezer's estate, the house of Shaws, is clearly modeled on the old Earnshaw mansion which Lockwood describes in the first chapters of Emily Brontë's romance. Both houses are old and in ill repair, ruled by close-fisted men who are hated and feared by their neighbors. Moreover, David Balfour is treated with the same discourtesy at Shaws as Lockwood encounters at the Heights. When the latter sug-gests that he be permitted to sleep in the sitting room, Heathcliff answers, "No, no! A stranger is a stranger, be he rich or poor—it will not suit me to permit anyone the

range of the place while I am off guard."[4] Similarly Ebenezer Balfour locks his nephew David into his room for the
night, and on the next morning, since he himself has an
errand to perform in the town, Ebenezer orders David un-
ceremoniously from the house. "I canna leave you by
yoursel' in the house. . . . I'll have to lock you out" (IX, 39) .[5]

Heathcliff has degenerated into the character Lockwood
encounters in 1801 because of the role which the circumstances of the story had forced him to assume. Ebenezer
Balfour's nature has also undergone radical change. When
we meet the once gallant young man, he is a dried-up old
miser, a Lowlander villain, one of the least attractive characters in all of Stevenson. Moreover, according to the
lawyer Rankeillor, who tells Ebenezer's story, the change
in him was also wrought by the part he had to play, by the
mean bargain he had made with his brother. The lawyer
explains:

> He could not think that he had played a handsome part.
> Those who knew the story gave him the cold shoulder;
> those who knew it not, seeing one brother disappear, and
> the other succeed in the estate, raised a cry of murder;
> so that upon all sides he found himself evicted. Money
> was all he got by his bargain; well, he came to think the
> more of money. (IX, 318)

Thus abstracted from the more colorful adventures of
Kidnapped, this small vignette may be seen as a practice
piece for Stevenson's major completed romance, *The Master of Ballantrae.* Here again, two brothers contend for a
woman and an inheritance, and here again a man's nature
is inevitably altered by the bargains he makes.

[4] *Wuthering Heights* (New York, 1960), p. 15.
[5] If we wish to look farther back in the tradition, it is likely that
the situations in Stevenson and Brontë both stem from the opening
chapters of *Melmoth the Wanderer,* where John Melmoth arrives at the
ramshackle house of his miserly uncle.

The influence of *Wuthering Heights* is evident also in this story, although with certain necessary modifications. In both works the cuckoo, the man without natural rights, succeeds to the estate and to the hand of the woman. And as in the dual plot of *Wuthering Heights,* the plot involving the second generation of characters, the woman wishes to give herself to one man because she loves him and to the other for the sake of pity and for the relief of her conscience. "I bring you no love, Henry," Alison Graeme says as she offers herself in marriage, "but God knows, all the pity in the world" (XIV, 41). In both works, one rival disappears as though from the face of the earth, only to return more formidable, more evil, and more revengeful than he departed. This man, moreover, is dark and diabolical, and tries in both stories to get at his enemy by subtly and treacherously undermining him with his wife and his child. Even the terms of contempt are similar. Henry Durie castigates himself as "the cipherer," while Heathcliff scorns Edgar as "the cipher at the Grange."[6]

But, of course, there are differences, as well; differences which are more instructive perhaps than the similarities. In Stevenson, we must never expect the savage to overcome the civilized man. Imagine, for instance, David Balfour outfaced by Alan as Edgar Linton is by Heathcliff. Neither must we expect the civilized man in Stevenson to possess so much beauty as he does in Brontë. Again Stevenson insists on the difference between the Englishman and the Lowland Scot. Henry Durie is unlovely and unloved, while his savage brother James has all the good looks and all the clever lines. Nevertheless, with these important modifications, Henry and James Durie act out a variant on the *Wuthering Heights* drama of Edgar Linton and Heathcliff. What stamps *The Master of Ballantrae* as characteristically Stevenson's is the fact that Henry, who corresponds

[6] *Wuthering Heights,* p. 220.

to the weak and helpless Edgar, emerges quite distinctly as the protagonist, and, indeed, as the tragic victor.

The narration, we have already noted, is handled similarly in the two romances. The Chevalier de Burke, a moral featherweight like Isabella Linton, is attracted at first to James Durie's fascinating villainy. And again, as with Isabella, Burke's infatuation changes to horrified rejection once he discovers that James means to treat him with the same amoral cruelty and indifference with which he has treated the rest of the world. Each narrator embraces what he takes to be a typical romantic figure, a seemingly bad man with a heart of gold beneath a rough exterior, and each recoils as from a serpent. Moreover, turning to the principal narrators of the two stories, Nelly Dean and Ephraim Mackellar, we note that both are faithful servants who give all of their own loyalty, and consequently turn a good deal of ours, to their masters. Mackellar is Henry's man and James' enemy from the very first moment. Nelly, although she has been brought up in the Earnshaw household, considers herself irrevocably a Linton.

All the narrators we have considered are essential to both romances. Without the sympathy which Nelly and Mackellar afford them, Edgar Linton and Henry Durie might appear to the reader as despicably weak; on the other hand, without their rejections by Isabella and by Burke, Heathcliff and James might look to us like typical Victorian translations of the Byronic hero, with one single vice and a thousand redeeming virtues.

But perhaps in Stevenson's story, these uninvolved narrators are not skillfully enough handled, and the narrators' distortions are too easily mistaken for the author's. Perhaps this is why so many critics have seen this romance as another of Stevenson's good versus evil allegories. Unfortunately, such an analysis will not take us very far into the meaning of the work. Henry Durie, as we shall see, is even less of a St. George figure than were the other protagonists.

Only the wicked brother, James, could find a proper home in a morality play. With him, there can be no question of narrator distortion, for James Durie is purely evil, far more wicked, in fact, even than Heathcliff. If we find James at all attractive, as even Mackellar does, it is perhaps because "Hell may have noble flames" (xiv, 353). James would himself offer a more perverse motivation. In *The Young Chevalier*, another work in which he appears, he reasons that "the height of beauty is in the touch that's wrong, that's the modulation in a tune. 'Tis the devil we all love; I owe many a conquest to my mole. . . . We are all hunchbacks, and beauty is only that kind of deformity that I happen to admire" (xviii, 419). And if his beauty is not a virtue, then James has no redeeming qualities at all. Stevenson called him "an INCUBUS"[7] and "all I know of the devil."[8] He fits perfectly the definition of the evil man which Stevenson applied to Hyde: he is malicious, cruel, and selfish. Mackellar will not hear of it, but perhaps he is even cowardly, as his flight from Alan Breck Stewart and his moment of panic in the Adirondacks may be intended to prove. At only one point in the story, during his voyage to New York with Mackellar, does he begin to look like the Victorian Byronic villain, the victim of a cruel Fate; but we are brought around quickly when James coolly admits that it was indeed part of his villainy to create this pathetic impression. He had set himself the task of winning the sympathy of Mackellar, his brother's strongest advocate. "I never yet failed to charm a person when I wanted; even you," James boasts. Then he shows his teeth: "Judge by

[7] Letter to James, Mar. 1888, *Henry James and Robert Louis Stevenson*, p. 171.

[8] Letter to Colvin, Dec. 24, 1887, *Works*, XXII, 57.

this little interlude how dangerous I am; and tell those fools . . . to think twice and thrice before they set me at defiance" (xiv, 284). This charm of his may strike us as a virtue, but if it does, so should Satan's in the Garden of Eden. Leslie Fiedler is perfectly correct when he writes there is no question of James "having some good qualities and some bad; it is his essential quality, his absolute evil, that is *at once* repellent and attractive."[9]

Unlike even Edward Hyde, James Durie has nothing of the voluptuary in his nature. As Quartermaster aboard the pirate ship he dispenses rum to the other men, but he keeps perfectly sober himself. He "had the name in the country of 'an unco man for the lasses' " (xiv, 27), but his one recorded sexual adventure, which took place before the action of the story began, is intended to show the Master's cruelty rather than his weakness for women: he abandons his mistress without provision of support; later he beats her with his cane. Only twice during his wanderings does he speak of his fiancée, Alison Graeme: first in a fit of envy directed at his brother—"he courts my wife" (xiv, 107)—and again to note that she owns extensive property in the province of New York (xiv, 107). In no way is his evil related to what Stevenson would have called the sense of joy in life. Even the hellish pleasure Hyde felt when mauling Danvers Carew's body is absent from James Durie's malice.

Chesterton writes that the "episode of Blackbeard" in *The Master of Ballantrae* is "a sort of fizzling anticlimax, spluttering like the blue matches in that fool's hat. Such a shoddy person had no claim to be so much as mentioned in that spiritual tragedy of the terrible twin spirits; the brothers Durrisdeer."[10] Artistically speaking, Chesterton is undoubtedly right: the pirate section creates an unfortu-

9 *"The Master of Ballantrae,"* p. 289.
10 *Robert Louis Stevenson,* p. 130.

nate change of tone in the story. But whatever the effect, Stevenson's motive for including the pirates is certainly valid enough; he wanted to contrast the childish, exuberant, largely ineffectual wickedness of the pirates with the Master's much more serious evil.[11] It is a question of trivial hellhound against devil. James handles Blackbeard like the child he is, actually ordering the blustering pirate captain to go below to his cabin when he misbehaves. James, indeed, masters him, and eventually betrays him, as he betrays nearly every other character in the romance. Often in Stevenson, evil and innocence are seen to be paradoxically connected; James Durie is one of the few Stevenson villains whose wickedness is presented in strictly Christian terms. His evil is sophisticated, prideful, joyless, and fully conscious. He is related to the serpent in the tree of the knowledge of good and evil—he is actually referred to once as Satan in *Paradise Lost* (xiv, 236). Emphatically, he is not related to Stevenson's probably arboreal ancestor, whom we shall meet in the next chapter.

In all other respects, the Master is like most of Stevenson's savages. He operates free of any kind of moral constraint. "I have always done exactly as I felt inclined" (xiv, 70), he says at one point in the story, and at another, "I go my own way with inevitable motion" (xiv, 131). Like Deacon Brodie, he believes that the essential nature of man is evil and that all virtue is a hypocritical disguise. "I am a pretty bad fellow, at bottom," he says, "and I find the pretence of virtues very irksome." Therefore, he suggests to the Chevalier Burke, "let us each dare to be ourselves like savages" (xiv, 67). His practice of settling all questions of choice by tossing a coin is calculated "to express . . . [his] scorn of human reason" (xiv, 108). And this scorn makes him, like so many of Stevenson's antagonists—Sir Daniel, James More Macgregor, Alain St. Ives, Madame von Rosen,

[11] See Leslie Fiedler, "*The Master of Ballantrae*," p. 288.

Alan Breck Stewart—absolutely inconsistent in his political allegiances. James begins the romance as an officer in the Stuart army; later he is a spy for the Whigs. Of course, like all of the savages, he is capable of any amount of energy and action. Stevenson even contemplated using him like Madame von Rosen or Alan Breck as the *deus ex machina* who was to save the hero of *The Young Chevalier*.[12]

David Daiches writes that "the Master is Long John Silver given psychological reality and subtlety—the attractive bad man."[13] Certainly there are many points of similarity. The image of maimed masterfulness, supposed by Stevenson to be the essence of Silver, applies to James as well. The inaccurate title, *Master* of Ballantrae, serves to remind us of the man's power and pride. And while the closest the handsome James Durie comes to physical deformity is in the mole on his cheek, Mackellar reports that "sometimes my gorge rose against him as though he were deformed" (XIV, 263). Both Durie and Silver, moreover, began as quartermasters and then rose to become captains of pirate crews, and in each case the differences between their own natures and the wild and ineffectual natures of other pirates is emphatically presented.

In another sense, however, James is not so subtle, or at least not so complex a character as Silver. James Durie is not a man of substance. If he has bank accounts, which is unlikely, they have certainly been overdrawn a number of times. James is, as a matter of fact, the most simplified major character in all of Stevenson. He has nothing of the civilized man in him, and as we have seen, he differs from the other savages only in that he lacks some of the elements of their character, notably their voluptuary passions. None of this is said in dispraise of Stevenson's creation. Stevenson was aiming, let us always remember, at "significant simpli-

12 Letter to Colvin, March 9, 1892, *Works*, XXIII, 49.
13 *Robert Louis Stevenson*, p. 81.

fication," and that the "INCUBUS" James Durie, who is called the devil on nearly every other page, comes across to some readers as a rather convincing eighteenth century character is perhaps one of Stevenson's highest artistic achievements.

In *Wuthering Heights*, Edgar Linton and Heathcliff are meant to represent the poles of a single mind, Catherine Earnshaw's mind. The allegory, however, is not of good and evil, but, like most of the allegories we have seen in Stevenson, of civilized and savage. Heathcliff, like Edward Hyde, is a wild man who turns positively evil; Edgar, like David Balfour, is a civilized man who freezes into paralysis. Emily Brontë's sister Charlotte presents the same kind of dichotomies in *Jane Eyre, Villette,* and in a number of the Angrian stories. But while Stevenson's duality is usually Brontëan, there is a significant difference in *The Master of Ballantrae,* for, as we have just finished seeing, James Durie is not a bestial frog prince who can be redeemed by a kiss from enthusiastic Catherine or passionate Jane, nor can he be maimed forever by a rejection. He is a static figure, incapable of becoming more evil, because as we have just seen, his evil is pure and absolute at the outset.

On the other hand, while it is perfectly proper to regard the other Durie brother, Henry, as a good man (for at least in the early part of the romance, he is as good a man as Stevenson found it possible to conceive) Henry is never virtuous enough to stand for Good in a moral allegory. James' character has only one facet to it, it has been got out clean, as Stevenson would say, without a single distracting embellishment.[14] Henry Durie, however, is quite another matter; he is the most complex figure to appear in Stevenson's fiction. His problem, moreover, is a perplexing

[14] Stevenson wrote to Colvin in August 1892, "I have in nearly all my works been trying one racket: to get out the facts of life as clean and naked and sharp as I could manage it *(Works,* XXVI, 501).

one, worthy of a Kafka or a Dostoyevsky: It concerns what happens to a rather ordinary young man, "neither very bad nor yet very able, but an honest, solid sort of lad like many of his neighbours" (xiv, 28) who discovers quite gradually that his brother is the Devil. Basically, this is the same question we have been tracing throughout Stevenson. The difference is simply that *The Master of Ballantrae* gives this problem its fullest and most dramatic treatment.

We have said that Henry is not virtuous enough to represent Good in a moral allegory; neither is he static enough. Henry's character is in the process of change throughout the action. And, indeed, these changes are the best part of the story's vision. In the course of his adventures we shall see Henry driven to both extremes of his nature. But in the beginning, he is, as we have just said, a "solid sort of lad like many of his neighbours." When the rebellion of 1745 breaks out, he is as anxious as his brother to join the forces of Charles Stuart. Perhaps he is even more anxious, for he understands the consequences to himself should James be attainted. Thus he tells his brother: "If you go, and the expedition fails, we divide the right and the title. . . . I shall be left in such a situation as no man of sense and honour could endure" (xiv, 30). He acquits himself in the first scene with both strength and spirit.

Nevertheless, James has his way. He is permitted to join the rebels, while Henry is forced to remain home and pretend loyalty to the Whigs. The result is exactly as Henry feared. After the false report of James' death, Alison, who is soon to become Henry's wife, blames Henry for "sitting there in safety when his brother lay dead" (xiv, 35). The neighbors throw stones at him and call him "the Judis" (xiv, 37), and even James, when he reappears from the dead for the first time, addresses his brother, "My dear Jacob" (xiv, 113). The consequence, even though he did not accept the bargain but had it forced on him, is that Henry becomes a good, exacting businessman, a staunch guardian of the family reputation, and a dutiful doer of good, who insists on receipts for his charity.

Up to this point Henry's case is much like Edgar Linton's. Both men have been given ignoble parts to play, and their natures shrink accordingly. But the change in Henry's character is not entirely caused by circumstances. Nor is it caused by stupid misunderstandings either. Mackellar, who we should remember is Henry's partisan, likes to point out the ironies of his master's bad reputation— that he is accused of ambition at the very moment he tries desperately to insure his not succeeding to his brother's title, that he gains his worst reputation for miserliness while he is ruining his estate in an effort to satisfy James' every unjust demand for money. But Henry is not acting nobly or generously in either of these instances. One of the reasons for his attempt to thwart James' plan of joining the rebels is his jealousy. The motive slips out in the heat of argument. "It is your duty to be here with my father," Henry says. "You know well enough you are the favourite." The Master replies, and with some justice, "And there spoke Envy! Would you trip up my heels—Jacob?" (xiv, 30). Moreover, the large sums of money which James later gets from Henry are given in a similar spirit of hatred.

> "They think it only natural. I have shameful proclivities. I am a niggardly dog," and he drove his knife up to the hilt. "But I will show that fellow," he cried with an oath, "I will show him which is the more generous."

At this point even Mackellar is driven to comment, "This is no generosity . . . this is only pride" (xiv, 120). And Henry finally develops into another Ebenezer Balfour only after he believes he has killed James and has thus fully satisfied his hatred. In the delirium which follows the duel between the two brothers, Henry babbles "of the garden, the salmon nets, and . . . continually of his affairs, ciphering figures and holding disputation with the tenantry" (XIV, 192).

When Alison Graeme tells Henry that he was a traitor to James in his heart, she is speaking the truth on two levels. On one hand, Henry hated the actual James, and on the other, he hated a part of his own character which he roughly equated to James. All of Stevenson's conscientious heroes have, as we have seen, some residue of a wild or savage nature from which they shrink. Richard Shelton had a strong appetite for action, at least until it was set down before him. Loudon Dodd, on his way to the wreck, positively looked forward to bloodshed. And even David Balfour, the purest of Stevenson's Lowlanders, felt his heart thrill when he saw uniformed men marching. Similarly Henry Durie sighs when he happens to see a party of smugglers, and in his painful isolation wishes he could join "these lawless companions" (XIV, 45). On the other side of fascination, however, there is always repulsion, and Henry despises and rejects the lawless smuggler whom he recognizes both within his heart and outside of it.

But the rejection works differently in *The Master of Ballantrae* than in the other works. Henry does not hate his brother's wickedness only because he is repelled by, or ashamed of it. And he does not turn aside from his own active nature because he is convinced of the futility of all action. These have been the causes of life-resignation which we have examined heretofore. Henry has a stronger constitution than the others, and the psychology that motivates him is more subtle. Mackellar writes that when Henry had moved to his Lowland extreme, "it seemed he had set out to justify his brother's calumnies; as though he was bent to prove himself a man of a dry nature, immersed in money-getting" (XIV, 192).

This is what Henry, at least subconsciously, has been attempting right along: "to justify his brother's calumnies." One of the strongest features of his character, as of the character of Henry Jekyll, is self-hatred. The part of him that wants to join the smugglers, to live the lawless life, hates the part of him that ciphers figures. And a great deal of Henry's patience in accepting affronts—a patience for which, to complicate matters, he despises himself—is to be read in this light. So is his statement, "The weakness of my ground . . . lies in myself, that I am not one who engages love" (XIV, 159).

We have encountered this attitude towards self once before in Stevenson's fiction when we examined *Prince Otto*. The earlier work was written at the time when Stevenson was least content with his own political morality. It is probably also worth noting that the bulk of *The Master of Ballantrae* was composed when Stevenson was most troubled over problems of personal honesty. During the writing of the romance, Henley sent the foolish letter that accused Fanny of plagiarism; almost at the same time, Stevenson himself promised to write for McClure after he had signed an exclusive contract with Scribner's. Henley's charge brought about the end of a long and very close friendship, and it disturbed Stevenson so much that he was obliged to take opium for relief.[15] Stevenson's concern over the doubledealing with Scribner's is reflected in a letter to J. A. Symonds, where he writes, "It is hard work to sleep; it is hard to be told you are a liar, and have to hold your peace, and think, 'Yes, by God, and a thief too!' "[16] Certainly a great deal of Stevenson's own torment, self-doubt, and self-hatred is mirrored in Henry Durie's character.

But with Henry, the situation is more complicated than with Stevenson; for just as the smuggler in him despises the

---

[15] *RLS: Stevenson's Letters to Charles Baxter*, Apr. 5, 1888, p. 201.
[16] Letter to J. A. Symonds, Nov. 21, 1887, *Works*, XXII, 43.

cipherer of figures, so Henry, the whole man, bitterly re-
sents the smuggler's contempt. This is an odd twist for
Stevenson. In *Jekyll and Hyde*, remember, Hyde grew to
hate Jekyll because he resented the latter's disapproval of
him, and this disapproval pushed Hyde farther towards
the extreme of pure evil and wildness. In *The Master of
Ballantrae* the exact opposite occurs, for here it is the conscientious man who reacts to the smuggler's contempt and
who is consequently pushed towards the other end of his
character, to the extreme of meanness. What we have, in
effect, is the lawless man acting as a kind of a jeering, insulting conscience; a Freudian turnabout perhaps, but a
very effective dramatization of Stevenson's continual discom-
fort at the passive solutions of his overcivilized heroes.

Henry externalizes the smuggler in the person of James,
who has, indeed, provided most of the barbs with which
Henry habitually wounds himself. The smuggler's attitude
towards the cipherer and James' attitude towards Henry
are perfect replicas of one another. On the night of the
duel, James' contempt for Henry reaches its high point;
yet James says nothing of Henry which Henry has not previously said or thought of himself. James calls Henry a
lourdeau.

"A *lourdeau*, my dear brother, is as we might say a bump-
kin, a clown, a clodpole: a fellow without grace, light-
ness, quickness; any gift of pleasing, any natural
brilliancy: such a one as you shall see, when you desire,
by looking in the mirror. . . . Do you not see the applica-
bility of the epithet I have just explained, dear Henry?
Let me show you. For instance, with all those solid qualities which I delight to recognise in you, I never knew a
woman who did not prefer me—nor, I think," he continued, with the most silken deliberation, "I think—who
did not continue to prefer me." (xiv, 162-163)

Later when Mackellar describes the quarrel to Alison and the old Lord Durrisdeer, he will present Henry as a man carried away by anger at this insult to his wife. But the scene as Mackellar narrates it stresses Henry's coolness and deliberation. It is the Master who is moved to Satanic rage. After Henry's blow, "The Master sprang to his feet like one transfigured; I had never seen the man so beautiful. 'A blow!' he cried. 'I would not take a blow from God Almighty.' " Henry answers these Melvillean heroics in a much calmer tone. " 'Lower your voice,' said Mr. Henry. 'Do you wish my father to interfere for you again?' " Moreover, the blow was delivered "with neither hurry nor any particular violence." A moment later Henry says of it, "It was the most deliberate act of my life" (XIV, 163-164). Henry is acting as a whole man throughout the quarrel and the duel. His behavior is indeed deliberate, carefully thought out, perhaps even premeditated. Previously he had tried to destroy the Master with evidence and argument: he had produced letters demonstrating that James was a Whig spy. But the Master's charm had been ample proof against logic and truth. Henry has determined now to get rid of his brother; he has been simply waiting for a proper justification. "Some method must be found, Mackellar," he has said only the day before, "some way must be found. . . . I am far past anger now" (XIV, 159).

But the killing of James represents even more than the murder of a brother. Henry is trying to eliminate his interior critic as well as the critic's physical manifestation. The situation is again analogous to *Jekyll and Hyde*, and it is significant that Henry's blow is delivered on the Master's mouth and that eight or ten years later he will say in his prayer, "Smite him, O Lord, upon the lying mouth!" (XIV, 211). At the conclusion of the story, moreover, Henry will force James literally to swallow his offending tongue.

Such a rejection of self is as bound to fail in *The Master of Ballantrae* as it did in the *Strange Case of Dr. Jekyll and Mr. Hyde*. It is particularly bound to fail in *Ballantrae* because it was an element of the smuggler—Henry's hatred for James—which motivated the experiment in the first place. Consequently, although Henry can be a pure cipherer while his fevered delirium lasts; when at length the sickness passes, he stands forth as predominantly the smuggler, in the same way that Jekyll, after the experiment, stood forth as Hyde. His hatred for James continues, but paradoxically he begins now to resemble his brother. We remind ourselves at this point that Henry has been stepping into James' shoes from the start of the romance. Previously he had taken his brother's bride and his estate. After the duel he was gratified to hear his father call him "My son" (xiv, 183) for the first time. But now he begins to assume James' character. He becomes more lively, he refuses to dwell on painful matters, and he turns slack in business affairs. Although he still believes that he has murdered his brother, he feels no guilt. The civilized paralysis has entirely passed, and Henry develops now into the kind of master who beats his servants. We have already seen Henry move to one extreme of his character; what we witness now is his progress to the other pole. The pillar of respectability, whom we observed at the halfway point in the story, is on his way to becoming "a poor, muddled toper" (xiv, 317), who thrives on hatred. Both poles, it seems hardly necessary to repeat, are of the same character, and both have been present from the start.

Henry begins now not only to resemble James, but indeed even to affect his family in the same ways which James had. In the early part of the story Mackellar delivered two lectures: one to Alison, on the coldness with which she treated Henry, and a second to the old Lord Durrisdeer on the partiality he showed for James. In the latter part of the story Mackellar must take Henry to task, on one occasion, for his coldness to Alison and on another for his absorption in his son Alexander and his consequent neglect of his daughter Katharine. Mackellar and Alison both fear that Henry is breeding another James in Alexander, and while this fear is never fully justified, it is certain that Henry is breeding another Master in himself. He remains a whole man for some time yet—Mackellar can usually bring him around to some sort of repentance—and it is not until very late in the book, when Henry literally loses his reason, that the two brothers are exactly alike.

Nevertheless, Henry's degeneration is continual, and the engine that develops the Master in him is his hatred, again as in *Jekyll and Hyde*. Near the middle of the story, Henry justifies and builds this enmity by a belief that the Master is not only diabolical, but quite literally the devil. He brings his son to the spot where the duel took place and tells him of "a man whom the devil tried to kill, and how near he came to kill the devil instead" (xiv, 209). Nor is he speaking in metaphor. His belief in the Master's supernatural character is perfectly serious:

Nothing can kill that man. He is not mortal. He is bound upon my back to all eternity—to all God's eternity! . . . Wherever I am, there will he be. (xiv, 203)

And the greater the hatred grows, of course, the more completely Henry creates himself as a reflection of his brother. In the New York scenes of the romance, when he has it in his power to destroy James, Henry begins to go out into society for the first time. He becomes so happy and so healthy that Mackellar begins to suspect he keeps a mistress. But, as Mackellar discovers, "it was hatred and not love that gave him healthful colours" (xiv, 294-295). Henry boasts, "I grow fat upon it" (xiv, 295). Moreover, now Henry no longer worries about the family reputation. Formerly this lack of concern had characterized James. Time and again he had extorted money by playing on Henry's almost morbid fear of a family scandal. In the New York scenes James tries this weapon once more: he opens a tailor shop in order to embarrass his respectable relatives. Alison is indeed properly mortified, but Henry positively glories in his brother's and indirectly in his own degradation. He spends each morning sitting outside his brother's shop, "tasting" the Master's neighborhood. "If any of my lord's friends went by, he would hail them cheerfully, and cry out he was there to give some good advice to his brother, who was now (to his delight) grown quite industrious" (XIV, 296).

Here in this war of wills over the tailor shop James admits for the first time that Henry has beaten him. Actually the tables have been turning for some time, and the sympathy we begin to feel for the Master in the last chapters does not stem from any improvement in his character—he still hopes to destroy his brother if he can—but from our growing recognition that he is being matched now with another wild and evil force, fully as destructive as his own. And since Henry is not completely deranged, James is even overmatched, for a little civilization, as we have seen a number of times now, serves only to make a savage more formidable. Henry is particularly dangerous, for, like Victor Frankenstein and the other justified sinners, he has set out piously on a holy war to destroy his devil.

Stevenson had not intended us to pity James. Even after he began composition, he wrote that the action of the story was supposed to lead up to "the death of the elder brother at the hands of the younger in a perfectly cold-blooded murder, of which I wish (and mean) the reader to approve."[17] Henry Durie, however, grew in the writing until he became, as Walter Allen states, "one of the most absorb-

17 Letter to Henry James, Mar. 1888, *Henry James and Robert Louis Stevenson*, p. 171.

ing psychological studies of degradation in our fiction."[18] Consequently, our sympathies are all with James as we see how easily he can be duped into going to the wilderness with a band of cutthroats whom his brother has hired to be his murderers, and as we note how gleefully Henry looks forward to the issue.

The last two chapters of *The Master of Ballantrae* have always been the most highly criticized. We have already seen that Stevenson apologized for them long before they were written.[19] In a similar vein, his wife explains the difficult conditions in Honolulu under which they were composed.[20] Stevenson's fears were that the flight through the American wilderness might prove too picturesque, and that the Master's final death-and-resurrection would jar the reader's suspension of disbelief if it depended entirely on supernatural occurrences. This second problem he tried to solve by introducing the Master's servant, Secundra Dass— even Jos Sedley of *Vanity Fair* had come back to England with a faithful Indian servant—and by explaining the "death," as Hawthorne might have done, as a Yogi tongue-swallowing trick. It was not supposed to be magic at all, if you prefer, since it depended upon the climate for its success or failure and since, after all, it did not work. Nevertheless, as Morton Zabel explains, "*The Master of Ballantrae* has become for its critics a typical example of the conflict of the realist and the fabulist in its author's talent."[21]

But the critics do Stevenson very doubtful service when they jettison the ending of *Ballantrae* in order to salvage the rest of the book, along with *Weir of Hermiston,* for the realistic tradition. *Hermiston,* these critics thank God, was

[18] *The English Novel* (London, 1954), p. 270.
[19] See Chapter I, pp. 34-35.
[20] Fanny Stevenson, "Prefatory Note" to *The Master of Ballantrae, Works,* XIV, 3-8.
[21] "Introduction," *The Two Major Novels,* p. xx.

left without an ending to apologize for. But this is a false approach; after failing with *Prince Otto*, Stevenson never practiced realism, and *The Master of Ballantrae*, of all his works, certainly never set itself up to be a realistic novel. If it had, then the whole character of James Durie would have been strangely out of place in it. Moreover, the highly romantic duel by candlelight and the chapter on piracy at the beginning of the book are far from realistic and should be ample preparation for a handful of American Indians and a single mystery of the Orient. The flight, the highly-pitched incidents, the wilderness locale, the mixture of races, the tendency to send the characters racing about the globe, all these are conventions of the tradition of the pursuit romance in which *The Master of Ballantrae* unmistakably partakes. We find these elements quite natural in *Frankenstein, The Scarlet Letter, Moby Dick,* and in Marryat's *The Phantom Ship,* which, after all, Stevenson claimed as the immediate influence on his story (XIV, 15).

One feels that what most of the critics found objectionable in the last chapters of the book, however, was not so much the picturesque scenery or even what David Daiches calls the trick conclusion, but the seeming ambiguity of the action. For both intellectually and morally, in the last chapters the story swims out of the grasp of the critic who has continued to regard it either as a realistic novel or as an allegory of good and evil. Even the most stubborn moralist can no longer maintain that Henry Durie, who has degenerated into a hate-filled, self-pitying, drunken sot, whom even Mackellar begins "to shrink from" (XIV, 358), is Stevenson's representation of the good angel.[22] Melvin Orth presents the difficulty of such critics when he wonders, "If

[22] Lettice Cooper writes that Henley and Leslie Stephen "were displeased because the good man was not more attractive" (*Robert Louis Stevenson,* p. 77).

evil is to be destroyed by good working through evil, is good, then, so desirable a characteristic?"[23]

David Daiches believes that the story ends as it does so that Stevenson may "force a solution to a situation which is in fact insoluble. He had delved too deeply into character and destiny to be able to come easily again to the surface."[24] The ending was, as we have seen, carefully planned before Stevenson began the writing. Nevertheless, Daiches has put his finger on Stevenson's primary failing as a writer of fiction, a failing which, as we have seen, Stevenson himself recognized since the time of *Prince Otto*. Daiches writes:

It seems that always in the last analysis, Stevenson shied away from the full implications of his tragic vision. In some of his short stories he could sustain it, but in a novel of any length, where the narrative line had to carry the surface interest to the end, he tended to bend the line towards its conclusion with an almost ironic shrug, which corresponded, on the level of art, to what superficial observers considered to be his optimism on the level of life. Just as his optimism represented a quietly wry acceptance of the inevitable, thus masking a profound pessimism, so even his apparently lighthearted works often represent a shrugging off of the tragic vision.[25]

This criticism is valid for almost every one of Stevenson's romances. Recall for a moment the long series of casual resignations from life which we encountered in the second and third chapters of this study. And, one fears, the criticism would also have been valid for *Weir of Hermiston*,

[23] "Robert Louis Stevenson as a Novelist" (diss. Univ. of Colorado, 1953), p. 130.
[24] "Introduction," *Robert Louis Stevenson* (Laurel Reader edition, New York, 1959), p. 16.
[25] *Ibid.*, pp. 16-17.

if that work had been completed. *The Master of Ballantrae,* however, is the one full-length work of Stevenson's to which Daiches' observation does not apply. There is no shrugging off of the tragic vision here. The story ends in the only way it could end: with Henry's murder of his brother and the death which that murder brings to Henry himself, a simultaneous death like those in "The Merry Men" and in *Dr. Jekyll and Mr. Hyde.*

Henry is killed by the momentary flutter of the Master's eyelids, which is the last act of James Durie's life, but confirmation enough for Henry of his belief that "nothing can kill that man." James, on the other hand, is killed not by his brother in the final stage of his disintegration, but by the machinery which Henry had set in motion when he had something of his reason left, when he was still a man with two parts to his nature, something of a "Highlander civilised." In his final stage, Henry, except that he is less attractive, is indistinguishable from his brother. He has the will to evil, but, since he is another wolf now, he lacks the stamina to make his evil effective. He is "a maimed soldier, looking vainly for discharge, lingering derided in the line of battle" (XIV, 357). The party of hired murderers, however, which contains at least one canny Scot with all his wits about him, represents Henry the whole man. So it is actually a Henry no longer in existence who murders his brother.

The party of murderers is analogous to the group of bystanders in *Jekyll and Hyde.* Again there is a circle of hateful faces, this time around a campfire in the American wilderness, and again the lawless man, like Satan, is terrified, but tries to brave it out. James, aware now of the plot, attempts to convince the murderers to depose their leader and follow him instead. In *Jekyll and Hyde* the fiercest member of the group that attacked Hyde was the normally unemotional Edinburgh doctor. In *The Master of Ballantrae,* James' most serious opponent is again an Edinburgher. James almost succeeds in seducing the wilder of the killers, "but the rock he split upon was Hastie. This fellow was not well liked, being sour and slow, with an ugly, glowering disposition, but he had studied some time for the Church at Edinburgh College, before ill-conduct had destroyed his prospects, and he now remembered and applied what he had learned" (XIV, 337). Hastie is Henry at his Lowland extreme, just as the Edinburgh doctor was Jekyll at his most respectable, and in both cases the repressed savagery of these men shows itself most clearly when they are confronted with savagery in its purest form, with Hyde or with James Durie. After Hastie, there is nothing left for the Master but the tongue-swallowing trick, in which neither he nor Secundra Dass has any real confidence.

As for Henry, his death and Dr. Jekyll's are remarkably similar. Both die at the moment they have totally rejected their doubles, their outward projections. Jekyll dies when he writes that Hyde is another than himself; Henry Durie dies when the Master's fluttering eyelid convinces him that James is in fact the devil. A clarification is in order here. James Durie has been presented as objectively diabolical. Yet we have maintained that Henry Durie destroys himself because he recognizes his double as evil, which sounds a bit like saying that Henry is destroyed because he sees things as they really are. There is something in this— clearly Henry Durie cannot live with the vision of evil which has been vouchsafed him—but this is not Stevenson's main point. Where Henry goes wrong is not so much in his understanding of the Master's character—although again perhaps he goes too far when he confuses the diabolical with the devil. Henry errs most seriously when he accepts James as the projection of an element in his own character, as his double, in fact; thus equating the smuggler or lawless element in himself to the devil in James. The fact that pure evil actually exists in the world simply facilitates such an equation. We have already seen that the smuggler and the devil have strong points in common and that they are very easily confused, especially by a nature which has been schooled in a Lowland theology of negative values. But in Stevenson's fiction, to make this confusion is to simplify fatally. It was the fault of Dr. Jekyll and of Henry Durie that they could not distinguish between the lawless and the wicked, and that they were therefore unable to live with themselves.

IN THE LAST five chapters we have considered some of Stevenson's comedies and some of his tragedies. The essential difference between the comic and tragic views, besides the obvious differences in tone, seems to be that in the comedies the hero will simply and ingloriously retreat from his life when he recognizes the savage forces in himself or in his projected double; in the tragedies—the romances and stories we have looked at in the last three chapters—the protagonist will alternately glory in and reject his discovered "evil" nature. Generally, he will continue in this course until, in truth, his wild nature is driven to evil depravity, and he becomes one with it and dies. This is precisely what happens to Emily Brontë's Catherine Earnshaw, who cannot bring herself fully to accept or fully to reject either of her lovers. However, when the *Wuthering Heights* story is told for the second time in terms of the life of Catherine's daughter,[26] the author is able to fashion a much more hopeful conclusion. So is her sister Charlotte capable of some optimism when Jane Eyre succeeds finally in giving herself without reservation to Edward Rochester.

[26] See William Empson, *English Pastoral Poetry* (New York, 1938), p. 86.

But in Stevenson neither the comic nor the tragic views can muster even *so* much reassurance. The first view, as we have heard Daiches say, "masks a profound pessimism" with an ironic shrug; the second, the tragic view, unblinkingly strips it bare.

CHAPTER VII

A CONVULSION OF BRUTE
NATURE

WE HAVE SEEN that the projected doubles in Stevenson's tragic romances and plays oftentimes appear as clearly defined devil figures. Alain St. Ives and James Durie are called devils, and Satanic pride is the greatest temptation to evil in the play *Deacon Brodie,* where the nighttime identity glories in feeling itself a bolder and a craftier rogue than other men. In the shorter fiction, Markheim's evil nature is reflected by a mysterious visitant who speaks and acts like the Prince of Darkness, and some characters, Gordon Darnaway and Huish, for instance, regard themselves as the enemies of God. Indeed, all of the villains we have discussed so far have something of the diabolic in them. Edward Hyde is a Gothic gnome, but even he can appear at times like Lucifer.

Moreover, what we have seen has been in strict keeping with the Romantic notion that the heart of man is radically evil and that his wickedness may be defined in Christian terms. But we have seen also in observing Alan Breck Stewart that for Stevenson theologically defined evil is only one direction in which man's primitive nature may go, if properly pushed. No doubt Alan is capable of great wickedness; actually, though, he performs very little of it. He never fights without just provocation, and he is emphatically not the Appin murderer. The worst that can be said of him is he takes too much pleasure and pride in the exploits of his sword. Be this as it may, we can understand why David Balfour is disturbed by his Highland friend, for Alan represents everything that is antithetical to David's highly civilized nature. It would be a positive relief for David if he could dismiss Alan as merely diabolical; the notion of the devil is, for many of Stevenson's characters, a simplification of experience, a convenient explanation for all the things in life they find least attractive and yet most irresistible. We have seen Dr. Jekyll, Gordon Darnaway, and Henry Durie indulge themselves in just such a comfortable simplification, and we have also seen the fatal consequences.

In Romantic literature, however, Christ was sometimes opposed not by the Christian devil, but by the Greek god Pan.[1] Schiller and Elizabeth Barrett Browning, to name two very different writers, had each produced works dealing with this less traditional rivalry.[2] Further along in the century, as Douglas Bush writes, "Swinburne's intoxicating neo-paganism gave a fresh and powerful stimulus and a whole new vocabulary to the old conflict."[3] Of course, the goat-god and the enemy of man are similar in a number of ways, and many writers tended to confuse them with one another. In the twentieth century D. H. Lawrence very consciously equated them.[4]

Stevenson, who was always an enthusiastic admirer of Swinburne, was interested in the Pan myth from the 1870's until the end of his life. That he too saw a likeness between Pan and Satan is perhaps apparent in one of the early letters to Sidney Colvin, where he writes, "There is more

[1] See W. R. Irwin, "The Survival of Pan," *PMLA*, LXXVI (June 1961), 159-167.

[2] See Schiller's *Die Götter Griechenlands* (1788) and Mrs. Browning's *The Dead Pan* (1844).

[3] *Mythology and the Romantic Tradition* (Cambridge, Mass., 1937), p. 352.

[4] *The Plumed Serpent* (London, 1955), pp. 308-309.

sense in that Greek myth of Pan than in any other that I
recollect except the luminous Hebrew one of the Fall."[5]
But while Stevenson's Pan is related to the devil on the one
side, he is quite as closely linked on the other with the
savage or the lawless Highlander. Stevenson makes Pan his
symbol for the beauty, horror, and joy in the world, for the
combination of the divine and the brutal. In the poem
Et Tu in Arcadia Vixisti he writes:

> There hast thou seen
> Immortal Pan dance secret in a glade,
> And, dancing, roll his eyes; these, where they fell,
> Shed glee, and through the congregated oaks
> A flying horror winged; while all the earth
> To the god's pregnant footing thrilled within.
> Or whiles, beside the sobbing stream, he breathed,
> In his clutched pipe, unformed and wizard strains,
> Divine yet brutal.[6]

Elsewhere, when Stevenson describes the shivering reeds of
the river Oise, he writes, "*Pan* once played upon their
forefathers; and so, by the hands of his river, he still plays
upon these later generations . . . and plays the same air,
both sweet and shrill, to tell us of the beauty and the terror
of the world."[7]

All of Stevenson's ballads were deeply psychological in
intention, juxtaposing contradictory elemental emotions in
their savage heroes.[8] The Pan-like combination of joy and
terror gets fullest development in *The Song of Rahéro*,
where the heroine, Tamatea "shook for terror and joy
like a girl that is a bride"[9] as she prepared to carry out a
bloody revenge. Stevenson argued strongly for the validity

[5] January or February 1878, *Works*, XX, 372.
[6] *Collected Poems*, p. 125.
[7] *An Inland Voyage*, *Works*, I, 70.
[8] See especially *Heather Ale* and *The Feast of Famine*.
[9] *Collected Poems*, p. 200.

of the psychological insights he believed he had made in this ballad. "The *Spectator*," he wrote, "said there was no psychology in it; that interested me much: my grandmother (as I used to call that able paper . . .) cannot so much as observe the existence of savage psychology when it is put before it. . . . The tale seized me one-third because of its picturesque features, two-thirds because of its astonishing psychology." And if there is primitive psychology in *The Song of Rahéro*, then there is pre-Christian morality in it, too, morality which Stevenson described as "tail-foremost" and "ancient as the granite rocks."[10]

Stevenson, we may be sure, did not reserve his insights into primitive psychology and morality for works about literal, bare-breasted savages. Indeed, in 1884, before he had created his first aboriginal character, he commended the genre of comedy largely because he felt it "keeps the beauty and touches the terrors of our life" at the same time, and is therefore, "the last word of moved representation."[11] In his fiction, this amalgam of joy and terror appeared as early as "The Suicide Club," where Prince Florizel, we are told, recognized "almost with astonishment that there was a degree of pleasure in his sensations" (III, 44) as he waited for the turning of the card which would tell him whether or not he was to be murdered. In the same story Mr. Malthus also played the suicide game, but not like Florizel, out of curiosity, or like the other members, because he really wished to die; Mr. Malthus played because he derived emotional satisfaction from the act of putting his life in jeopardy. His great cowardice only added spice to his pleasure. As the cards were being dealt, "His eyes protruded; his head kept nodding involuntarily upon his spine; his hands found their way, one after the other, to his mouth, where they made clutches at his tremulous and

---

[10] Letter to H. B. Baildon, 1891, *Works*, XXII, 341-342.
[11] Letter to Henley, May 1884, *Works*, XXI, 273.

ashen lips" (III, 43-44) .[12] This picture of Mr. Malthus is disturbing enough to have caused the critic H. C. Beeching to note with some distaste a "strain of brutality . . . in Stevenson's fine nature, which cropped out once and again, even in the later books."[13] Stevenson himself had always at least affected a finicky concern over the nastiness which he claimed to find in all his stories.[14]

Sometimes in nineteenth century literature, this Pandevil notion of evil as the primitive, the savage, or the irrational in man is given a scientific cast, as, for instance, in James Thomson's "Great Christ is Dead!" (1875) . Darwinism, of course, tended to encourage such a conception, and Stevenson belonged to the first generation of Victorians brought up on *Origin of Species*. He liked to consider himself something of a disciple of Darwin.[15] Moreover, George Meredith, whose egoist is a type of the primitive man, had shown some of the literary and philosophical possibilities in the new biology. Consequently, Stevenson, as we might expect, appropriated much of Darwinism for his own conception of man's duality. He presents such material whimsically in the essays, where he keeps up the optimistic front, and quite seriously, even tragically, in the fiction.

In the essay "The Character of Dogs," for instance, he explains the disrespectful canine as "an exception, a marked reversion to the ancestral type; like the hairy human infant" (XII, 157) . And the love which the conscientious gentleman has for argument, he writes in "Talk and

---

[12] Another such character appears in the fragment *When the Devil Was Well*, where the villain "was never content unless he were strongly moved, whether by passion or religion, or the uncertain issue of some piece of perilous or desperate policy. This avidity for violent sensation was with him a mode of cowardice" (*Works*, XXV, 470).

[13] "The Works of Robert Louis Stevenson," *Robert Louis Stevenson: His Work and His Personality* (London, 1924), p. 95.

[14] On August 10, 1874, he wrote to Mrs. Sitwell, "I wonder why my stories are always so nasty" (*Works*, XX, 273).

[15] See his letter to Mrs. Sitwell, Sept. 1, 1873, *Works*, XX, 135.

Talkers," is an instance of "the aboriginal man within us, the cave-dweller, still lusty as when he fought tooth and nail for roots and berries" (XII, 131). In still another essay, "The Manse," Stevenson is amused to speculate that the very Lowland and very reverend Dr. Balfour, his maternal grandfather, is "a *homunculus* or part-man" of his own (XII, 90) who "no doubt, and even as I write the phrase . . . moves in my blood, and whispers words to me, and sits efficient in the very knot and centre of my being" (XII, 89). But he is even more amused to think about the part-man whom poor Dr. Balfour must have had to put up with:

> As he sat in his cool study, grave, reverend, contented gentleman, there was an aboriginal frisking of the blood that was not his; tree-top memories, like undeveloped negatives, lay dormant in his mind; tree-top instincts awoke and were trod down; and Probably Arboreal (scarce to be distinguished from a monkey) gambolled and chattered in the brain of the old divine. (XII, 93)

All this adds up to a humorously presented theory of duality in which our ancestors, cavemen or Probably Arboreal, act as our doubles, or we as theirs. The theory is developed, to some extent, in the fable "The Poor Thing," where a spirit who announces, like the ghostly visitant in "Markheim," that he is neither of God nor of Hell, comes to act as a matchmaker for the hero.

> My name . . . is not yet named, and my nature not yet sure. For I am part of a man; and I was part of your fathers, and went out to fish and fight with them in the ancient days. But now is my turn not yet come; and I wait until you have a wife, and then shall I be in your son, and a brave part of him, rejoicing manfully to launch the boat into the surf, skillful to direct the helm, and a man of might where the ring closes and the blows are going. (XXV, 240)

But the theory is treated most completely and most seriously in the short story "Olalla," a work of the middle 1880's, in which atavism is, indeed, the central idea. The theme was by no means a new one to the century, and, as usual, Stevenson did not hesitate to borrow characters, incidents, and even ideas from the Romantic literature which came before him. In this case he borrowed chiefly from Bulwer's *A Strange Story*[16] and Hawthorne's *The Marble Faun*, both important works in the romance tradition, and both involving actual *Doppelgänger*.

The most obvious borrowing from Hawthorne is the Pan-figure, Felipe, Olalla's brother. Hawthorne writes that Donatello gave "Miriam the idea of being not precisely man, nor yet a child, but, in a high and beautiful sense, an animal."[17] We shall see that Stevenson's Felipe is described in similar terms. The debt to *A Strange Story* is also evident through this character, which is perhaps hardly to be wondered at, since Bulwer, whose romance appeared two years after *The Marble Faun*, had also appropriated Donatello. Stevenson's Felipe owes a debt to both works; he has traits of Donatello which Bulwer did not imitate, and also characteristics which were original in *A Strange Story*.[18]

16 For a somewhat more expanded treatment of this significant work see Chap. I, pp. 28-29.

17 *The Complete Writings of Nathaniel Hawthorne*, 22 vols. (Boston, 1900), IX, 104. Subsequent references to this edition will be to *Hawthorne's Works*.

18 By dwelling for a moment on a few of the works that influenced *The Marble Faun*, and a few of those it influenced, we can perhaps appreciate something of the extent to which these Romantic writers worked with one another's materials. *The Marble Faun* shows very clear traces of three works of the 1850's—*Villette, Men and Women*, and *Pierre*. It also owes much to *The Cenci*. Harry Levin (*The Power of Blackness*, p. 61) comments on the fascination which Beatrice Cenci seems to have exercised over both Hawthorne and Melville. In addition to the works we have already mentioned, "Olalla" and *A Strange Story*, Hawthorne's story must certainly have been an important in-

Bulwer's Pan-figure, Margrave, is evil in the fullest sense. As the story develops we learn that he is a wicked magician and a dangerous psychopath, literally lacking a conscience. But in the early part of the romance his freedom from restraint makes him appear charmingly child- or animal-like. The narrator writes, "In Margrave's character there seemed no special vices, no special virtues; but a wonderful vivacity, joyousness, animal good-humor."[19] Stevenson gives Felipe these general characteristics, which are, of course, also characteristics of Donatello, but he also borrows two incidents from Bulwer which did not come from *The Marble Faun*. Felipe, like Margrave but very much unlike Donatello, is revolted at the idea of drinking wine. He and Margrave, moreover, share a strain of gratuitous cruelty, which again does not belong to Hawthorne's Faun. Both Felipe and Margrave catch squirrels and brutally crush them to death.

But Stevenson is not preparing a complicated villain in Felipe, as Bulwer was in Margrave. Felipe is like Donatello, a throwback—"quick and active" (xi, 177). He is "superlatively well-built, light, and lithe and strong . . . well-featured; his yellow eyes . . . very large, though, perhaps, not very expressive . . . a pleasant-looking lad . . . of a dusky hue, and inclined to hairiness" (xi, 178-179). He is called "an innocent" (xi, 176), "a child in intellect" (xi, 180), and a person "who seemed to live . . . by the senses" (xi, 178).

And yet Felipe is not entirely an animal; he has some tincture of a conscience, although it is largely imposed by his sister, and he spends at least part of his day at her behest dutifully laboring in the garden. Moreover, he is full of remorse when the narrator lectures him about killing the squirrel—" 'Oh, I try so hard,' he said. 'Oh, comman-

---

fluence on *The Ring and the Book*, which Browning began the year of *The Marble Faun*'s publication.
19 *A Strange Story, Bulwer's Works*, VII, 66.

dante, bear with Felipe this once; he will never be a brute again!' " (XI, 188).

Stevenson presents a much purer instance of atavism in Felipe and Olalla's mother. The Señora seems to have been based on Hawthorne's description of Donatello's ancestors as they appear in their middle or old age. After describing the pleasant qualities of the Faun, Hawthorne mentions some of his defects:

> On the other hand, there were deficiencies both of intellect and heart, and especially, as it seemed, in the development of the higher portion of man's nature. These defects were less perceptible in early youth, but showed themselves more strongly with advancing age, when, as the animal spirits settled down upon a lower level, the representative of the Monte Benis was apt to become sensual, addicted to gross pleasures, heavy, unsympathizing, and insulated within the narrow limits of a surly selfishness.[20]

Stevenson's Señora is beautiful, but perfectly nonintellectual. "A look more blankly stupid," comments the narrator, "I have never met. . . . Her face . . . was devoid of either good or bad—a moral blank expressing literally naught" (XI, 192). She goes violently mad when the wind blows, and she has an uncontrollable blood lust. When the narrator shows her his badly cut and bleeding hand, the wild animal in her nature flames out as she attacks him, savagely biting him to the bone.

Although the Señora's more normal behavior is much less fierce than this, it is never quite human. She spends her days lying on animal skins in the warm sun, making "infinitesimal changes in her posture, savouring and lingering on the bodily pleasure of the movement." The narrator writes that he "was driven to wonder at this depth

20 *Hawthorne's Works*, X, 31-32.

of passive sensuality. She lived in her body; and her consciousness was all sunk into and disseminated through her members, where it luxuriously dwelt" (XI, 212). Although she is the daughter of a very old and noble Spanish family, she married a muleteer or took him as her lover. The attraction was entirely physical, and the picture Stevenson gives us of the Señora standing at the gallery with a lamp in her hand, smiling at the muleteer, luring him into the house, is perhaps the most frankly sexual scene in all of his works. The other muleteer, who describes this temptation as an instance of the utterly diabolic, clearly does not share Stevenson's definition of the evil in man. For him, illicit sex and Satanic evil appear one and the same.

Nearly all of Stevenson's critics have commented, either favorably or otherwise, on the avoidance of sex in his stories. And yet Stevenson was certainly no prude, nor was he ever comfortable at this exclusion. A sexless Pan, as D. H. Lawrence would have found it unnecessary to tell him, has to be something of a mockery. What kept him back was a fear that with his talent for realistic descriptions he would overdo the grossness in his treatment,[21] and, more practically, he hesitated because he made a canny appraisal of just what British and American publishers would and would not print. In the essay "A Chapter on Dreams," he outlines the appealing plot of a story involving the adulterous love of a son for his step-mother, a story he never attempted because he felt it was unmarketable. Yet towards the end of his career Stevenson began to regret having been so timid. In June of 1892 he wrote to Colvin, "Think how beautiful it would be not to have to mind the critics, and not even the darkest of the crowd—Sidney Colvin. I should probably amuse myself with works that would make your hair curl, if you had any left" (XXIII, 100). A few months earlier, he had refused the "plaintive

[21] See Chap. III, note 31.

request . . . to make the young folks [of *The Beach of Falesá*] married properly before 'that night.' "[22] And in one of his last letters he wrote:

> If I had to begin again . . . I believe I should try to honour Sex more religiously. The worst of our education is that Christianity does not recognize and hallow Sex. It looks askance at it, over its shoulder, oppressed as it is by reminiscences of hermits and Asiatic self-tortures. It is a terrible hiatus in our modern religions that they cannot see and make venerable that which they ought to see first and hallow most. Well, it is so; I cannot be wiser than my generation.[23]

There were even times throughout his career, when Stevenson kicked at the "little box of toys"[24] which, he felt, had been given him to play with. *The Bloody Wedding* contained an "indiscretion";[25] *Sophia Scarlet* was to offer "a kind of love affair between the heroine and a dying planter who is a poet! large orders for R.L.S."[26] *When the Devil Was Well*, perhaps the most daring, features an adulterous affair in which the lovers' "mouths joined, with a shudder, in one long kiss" (xxv, 428). And the heroine of *Weir of Hermiston* was actually to be seduced and made pregnant. The following passage, a description of Marie-Madeleine of *The Young Chevalier*, reads, with its heavy breath, like the work of one of the sex prophets of our own century:

[22] Letter to Colvin, Jan. 31, 1892, XXIII, 23.

[23] Letter to R.A.M. Stevenson, Sept. 1894, XXIII, 438.

[24] Lloyd Osbourne quotes Stevenson as saying, "What books Dickens could have written had be been permitted! Think of Thackeray as unfettered as Flaubert or Balzac! What books I might have written myself! But they give us a little box of toys, and say to us: 'You mustn't play with anything but these'" (*An Intimate Portrait*, p. 133).

[25] Letter to Colvin, Mar. 1891, *Works*, XXII, 353.

[26] Letter to Colvin, May 17, 1892, *Works*, XXIII, 71.

She was of a grave countenance, rarely smiling; yet it seemed to be written upon every part of her that she rejoiced in life. Her husband loved the heels of her feet and the knuckles of her fingers; he loved her like a glutton and a brute; his love hung about her like an atmosphere; one that came by chance into the wine-shop was aware of the passion; and it might be said that by the strength of it the woman had been drugged or spellbound. She knew not if she loved or loathed him; he was always in her eyes like something monstrous—monstrous in his love, monstrous in his person, horrific but imposing in his violence; and her sentiment swung back and forward from desire to sickness. But the mean, where it dwelt chiefly, was an apathetic fascination, partly of horror; as of Europa in mid-ocean with her bull. (XVIII, 414)

But all of these works are fragments, most of which Stevenson never even intended to finish. Turning to completed works, there is some mild sexual suspense generated in *David Balfour* when the hero and Catriona are sharing quarters; and the marriage laws seem at first to be made very little of in *The Beach of Falesá*. Of all the completed works, however, only "Olalla" deals with sex as an animal passion.

As we have seen, such a treatment of sex is evident in the Señora, but the Señora is far past her prime when the principal action of the story takes place. The incident with the muleteer is a briefly described scene from her youth. Sexual attraction as an animal passion finds its fullest expression in Olalla herself and in the love she shares with the narrator. At their second meeting, before they have ever spoken to one another:

She drew back from me a little as I came; but her eyes did not waver from mine, and these lured me forward. At last, when I was already within reach of her, I stopped. Words were denied me; if I advanced I could but clasp her to my heart in silence; and all that was sane in me, all that was still unconquered, revolted against the thought of such an accost. . . . Was this love? or was it a mere brute attraction, mindless and inevitable, like that of the magnet for the steel? . . . Of me she knew nothing but my bodily favour; she was drawn to me as stones fall to earth; the laws that rule the earth conducted her, unconsenting, to my arms. (XI, 214-215)

Elsewhere the narrator calls their love "a thing brutal and divine, and akin at once to the innocence and to the unbridled forces of the earth" (XI, 219). Here again we may be dealing with an influence from *The Marble Faun*, where Miriam is blankly told "you are yourself, and I am Donatello. . . . Therefore I love you! There needs no other reason." And Hawthorne supports this view by commenting, "Certainly, there was no better or more explicable reason."[27]

But for all her full-bloodedness and passion, Olalla is not simply a younger version of her sensual mother. Indeed, she is more complicated even than Hawthorne's Miriam. We have already noted that Olalla acts as a conscience for her brother. She is, in fact, a very devout Catholic, a favorite of her confessor, and a writer of religious poems of austere renunciation. The civilized or Christian side of her character is at least as strong as, and indeed much more fully developed than the savage side. Her conscience, moreover, seems to belong to herself, or perhaps she got some of it from the sturdy though fallible muleteer, her father; she derived her primitive, savage passions from her mother's family. In any event, to speak again in terms of *The Marble Faun*, Olalla is both Miriam and Hilda in one. She is a complete person, in whom what we have pre-

27 *Hawthorne's Works*, IX, 106.

viously called Highland and Lowland passions are violently at war.

At the beginning of the story, in a scene which is again reminiscent of Hawthorne's romance (where a character resembles a work of art), the narrator looks at the portrait of one of Olalla's ancestors. He is struck at once by the beauty and vivacity of the face, but he notes also its "cruel, sullen, and sensual expression" (xi, 183). And his attitude expresses the same ambivalence we have come to expect in a Stevenson narrator. "I knew that to love such a woman were to sign and seal one's own sentence of degeneration, I still knew that, if she were alive, I should love her." He writes that he "had a half-lingering terror that she might not be dead after all, but re-arisen in the body of some descendant" (xi, 184).[28]

When the narrator sees Olalla, he immediately recognizes her as the double of the woman in the portrait. This recognition accounts, to some extent, for his immediate attraction, and, while he argues for a while that the instinct which makes them love must be the will of God, the recognition accounts also for some of his revulsion. He pulls back from the savage and irrational. After Olalla's mother has fully exposed her own animal nature by attacking the narrator, his pain and disgust turn her wild screams for more blood into "the death-cry of my love; my love was murdered; it was not only dead, but an offence to me" (xi, 223). He then begins to doubt whether or not Olalla, the daughter of this woman, can be truly human. This is the same kind of rejection which we saw in *Dr.*

[28] Eino Railo, in *The Haunted Castle* (pp. 304-307), traces a regular portrait *motif* from Walpole to Wilde, and then relates it to the idea of double identity as expressed in *Dr. Jekyll and Mr. Hyde.* One work which Railo does not mention in this context, Maturin's *Fatal Revenge*, contains a scene very close to the incident we have just noted in "Olalla." In Maturin's romance the hero falls in love with the portrait of a woman whom he is advised to flee, should he ever meet her.

Jekyll and Mr. Hyde and *The Master of Ballantrae*. It is also the sort of rejection which Miriam, in *The Marble Faun*, receives from Hilda. "Your very look," Miriam says, "seems to put me beyond the limits of human kind."[29] What the narrator feels for Olalla thereafter, he calls not love, but "infatuation," for the conviction that the Señora's bite and Olalla's love are tokens of the same "savage and bestial strain" (xi, 223) proves too much for the narrator's predominantly Lowland or civilized soul.

The savage and bestial strain which she finds in her own nature is also too much for Olalla's own conscience to accept. Once again the narrator's attitudes serve primarily as a mirror for the protagonist's. We see in her the same kind of self-hatred we saw in Dr. Jekyll, in Henry Durie, and in Gordon Darnaway, although certainly not the same indulgence. Olalla describes herself to the narrator "as one who loved you indeed, but who hated herself so deeply that her love was hateful to her" (xi, 229). Olalla despises herself because she sees "the horror of the living fact" (xi, 225), and because she regards herself as the embodiment, the double, of her entire evil race.

> Not a gesture that I can frame, not a tone of my voice, not any look from my eyes, no, not even now when I speak to him I love, but has belonged to others. Others, ages dead, have wooed other men with my eyes; other men have heard the pleading of the same voice that now sounds in your ears. The hands of the dead are in my bosom; they move me, they pluck me, they guide me; I am a puppet at their command; and I but re-inform features and attributes that have long been laid aside from evil in the quiet of the grave. (xi, 226-227)

Hawthorne's Hilda had spoken words similar to these. "It is very dreadful," she had said. "Ah! now I understand

[29] *Hawthorne's Works*, IX, 288.

how the sins of generations past have created an atmosphere of sin for those that follow."[30] And Hilda, like Olalla and so many other of Stevenson's protagonists, abhorred more than anything else the duality of man's nature. "If there be any such dreadful mixture of good and evil as you [Kenyon] affirm,—and which appears to me almost more shocking than pure evil,—then the good is turned to poison, not the evil to wholesomeness."[31]

Olalla depicts the hereditary forces that control her in almost the same imagery which Markheim had used to describe the giants of circumstance. Markheim, we recall, was trying to dissociate what he believed to be his essential personality from the character of the man (himself) who had just committed murder. His essential identity, he believed, was innocent, but it was helpless in the hands of these giants. Olalla is trying to accomplish the same sort of dissociation, although what she characterizes as her evil self is guilty of no worse a crime than falling irrationally in love. She calls herself an "impotent prisoner . . . carried about and deafened by a mob that I disown," her evil or brutal ancestors (XI, 225).

Olalla finally frees herself from this mob with a Stevensonian solution which should be familiar enough to us by now: she resigns from life. She vows never to marry or to have children—"the race shall cease from off the earth" (XI, 228), she declares. Given Olalla's conviction that her identity lies not in herself but in her race, the fulfillment of such a vow is tantamount to suicide. There is, however, no expression of contempt on Stevenson's part. He remains outside the story, and, as in "Markheim," allows his character to drape her renunciation with the gaudiest of theological implications. With her hand upon a crucifix Olalla explains her vow: "We are all such as He was—the

30 *Ibid.*, IX, 294.
31 *Ibid.*, X, 244-245.

inheritors of sin; we must all bear and expiate a past which was not ours. . . . Like Him, we must endure for a little while, until morning returns bringing peace" (XI, 238).

Here again, at this most crucial turning, the Stevenson story differs characteristically from its source. Hilda, the daughter of the Puritans, also refuses to compromise with evil, but after all, she recognizes sin only in her friend's nature, not in her own. On the other hand, the actual sinners in *The Marble Faun*, as we are specifically told, have far too much life to renounce any of it. Indeed, they contemplate renunciations—Miriam thinks of suicide, and Donatello wishes to become a monk—but their natures are too strong to allow this. They decide instead to acknowledge their evil and to live with it. This is pretty good Christian theology, by the way. Olalla's is twisted, as Stevenson must have meant us to understand. Certainly Christ accepts responsibility and pays for sins which are not his own. But to be an animal is not quite the same as to have eaten from the tree of knowledge, and to eliminate the evil in us along with the good by refusing to go on living is surely not the same as to expiate sin. But no one undertakes to correct Olalla, who remains true to her sad vow, and once again, Stevenson, whom his contemporaries regarded as an optimist, is able only to despair in the same situation where another great romantic was capable of some hope. In another corner of Romantic fiction, Rose Maylie of Dicken's *Oliver Twist* takes a vow similar to Olalla's: that she will carry the disgrace upon her name into no blood except her own. At the end, of course, Rose relents; Olalla does not. Nor does she, like some of Hawthorne's characters, even toy with the notion that the Fall of Man may have been a fortunate occurrence.

After this emphasis on ancestry, we would do well, perhaps, to look at the ancestors of the other heroes. But here

again we will be dealing with material which is not particular to the Romantic tradition. Indeed, Dorothy Van Ghent
speaks of a regular "theme of the 'fathers' " and illustrates
it from such realistic works as *Tom Jones* and *Vanity
Fair*.[32] The tyrannical or evil father, out of *Romeo and
Juliet, King Lear,* and *Hamlet,* had his influence also on
the romances of the eighteenth century: on *Clarissa,* on
The Castle of Otronto, on *A Sicilian Romance,* on *The
Romance of the Forest,* and on *The Italian.* Once again,
as with the brothers in the last chapter, we must proceed
somewhat cautiously. Nevertheless, fathers or foster fathers
had been important and significant in the nineteenth century romance tradition at least since *Great Expectations,*
where the hero, after conveniently dividing all the world
between the ethereal Estella, to whom he aspires, and the
animalistic Magwitch, whom he would like to reject, must
acknowledge the latter not only as his own benefactor but
even as Estella's fleshly father.

Parents, however, are not very easy to come by in Stevenson's fiction. Almost all of Stevenson's heroes are
orphans, or at least half-orphans, and not a single one of
them keeps both his parents until the end of the story.
Usually, in the rare instances when a parent is left living,
he does not appear and is referred to only briefly. On the
other hand, there are a great many fathers-in-law, who,
considering the absence of actual fathers, particularly in
the works published before Thomas Stevenson's death in
1887,[33] may be regarded perhaps as psychological evasions
and given some attention here.

[32] *The English Novel: Form and Function* (New York, 1959), p. 147.
[33] The central characters are provided with fathers who survive the
story in the comic works "The Adventures of John Nicholson" and
"The Story of a Lie." "John Nicholson," however, was not published
during the author's lifetime, and "The Story of a Lie," which had
originally appeared in the *New Quarterly Magazine,* October 1879,
was not republished until after Thomas Stevenson's death. The only

Stevenson's heroes have remarkably bad luck in their choice of fathers- or guardians-in-law. The line of them begins with the evil Sire de Malétroit, who constructs a trap for the hero and offers him his choice between marriage and execution; it ends with the two fathers-in-law of Keola in "The Isle of Voices"—the first, an evil magician who tries to drown the young hero; the second, a cannibal who tries to eat him. In between, we find James More Macgregor of *David Balfour*, Gordon Darnaway of "The Merry Men," Van Tromp, the derelict artist of "The Story of a Lie," and Bernard Huddlestone, the cowardly desperado of "The Pavilion on the Links." Sir Daniel, the chief villain in *The Black Arrow*, is the guardian of Richard's beloved. Most of these fathers-in-law are what we have called savages or Highlanders, and the mixed natures of the two exceptions, Huddlestone and Darnaway, are drawn towards wildness and violent death.

An extremely interesting example of the Highlander turned Lowlander, that is, the Highlander civilized during his own lifetime, occurs in John Gaunt, the father-in-law in the Stevenson–Henley play *Admiral Guinea*. Gaunt was formerly a slaver and a great sinner—"there was none worse that sailed to Guinea" (VI, 206). When we see him, however, he is a pious convert, and as we might expect, he is a more forceful figure now than he was in his more positively evil youth. He has become a religious fanatic who pronounces stern dicta and emphasizes them, like Alan Breck, with his fist on the table. All of the energy which was incident to his former Highland life has been brought along into his pious retirement, even the hellish energy. As his daughter's exasperated suitor tells him, "You spoke just now of a devil; well, I'll tell you the devil you have: the

---

other fathers of central characters in the works written before 1887 are the senile father of Deacon Brodie and Jim Hawkins' father, who dies in the third chapter of *Treasure Island*.

devil of judging others" (vi, 223) . John Gaunt is a particularly important character because he is the first version in
the development of Stevenson's most significant father, the
hanging judge, Adam Weir.

The next step in this development occurs in *The Ebb-
Tide*, another collaboration, this time with Lloyd Osbourne. The story concerns a group of Stevenson's most
dismal life-failures, three men who have been defeated in
literally everything they have ever tried to do. At the beginning of the story they find themselves on the beach at
Tahiti, getting bad food, when they can, by singing and
dancing before low Hawaiian sailors. "Each had made a
long apprenticeship in going downward; and, each at some
stage of the descent, had been shamed into the adoption of
an *alias*" (xviii, 7) , "had struck his flag" (xviii, 10) .

Exasperated at their failures along respectable lines, they
determine to try a life of crime. They steal an old hulk
with a cargo of champagne, which they intend to sell in
South America. But they are as hopelessly inept in evil as
they were in good. For after they have drunk away the
top layer of their loot, they discover that the bottles under-
neath are filled with water, and that their act of piracy fell
in beautifully with the shipowners' plans to lose a worthless ship and thus collect the insurance. Next, the three
failures come upon an unregistered island, obviously a
pearl island, and discovering that there is only one white
man ashore, they resolve to despoil him of his treasure.
They have about as much chance here as Chaucer's repro-
bates have of killing Death in "The Pardonner's Tale,"
which, we should note, *The Ebb-Tide* resembles in many
ways. Stevenson once suggested, as we have previously
mentioned in a different context, that the story should bear
the subtitle "*a tract by R.L.S. and L.O.*"[34]

One of the three failures is a sentimental sea captain

[34] See Chap. IV, pp. 118-119.

who is always mooning about his little girl, but the real
father-figure in this story is Attwater, the white man whom
the three pirates have determined to rob. Attwater sees
himself as a father to everyone, and by the end of the story
the other characters have gone far towards accepting him
pretty much at his own value. We have already spoken about
Huish's attempt on Attwater's life, a venture which was
presented as a rebellion against God. At the end of the
story the other two failures are on their knees before
Attwater. Indeed, the central character, Herrick, after
making a failure even of his suicide, throws himself before
Attwater, as an abject sinner in the hands of a stern but just
God.

> Can you do anything with me? . . . Here I am. I am
> broken crockery; the whole of my life is gone to water;
> I have nothing left that I believe in, except my living
> horror of myself. Why do I come to you? I don't know.
> You are cold, cruel, hateful; and I hate you, or I think I
> hate you. But you are an honest man, an honest gentle-
> man. I put myself helpless in your hands. What must I
> do? If I can't do anything, be merciful, and put a bullet
> through me; it's only a puppy with a broken leg!
> (XVIII, 175-176)

Attwater is a religious fanatic like John Gaunt. He
preaches and prays, and he speaks in parables. His religion,
moreover, like Gaunt's theology, is based upon a stern and
savage interpretation of justice. In this respect Attwater
looks especially forward to Adam Weir, who says to his
son, "Him that the law of man whammles is no' likely to
do muckle better by the law of God. What would ye make
of hell? Wouldna your gorge rise at that?" (XVIII, 263).
Similarly Attwater explains that "religion is a savage thing,
like the universe it illuminates; savage, cold, and bare, but
infinitely strong" (XVIII, 133). Adam Weir sees himself as

"the King's officer, bearing the sword, a dreid to evil-doers" (xviii, 262). Attwater calls himself "a judge in Israel, the bearer of the sword and scourge" (xviii, 133).

In physical appearance, Attwater might very easily be mistaken for a Biblical judge or prophet, perhaps even for the Presbyterian God himself. Note the features of this description:

> He was a huge fellow, six feet four in height, and of a build proportionately strong, but his sinews seemed to be dissolved in a listlessness that was more than languor. It was only the eye that corrected this impression,—an eye of an unusual mingled brilliancy and softness, sombre as coal, and with lights that outshone the topaz; an eye of unimpaired health and virility; an eye that bid you beware of the man's devastating anger. (xviii, 114)

The natives of the island treat Attwater as their god, and he treats the natives as though he were their creator. "I was making a new people here," he tells his visitors, and he describes the Old Testament justice he dispensed as giving "these beggars what they wanted" (xviii, 133).

Another of Stevenson's South Sea tales, *The Beach of Falesá*, has been suggested as a source for Conrad's "Heart of Darkness."[35] Certainly there are similarities. Both stories deal with man's ability or inability to remain decent when all the external restraints of civilization have been re-moved. As Stevenson's hero says, "It would be a strange thing if we came all this way and couldn't do what we pleased. The mere idea has always put my monkey up" (xv, 315).[36] But the savagery in *The Ebb-Tide*, especially

[35] See Albert J. Guerard, *Conrad the Novelist* (Cambridge, Mass., 1958), p. 43n.

[36] Stevenson may have got this idea from Thackeray, whose Sir Pitt Crawley says, "What's the good of being in Parliament . . . if you must pay your debts?" *Vanity Fair, Thackeray's Works*, I, 114.

the savagery found in Attwater's religion, is far closer to
Kurtz's darkness than are any of the stage magician tricks
of Case, the villain of *The Beach of Falesá*. Case simply
exploits the primitive superstitions of his native subjects;
Kurtz and Attwater go far beyond this: they share in the
savagery, and they outdo it.

Herrick, like the natives, confuses Attwater with God:
"He knows all; he sees through all," Herrick says. "We only
make him laugh with our pretences—he looks at us, and
laughs like God!" (xviii, 162). And the hero follows after
Attwater "as the criminal goes with the hangman, or the
sheep with the butcher.... He saw him now tower up
mysterious and menacing, the angel of the Lord's wrath,
armed with knowledge, and threatening judgment" (xviii,
144-145). Moreover, and this is an essential point, he feels
for Attwater all the emotions which we have come to expect the protagonist of a Stevenson story to feel for his
projected double: "Attwater intrigued, puzzled, dazzled,
enchanted, revolted him" (xviii, 139).

Most of these attitudes of Herrick towards Attwater parallel the attitudes of Archie Weir to his father. In both
cases there is the same respect, hatred, and fear for power,
the same reliance on the other's honesty, the same fascination, and the same revulsion. But Archie and Herrick
are most alike in their reactions to the savage justice which
their father or father-figure dispenses. Archie's public de-
nunciation of the execution of Duncan Jopp, whom his
father had condemned, is clearly previewed in *The Ebb-
Tide*. When Attwater amuses his guests with an account
of one of his administrations of justice, Herrick, like
Archie, cannot restrain himself. Archie shouts, "I denounce
this God-defying murder." Herrick is less eloquent, though
equally moved. " 'It was a murder,' he screamed. 'A cold-
hearted, bloody-minded murder! You monstrous being!

Murderer and hypocrite! Murderer and hypocrite! Murderer and hypocrite!' he repeated, and his tongue stumbled among the words" (xviii, 157).

In the fragment *Weir of Hermiston*, the last romance Stevenson worked on, the character whom the author calls Mephistopheles,[37] Frank Innes, is clearly the most superficial of all the personages. The devil-figure has shrunk in importance. Innes makes mischief everywhere in the plot. It is he who carries and improves the tale of Archie's pronouncement at the execution of Duncan Jopp, thus alienating Archie from his father; he who engineers the misunderstanding between Archie and Christina and who will capitalize on this estrangement by seducing Christina. But with all of this involvement, Innes is still peripheral to the story. "Poor cork upon a torrent, he tasted that night the sweets of omnipotence, and brooded like a deity over the strands of that intrigue which was to shatter him before the summer waned" (xviii, 372). At best, he is a catalyst to a combination of passions, diabolical perhaps, but old and powerful enough to pale the more modern Christian devil into insignificance.

Weir of Hermiston is a story of Lowlanders who keep fierce Highland passions under strenuous control. This conflict exists in all the characters, except the uncomplicated Innes, and it creates the tensions of the romance. The characters, again excepting Innes, are all dual, are all Highlanders civilized, and the fierceness in them can break out at any moment. Hob Elliott, the heroine's eldest brother, serves as example. Stevenson describes how in the night of his father's murder, Hob turned wild revenger, forcing his horse to walk back and forth over the prostrate body of the murderer. Yet this is far from the Hob Elliott we meet in Stevenson's story:

[37] The chapter that brings Frank to Hermiston is entitled "Enter Mephistopheles."

The figure he had shown on that eventful night dis-
appeared as if swallowed by a trap. He who had ecstati-
cally dipped his hand in the red blood, he who had
ridden down Dickieson, became, from that moment on,
a stiff and rather graceless model of the rustic proprieties; cannily profiting by the high war prices, and yearly
stowing away a little nest-egg in the bank against calam-
ity; approved of and sometimes consulted by the greater
lairds for the massive and placid sense of what he said,
when he could be induced to say anything; and particularly valued by the minister, Mr. Torrance, as a right-
hand man in the parish, and a model to parents. The
transfiguration had been for the moment only; some
Barbarossa, some old Adam of our ancestors, sleeps in
all of us till the fit circumstance shall call it into action;
and for as sober as he now seemed, Hob had given once
for all the measure of the devil that haunted him.
(XVIII, 299)

In no other fictional work of Stevenson, not even excepting "Olalla," is the influence of ancestry made so much of.
This influence is not presented only as a matter of "the
inheritance of cells"; tradition also plays an important
part. "If I buy ancestors by the gross from the benevolence
of Lion King at Arms, my grandson (if he is Scottish) will
feel a quickening emulation of their deeds" (XVIII, 291).
Thus both the blood *and* the tradition of the "Auld, auld
Elliotts, clay-cauld Elliotts, dour, bauld Elliotts of auld"
(XVIII, 344) inform the actions of Christina, just as the wild
and lawless "riding Rutherfords of Hermiston" (XVIII, 217)
still work strongly in Archie.

Stevenson emphasizes the instinctive, the aboriginal,
even the animal qualities of Archie's and Kirstie's love. On
the day of their meeting, Archie wonders at the "essential
beauty of the old earth. . . . His heart perhaps beat in time

to some vast indwelling rhythm of the universe" (xviii, 315-316) . "Brightness of azure, clouds of fragrance, a tinkle of falling water and singing birds, rose like exhalations from some deeper, aboriginal memory, that was not his, but belonged to the flesh on his bones" (xviii, 317). When he sees Kirstie, "Archie was attracted by the bright thing like a child" (xviii, 321). During the encounter, which takes place against the background of Mr. Torrance's dry Lowland sermon, Kirstie is described again and again in animal terms. Her skin is "tawny" (xviii, 322), her gaze is "like a tame bird" (xviii, 319), and her eyes are "great as a stag's" (xviii, 322). When Archie looks at her, she is "like a creature tracked, run down" (xviii, 323). Their "stealthy glances were sent out like antennae" (xviii, 325). And Kirstie runs home from church with "the tread of a wild doe" (xviii, 329). Where the animal metaphor fails, it is replaced by even more elemental comparisons from nature. Thus Kirstie comes to Archie "as a stone falls" (xviii, 339) , and their love is described as "simple and violent, like a disruption of life's tissue" (xviii, 333). Stevenson must apologize for his clumsiness in describing it, for "it is to be understood," he breaks his narrative to say, "that I have been painting chaos and describing the inarticulate" (xviii, 332).

Fate plays a very strong part in this love, but it is "a pagan Fate, uncontrolled by any Christian deity, obscure, lawless, and august—moving indissuadably in the affairs of Christian men" (xviii, 333). Kirstie's first thought on seeing Archie is "I wonder, will I have met my fate?" (xviii, 319). Of course, she is using the term colloquially, but the author is not. He uses it as seriously as Hardy does and in much the same way. For Stevenson, Fate and the aboriginal in man are closely bound up. "Fate played his game artfully with this poor pair of children," he writes. "The generations were prepared, the pangs were made ready, before the curtain rose on the dark drama" (xviii, 345-346). And in the last scene of the fragment, we are told that Kirstie "had accepted the command of that supreme attraction like the call of fate and marched blindfold on her doom" (xviii, 388). No doubt, if *Weir of Hermiston* had been completed, a comparison between it and *The Return of the Native* and perhaps *Tess of the D'Urbervilles,* another story of seduction and murder and of ancestry, would be very much in order here.[38]

Melvin Orth notes the primordial passions displayed in this love affair, and he interprets them as reinforcements of the major theme of the fragment, which he sees as "duty versus inclination." The word "inclination" seems rather a weak one to describe emotions such as Archie and Kirstie feel; but we have seen that this conflict runs all through Stevenson. Nevertheless, when Orth juxtaposes Archie against his father—"One succumbs to his inclinations, the other knows, almost wholly, only duty"[39]—he is simplifying out of all proportion.

To be sure, such juxtapositions exist in *Weir of Hermiston.* Sidney Colvin writes that the two Kirsties of the story, the hero's beloved and his housekeeper, "were to embody one the wavering and the other the heroic soul of woman."[40] They are indeed set up for such treatment. Like a pair of Scott heroines, the elder Kirstie is fair and the younger dark; moreover, Stevenson once proposed *"The Two Kirsties of the Cauldstaneslap"* as the work's title.[41] The four Elliott brothers—Hob, the stockish laird;

---

38 In a letter to James Barrie, Nov. 1, 1892, Stevenson, who had read *Tess* and reviled it in a letter to Henry James, describes his own heroine as "what Hardy calls (and others in their plain way don't) a Pure Woman" (*Works,* XXIII, 171-172).

39 "Robert Louis Stevenson as a Novelist," pp. 177-183.

40 "Epilogue," to *Vailima Letters, Thistle Edition* of Stevenson's works (Headings vary from volume to volume), 27 vols. (New York, 1911-1912), XVII, 303.

41 Letter to Sidney Colvin, Oct. 28, 1892, *Works,* XXIII, 164.

Gib, the religious enthusiast; Clem, the vulgar businessman; and Dandie, the sentimental poet—are presented like
figures from a morality play; together they form a com-
posite picture of mankind. And another proposed title for
the story was "*The Four Black Brothers.*"[42] But Archie and
Adam Weir, who are the principal characters, are not presented as simple opposites. They are both far too complicated for any such treatment, and, besides, they have too
many points in common.

Adam Weir is indeed presented as one going "up the
great, bare staircase of his duty, uncheered and unde-
pressed" (XVIII, 244). He is the "King's officer," remember,
and the need for order is as strong in him as in any Lowlander we have discussed. When he puts an end to his son's
legal career because Archie, by insulting him, has "flung
fylement in public on one of the Senators of the Coallege
of Justice," he is not merely reacting to a personal attack.
As he further says, "There is a kind of decency to be ob-
servit" (XVIII, 263). He is a faithful minister of the law and
a brilliant judge who earnestly and painstakingly prepares
his cases. His colleague Glenalmond calls him "two things
of price . . . a great lawyer, and . . . upright as the day"
(XVIII, 241).

But there is another side to Adam Weir's character, a
side emphasized by his first name, which we have already
seen used in this romance as a synonym for the primitive
in man. The painstaking lawyer is certainly not another
Gabriel Utterson; he is, in fact, something of an epicure
and a heavy drinker of port wine. Moreover, as we watch
him preside at the trial of Duncan Jopp, it is obvious that
he is moved by something more than a stern obligation to
duty. Stevenson writes that it was not possible "to see his
lordship, and acquit him of gusto in the task" (XVIII, 247).
"The words were strong in themselves; the light and heat

42 *Ibid.*

· 222 ·

and detonation of their delivery, and the savage pleasure of the speaker in his task, made them tingle in the ears. . . . The judge had pursued him [Jopp] with a monstrous, relishing gaiety, horrible to be conceived, a trait for nightmares" (XVIII, 248-249).

The savage and the civilized man both run strong in Adam Weir, as they did in Markheim, but they do not "hale" him both ways. Adam Weir has effected a truce, perhaps even a peace, between the contrary elements in his nature, for he has told himself that it is his duty to be a cruel judge, "a dreid to evil-doers." His is, at least temporarily, a successfully integrated character, like that of Prestongrange in *David Balfour,* who legally murdered James of the Glens and asked for no reward beyond the satisfaction of his duties done. As we have previously noted, in the mature works such characters, the Highlanders civilized, are the most terrifying to the ultracivilized protagonists, for it is not too difficult for the hero to dissociate himself from an out-and-out monster, unless the monster displays characteristics which the hero recognizes and indeed prides in himself.

Daiches points out that "Adam Weir stands alone without ancestry."[43] This is another implication of his name. He is the only character in the fragment without a tradition or a bloodline. In a sense, this integrated man is the ancestor of all the rest. At the very least, and of course in a quite literal way, he is Archie's ancestor, and Archie's character contains all the contradictions of his father's. We have already seen a fair sampling of the aboriginal in Archie's love for Kirstie. This impression is reinforced by Stevenson's references to his hero's "pugnacity" (XVIII, 228) and to his "Byronism" (XVIII, 285). But Archie is also very much the dutiful Lowlander. When he has been made to understand that the secret love affair is dangerous to

43 *Robert Louis Stevenson,* p. 111.

Kirstie's reputation, he becomes "a grey-faced, harsh schoolmaster" (xviii, 385) . In an encounter which is very reminiscent of the Leyden scenes between David Balfour and Catriona, Archie, "wound up to do his duty" (xviii, 386) , clumsily lectures Kirstie on the necessity of caution. "We must not wreck our lives at the outset. They may be long and happy yet, and we must see to it, Kirstie, like God's rational creatures and not like fool children" (xviii, 387) .

Moreover, Archie's inheritance is also mixed from his mother's side. From her *blood* he gets the wildness of the old Riding Rutherfords and from her *teachings* an "implanted" (xviii, 228) Lowland quietism, piety, and tenderness, "a shivering delicacy, unequally mated with potential violence" (xviii, 239) . Morton Zabel writes that Archie's abhorrence at his father's brutality represents Stevenson's "own protest of humane sympathy."[44] Perhaps so, but Stevenson, we should be careful to note, did not altogether approve of such sympathy. The aboriginal, whatever his faults, is always equated with life, which the civilized man in his delicacy and fear has rejected. Remember that Gordon Darnaway is "rejuvenated, mind and body," as well as damned, when he identifies himself with the Merry Men. And at least part of Stevenson does not go along with Archie Weir when he humanely denounces the execution of Duncan Jopp. In 1886, Stevenson wrote, "As for those crockery, chimney-piece ornaments, the bourgeois (*quorum pars*) , and their cowardly dislike of dying and killing, it is merely one symptom of a thousand how utterly they have got out of touch of life. Their dislike of capital punishment and their treatment of their domestic servants are for me the two flaunting emblems of their hollowness."[45]

44 "Introduction," *The Two Major Novels*, p. xxi.
45 Letter to J. A. Symonds, Spring 1886, *Works*, XXI, 400.

Archie understands his father very badly. As Stevenson writes, "He could not combine the brutal judge and the industrious, dispassionate student; the connecting link escaped him; from such a dual nature, it was impossible he should predict behaviour" (xviii, 255). Such a lack of understanding on the part of a son is unfortunate, but it is more than unfortunate when the son's nature so clearly parallels the father's. The facts are that Archie cannot understand himself and therefore cannot predict his own behavior. He thinks of himself as entirely his mother's son. He sees no evidence even of her wild Rutherford ancestry in his character. When Jean Weir dies, Archie takes the studious and gentle Lord Glenalmond as a spiritual parent and uses him, as previously he had used his mother, as an auditor for his speeches of revulsion at his father's character.

No doubt Archie is influenced by the "shivering delicacy," or, if you prefer, the "humane sympathy" of his mother when he cries out at the execution, yet we must note that when he does so, his father, "if he must have disclaimed the sentiment, might have owned the stentorian voice with which it was uttered" (xviii, 250-251). If this is a contradiction, it is at least a familiar one. His outcry at the execution is Archie's formal rejection of his father, and as we have noted, such dissociations are always accompanied by a movement of character in the very direction of the thing rejected. It is fitting that Archie should most resemble his father when he is in the act of disclaiming him. We might have noted this paradox early in the fragment. When Archie, at the age of seven, suggests that he and his mother ought to abandon Adam Weir because the latter, since he is a judge, has a sin for his trade, Jean quiets him by asking, "here are'na *you* setting up to *judge?*" Stevenson is right in calling Jean's defense a circumvention, but her point is well taken, nevertheless, as is her injunction, "Mind you upon the beam and the mote!" (XVIII, 231).

In spite of Archie's preferred identifications, first with his mother and then with Glenalmond, his contemporaries think of him as "a chip of the old block" (XVIII, 243). At the Speculative Club, a few hours after the execution, he plays his father most fully. He is making ready to propose as the subject of debate, "Whether capital punishment be consistent with God's will or man's policy?"; but before he can do this, he must preside over other debates. "At times he meddled bitterly and launched with defiance those fines which are the precious and rarely used artillery of the president. He little thought, as he did so, how he resembled his father, but his friends remarked upon it, chuckling" (XVIII, 253). When Archie has his first argument with Frank Innes, he is "completely Weir, and the hanging face gloomed on his young shoulders" (XVIII, 363). No doubt, if the story had been completed, the hanging face would have gloomed again at Innes' murder.

T H E R E is very little else which we can be certain of in the unwritten portion of *Weir of Hermiston*. We have a foretaste of "the aboriginal instinct" (XVIII, 387) for revenge in Kirstie which will cause her seduction. Probably she will fall victim to Frank in a twisted attempt to punish Archie. We know that the "Barbarossa" in the four black brothers was to be reawakened when they learn of their sister's fate, and that the "old Adam of our ancestors" was to come alive in Archie, as well. Everything else is guesswork. Most critics are concerned with fears that Stevenson, as he wrote to James Barrie, meant "at the cost of truth to life" to allow "young Hermiston [to] escape clear out of the country, and be happy."[46] No doubt, such an ending would

[46] Letter to J. M. Barrie, Nov. 1, 1892, *Works*, XXIII, 171.

have ruined the book. But a consideration of whether or not Stevenson would have had the courage to see his vision to the end is not crucial to this study. Neither conclusion, the comic or the tragic, tells us anything of how Stevenson meant to resolve the problem of duality which the fragment presents. More important to us, if they could only be found, would be hints which would tell us whether or not Adam Weir, as he presides at Archie's trial, was to recognize a reflection of himself in the murder Archie has committed, or whether Archie would eventually have acknowledged the influence of his father in his own violence. One would also like to know what these recognitions would do to the integrity of the father and to the shivering delicacy of the son, although perhaps it is possible to predict in these areas from what we have seen in other works.

Yet even without a conclusion, *Weir of Hermiston* stands as Stevenson's most complicated and most serious study of the problem of man's dual nature. It is indeed Stevenson's greatest work, not because, as has been so often stated, it is entirely different from anything else he ever wrote, but because it represents his most mature handling of the major theme of all his fiction. It is even fitting, in terms of Stevenson's career, that *Weir of Hermiston* was left unfinished, without a solution, for Stevenson had no solution to the problem of duality which he could bring himself to impose on his fiction. Moreover, this absence of solution puts him once again squarely in the Romantic tradition, at least in the company of the great American romantics — Hawthorne, Melville, and Faulkner — whose characteristic imagination, writes Richard Chase, is "not specifically tragic and Christian, but melodramatic and Manichaean. It does not settle ultimate questions; it leaves them open."[47] *Weir of Hermiston* presents Stevenson's last

47 *The American Novel and Its Tradition*, p. 114.

word on the primary theme of the nineteenth century prose romance—the *problem* of man's duality—just as the last words of this fragment, "a wilful convulsion of brute nature. . . ." (XVIII, 392), dictated on the very morning of Stevenson's death, present what had become to him the theme's most dramatic and most significant aspect.

CHAPTER VIII

A FOOTNOTE TO ROMANCE

IF ROMANCE is dead, concluded the realist Frank Swinnerton, then "Stevenson killed it."[1] Of course the kind of romance Swinnerton meant had never been very robust, at least where critics and serious readers of fiction were concerned. On the other hand, so long as children and childlike adults persist, escape romance will never become quite extinct, no matter how many Stevensons practice it. As for the other kind of romance, no doubt at the time Swinnerton wrote, when Bennet and Galsworthy looked like the memorable writers of the age, the tradition of romance that we have been treating must also have appeared far from healthy. Now, of course, we have a different perspective, and if, as we believe, the great writers of our century include Conrad, Lawrence, Hesse, Faulkner, Joyce, Kafka, and Thomas Mann, then romance probably has suffered very little from Stevenson's meddling with it.

It is more difficult to appraise just what romance gained through Stevenson. When themes and plots involving double identity occur in works written after Stevenson, critics, and sometimes even authors, are apt to mention something about Jekyll and Hyde, but such cursory and unthinking nods in Stevenson's general direction do not betoken a recognized influence; for Jekyll-and-Hyde is used on these occasions as nothing more than a convenient phrase, denoting some sort of loosely defined split person-

[1] *R. L. Stevenson: a Critical Study* (London, 1914), p. 209.

ality.[2] This study began by illustrating the frequency in nineteenth century literature of theories of duality and of plots involving *Doppelgänger*. No doubt, such plots and such theories would have continued into the twentieth century had Stevenson never written.

The works of Joyce, for instance, are characterized by a dualistic approach to experience. We need only think for a moment of the two sons of HCE in *Finnegans Wake* or of the contrast and identity established between Dedalus and Bloom of *Ulysses*. In *A Portrait of the Artist as a Young Man*, Stephen could be said to lead an Edward Hyde life in his dreams and, for a while at least, even outside of them. And he has another identity, where in his dreams he knows "the ecstasy of seraphic life."[3] Large parts of *Ulysses*, moreover, and the whole of *Finnegans Wake* are what Stevenson would have called the work of the Brownies. But probably Stevenson influenced Joyce very little, if at all, and what similarities we note, exist because both writers fed early on Romantic literature and hellfire sermons, and because both of them were strongly influenced by a century of dualistic thought.

Another factor that makes it difficult to judge Stevenson's influence is the fact that Stevenson did not, of course, have the only line open to the French doctors of abnormal psychology. Henry James was one of Stevenson's best friends and one of the strongest admirers of his fiction, but James had a brother who knew as much as any man in the English-speaking world about the subject of double identity. Consequently when Spencer Bryden, the hero of "The

[2] Violet Hunt writes, for instance, that Edward Ashburnham and Mr. Dowell of *The Good Soldier* are Ford's "Jekyll and Hyde." *I Have This to Say: The Story of My Flurried Years* (New York, 1926), pp. 202-203. Note how loosely she uses the term: "Edward Ashburnham and Mr. Dowell in *The Good Soldier* are Joseph Leopold's Jekyll and Hyde—or say two Mr. Jekylls for neither is really wicked."

[3] *A Portrait of the Artist as a Young Man* (New York, 1955), p. 169.

Jolly Corner," confronts the specter of the man he might have become, or when the narrator of "The Private Life" intrudes upon the artistic ego of Clare Vawdrey while Vawdrey's public identity is busy elsewhere, we are certainly dealing with *Doppelgänger*, but the influence is probably not Stevenson's. This is anyway not the manner in which Stevenson generally used his doubles.[4]

And then Sigmund Freud, who was certainly as much a product of the nineteenth century Romantic tradition as Stevenson was, read about and indeed shared in the work of the French psychologists. After Freud published, in the year following Stevenson's death, it was unlikely that writers would be much influenced by Stevenson's psychology, which tended anyway, though with lesser complexity, in the same direction. This is why one hesitates to speak very boldly of Stevenson's influence on D. H. Lawrence, even though Lawrence seems almost to have modeled a good deal of his life on Stevenson's, and even though the duality which Lawrence presents in his novels is very close to that which we have been considering. Mellors of *Lady Chatterley's Lover*, and Paul Morel of *Sons and Lovers* have double personalities of the Stevenson type. The alternate personalities of each man speak separate dialects of English, in fact. Moreover, the flower-picking scene in *Sons and Lovers* is strikingly similar to a vignette from "Will o' the Mill." But the doubles, as we have seen, could have come from practically anywhere, and the flowers of both writers probably belonged first to Hawthorne and *The Scarlet Letter*. The tradition is indeed a large one.

[4] There is a superficial similarity in the relationship between the two Clare Vawdreys and the collaboration of Stevenson and his Brownies described in "A Chapter on Dreams." The essential difference is that Stevenson, though he is "as common as any cheesemonger or any cheese" (See Chap. I, p. 38) does contribute the morality to the stories. The bourgeois Clare Vawdrey has no connection with the literary productions of his double. "He talks, he circulates, he's awfully popular; he flirts." *The Private Life and Other Stories* (New York, 1893), p. 42.

Nevertheless, it would not be presumptuous on the basis of his reputation for Stevenson to claim such influences. He was a very highly regarded writer at the time of his death, and, as we have noted, he corresponded with such brother craftsmen as James and Meredith on terms of perfect equality. Sir Arthur Quiller-Couch's dramatic lament for Stevenson—"Put away books and paper and pen. Stevenson is dead. Stevenson is dead, and now there is nobody left to write for"[5]—gives an emotionally exaggerated picture of this reputation, but it is nevertheless a simple truth that Stevenson was regarded in certain quarters as a major writer and that his work was certainly expected to survive. One modern historian of the novel lists three separate schools of minor writers which stem from Stevenson.[6] It would be surprising, therefore, if he had no influence at all on the important Romantic writers who followed immediately after him.

William Butler Yeats began his education, as he said, in the Henley group. He matriculated shortly after Stevenson left England for the last time, and so the two men just missed meeting one another, although they corresponded briefly and Yeats contributed a short item to the Stevenson bibliography.[7] The image of R. L. S. that Henley gave to Yeats had little in common with the "Seraph in Chocolate," the "barley-sugar effigy of a real man,"[8] created by the early biographers, and the impressionable young Irishman was taught to romanticize and rather to savor the wickedness

[5] "Robert Louis Stevenson," *Adventures in Criticism* (London, 1896), p. 184.

[6] Lionel Stevenson, *The English Novel: A Panorama*, pp. 408-412, 428-431.

[7] "Chevalier Burke and Shule Aroon," was published first in the Boston *Pilot* for December 28, 1889. It has been reprinted in *Letters to the New Island*, ed. Horace Reynolds (Cambridge, Mass., 1934), pp. 90-96.

[8] These phrases are Henley's; they come from his article "R.L.S.," *Pall Mall Magazine*, XXV (Dec. 1901), 508.

of the "wild and reckless early life of the Stevenson–Henley circle," which, he wrote Katharine Tynan, "would hardly do for the public press."[9] Yeats, moreover, recognized Stevenson as the chief of the Romantic writers. He thought, for instance, that Anthony Hope's *The Prisoner of Zenda* —which, by the way, contains a pair of doubles—was "a book certainly not to be laid down till one has got through it," but he felt it was "infinitely below Stevenson, from whom Hope has evidently learned all he knows—at least, in romance."[10] The highest praise Yeats could think to accord the conversational skills of the art critic R.A.M. Stevenson was to say that "he gave as good entertainment in monologue as his cousin Robert Louis in poem or story."[11]

Yeats, of course, thought of himself as a Romantic, and like the writers we have been considering, he took his romanticism from Shelley rather than from Wordsworth. For he rejected the entire Wordsworth tradition as "the poetry of the utilitarian and the rhetorician and the sentimentalist and the popular journalist and the popular preacher . . . not the poetry of 'the seer.' "[12] His own reliance for the basis of poetry was on vision, not experience; and the source for his visions, as for many of the Romantics, was the examination of his own psyche. "Poetry and romance," he wrote in 1896, can be made "only by looking into that little, infinite, faltering, eternal flame that we call ourselves."[13] Moreover, like many of the romancers we have been considering, Yeats preferred always to deal with

9 June 27, 1891, *The Letters of W. B. Yeats,* ed. Allan Wade (London, 1954), pp. 169-170.

10 Letter to Lily Yeats, Dec. 26, 1894, *Letters,* p. 244.

11 *The Trembling of the Veil, Autobiographies* (London, 1955), pp. 132-133.

12 "John Eglinton and Spiritual Art," *Literary Ideals in Ireland* (Dublin, 1899), p. 35.

13 "Dedication," *Stories of Red Hanrahan* (New York, 1914), p. 78.

simplified rather than full or rounded characters. Thus he wrote, "In literature . . . we have lost in personality, in our delight in the whole man—blood, imagination, intellect, running together—but have found a new delight, in essences, in states of mind, in pure imagination, in all that comes to us most easily in elaborate music."[14]

Yeats' conception of the anti-self, "always opposite to the natural self,"[15] is a Stevensonian notion and might be illustrated by Henry Durie's fluctuations in *The Master of Ballantrae*. But Stevenson's influence on Yeats is most easily perceived in a short story of the middle nineties, "Rosa Alchemica," for in this work Yeats presents a pair of *Doppelgänger*, Michael Robartes and Owen Aherne, who are clear Stevenson types, and who act out virtually the same drama we have followed in one after another of Stevenson's works.

"Rosa Alchemica" is much more Eastern and French than any tale Stevenson told; it belongs also to the Beckford–Bulwer-Lytton tradition of romance and contains the full range of rare incenses, mystic dances, swoons, and visions; but these colorful properties serve here only to make the Stevensonian problem more dramatic. The narrator, elsewhere named Owen Aherne, is akin to Stevenson's civilized man, who draws back from all involvement in life. Like Will o' the Mill, he gives active scope only to his imagination and is thus enabled, he believes, to experience all human passions "without their bitterness and without satiety."[16] But like all of Stevenson's would-be life-deserters, he has a double nature, he contains "two selves"; and even in the most perfect times of imagination, one

---

[14] "Personality and the Intellectual Essences," *The Cutting of an Agate* (New York, 1912), pp. 58-59.
[15] *The Trembling of the Veil*, p. 171.
[16] "Rosa Alchemica," *Stories of Red Hanrahan*, p. 193.

side of him watches "with heavy eyes the other's moment of content."[17]

It is this second and restless nature of Aherne which in student days had been fascinated by the "magnetic power" of the savage Michael Robartes. And now when Robartes suddenly reappears, with his "wild red hair, fierce eyes, sensitive, tremulous lips and rough clothes," and with an expression "something between a debauchee, a saint, and a peasant,"[18] he once more tempts this more lawless element of his friend's nature to enter life fully at last and without restraint. "You have shut away the world and gathered the gods about you," Robartes tells the narrator; "and if you do not throw yourself at their feet, you will always be full of lassitude, and of wavering purpose."[19]

When they were students together, Aherne had fled the kind of participation in life that Robartes would have forced upon him, but now, caught momentarily in a trance, he agrees to become a member in the Order of the Alchemical Rose, a mystic society, and even begins to go through the rites of initiation. But ultimately he rejects the offered vision. At the crucial moment of the ceremony he looks at the "immortal august woman" with whom he is dancing, and, like any hero out of Stevenson, draws back with distaste and horror.

> Suddenly I remembered that her eyelids had never quivered, and that her lilies had not dropped a black petal, or shaken from their places, and understood *with a great horror* that I danced with one who was more or less than human, and who was drinking up my soul as an ox drinks up a wayside pool; and I fell, and darkness passed over me.[20]

[17] *Ibid.*, p. 195. [18] *Ibid.*, pp. 197-198.
[19] *Ibid.*, p. 201. [20] *Ibid.*, pp. 227-228, my italics.

When he awakens he deserts the exhausted and now sleeping celebrants, leaving them to be murdered by a group of piously Christian and shrewdly commercial fishermen, Highlanders civilized, justified sinners, who believe the mystics are charming the fish away from their harbor. As we might expect, the narrator is driven by these violent experiences "to the verge of taking the habit of St. Dominic."[21]

"Rosa Alchemica" is not one of the great pieces of English prose fiction, but it was a work that seriously influenced the development of its author's thought and art. More than anything else in the story, the characters— Michael Robartes and Owen Aherne—are, as Richard Ellmann notes, "symbolic personages who recur in his writings during the rest of his life."[22] Out of the contrast between these two men, moreover, may have developed the statement from *The Second Coming* which has become so important to the literature and thought of our century: "The best lack all conviction, while the worst/Are full of passionate intensity." And certainly we have met with such a sentiment frequently enough in the writings of Robert Louis Stevenson.

Another of the young writers who made contact with the Henley circle shortly after Stevenson's departure from it was Oscar Wilde, who began and always remained a great admirer of Stevenson, "that delicate artist in language," as he called him.[23] In prison, Wilde was constantly asking his friends for the works of Stevenson, which he ranked in very high company. "You know the sort of books I want,"

---

[21] *Ibid.*, p. 191.

[22] *Yeats: The Man and the Masks*, p. 82.

[23] Letter to Oswald Sickert, May 1892, *The Letters of Oscar Wilde*, ed. Rupert Hart-Davis (London, 1962), p. 314. In "The Decay of Lying," he refers to Stevenson as "that delightful master of delicate and fanciful prose." *The Complete Works of Oscar Wilde*, 12 vols. (New York, 1927), V, 15.

he writes Robert Ross in 1897, "Flaubert, Stevenson, Baudelaire, Maeterlinck, Dumas, *père*, Keats, Marlowe, Chatterton, Coleridge, Anatole France, Gautier, Dante and all Dante literature; Goethe and ditto; and so on."[24] At one time he had a plan to give a set of Stevenson to the inadequately stocked prison library.

Of course Wilde, like Yeats and Stevenson, was a thoroughly self-conscious Romantic, and his contempt for realism was perfect. "It plays very cleverly upon one string," he wrote, "and this is the commonplace."[25] Wilde was also one of the most important contributors to the literature of the double. An article by Arthur Ganz, "The Divided Self in the Society Comedies of Oscar Wilde" (*Modern Drama*, III [May 1960], 16-23), shows how pervasive the idea of psychological dualism is to this author's works. Moreover, the double man, in much less subtle forms than Mr. Ganz considers, shows himself obviously enough to any reader of the plays. And what is treated lightheartedly as Bunburying in *The Importance of Being Earnest* takes on a different, more somber aspect when it appears in *The Picture of Dorian Gray*.

Eino Railo in *The Haunted Castle* (p. 307) and Richard Ellmann in *Yeats: The Man and the Masks* (p. 72) both point out similarities between Wilde's romance and Stevenson's *Jekyll and Hyde*. We shall see that there are indeed a number of points in common, but we should note first that Wilde, as a man of the theater and as an acquaintance of Henley, would have been almost as familiar with *Deacon Brodie* as with the novella that that play ultimately developed into. And indeed *The Picture of Dorian*

24 Letter to Robert Ross, Apr. 1, 1897, *The Letters of Oscar Wilde*, p. 521. This list puts Stevenson's influence in perspective and emphasizes what should really need no statement: that the present writer fully recognizes Wilde's debts to writers far different from Stevenson.

25 "Literary and Other Notes," *The Complete Works of Oscar Wilde*, XII, 246.

Gray seems to have profited from the familiarity. Wilde's
Lord Henry Wotton speaks at times the same philosophy
that characterized the early Brodie, who believed that conscience and cowardice were the same thing given different
names, and that all men would be evil if only they dared.
And Dorian, like Brodie of the later part of the play, finds
himself unmasked by a friend who starts with horror at the
evil suddenly revealed to him. " 'Each of us has Heaven
and Hell in him, Basil,' cried Dorian, with a wild gesture
of despair,"[26] and in a voice that echoes the Deacon's plea
to his friend Leslie: "Have you not ill thoughts yourself?
It must be; we have all our secret evil." At the end of the
story, moreover, Dorian, once again like Brodie, is calling
for "a new life!"[27]

Of course, *Deacon Brodie, or the Double Life* and *Dr.
Jekyll and Mr. Hyde* are so intimately related to one
another that it is hard to distinguish between the two in
matters of influence. Dorian, like both Brodie and Jekyll,
engages rooms in a disreputable part of town to house his
nighttime identity. And the pleasure Wilde's hero takes in
being able to sin blamelessly, because with a face or an
identity not strictly his own, could have come from either
of Stevenson's heroes. Like them, Dorian sits smugly and,
he believes, safely behind his mask of innocence and respectability. "Eternal youth," Dorian thinks, "infinite passion, pleasure subtle and secret, wild joys and wilder sins—
he was to have all these things. The portrait was to bear
the burden of his shame: that was all."[28] Moreover, like
Jekyll and Brodie, he is both fascinated and horrified by
his degradation and corruption—fascinated to the extent
of indulging and perverting his sensual appetites; and horrified to the extent of stabbing and killing the manifesta-

26 *The Complete Works of Oscar Wilde*, IV, 286.
27 *Ibid.*, p. 401.
28 *Ibid.*, p. 194.

tion of his way of life, the portrait. Finally, the simultaneous deaths of Dorian and his picture could have come from any one of a number of Stevenson stories and romances.

These two writers, Yeats and Wilde, are inferior as romancers to Stevenson himself. We have considered Stevenson's influence on them because, of course, they were not only writers of fiction and because Wilde, through his plays, and Yeats, through his poetry, have had far greater followings in the present century than Stevenson. But Stevenson influenced at least one writer, Joseph Conrad, who was a better writer, and who might even be said to have written some of the very books for which Stevenson's acknowledged disciples and critics had long been taking notes.[29]

If the incident had occurred in a novel instead of in life, it would no doubt be considered of the utmost significance that Joseph Conrad made his first important literary acquaintance when John Galsworthy ran out of money and was unable to complete his trip to Samoa where he intended to visit Stevenson. Galsworthy took passage home on the *S. S. Torrens*, where Conrad, the unfinished manuscript of *Almayer's Folly* in his drawer, was a mate. This is certainly not to suggest, even facetiously, that Conrad was a poor man's substitute for Stevenson, but it would certainly be accurate to say that he was thus regarded by the critics for a number of years. In the 1890's, when Conrad's first books were published, it was a commonplace to compare him with Stevenson. There seemed to be a similarity both in their subject matter and in their themes, and while these comparisons were generally friendly to Conrad,

[29] James Barrie describes the attitude of the note takers, who are so fascinated by Stevenson that "they are willing to judge him by the great works he is to write by and by." "Robert Louis Stevenson," *An Edinburgh Eleven, The Novels, Tales and Sketches of J. M. Barrie,* 12 vols. (New York, 1927), III, 248.

they were clear in according him a rank slightly below that which the recently dead master still occupied. The *Bookman* review of *An Outcast of the Islands* will serve as an illustration: "Mr. Conrad's chief power is psychological. It is a terrible psychology, realised with as awful an imagination as we can remember in present fiction excepting Stevenson."[30]

For Conrad, who feared Bohemian poverty, Stevenson stood as an example of a writer who had actually been able to support himself through his craft, and through writings which, as Conrad believed, had not given an inch to the low tastes of the public. "When it comes to popularity," he wrote Alfred Knopf as late as 1913, "I stand nearer the public than Stevenson, who was super-literary, a conscious virtuoso of style; whereas the average mind does not care much for virtuosity."[31]

Earlier we noted that Lionel Stevenson calls Conrad's most successful narrator, Marlow, a "Stevensonian on-looker."[32] But this technique, which belongs anyway to the more general romance tradition, does not represent Stevenson's most significant contribution to Conrad. Conrad's chief power, as we have just heard the reviewer for *Bookman* say, "is psychological," and it is in this area that we can expect the greatest influence from Stevenson.

J. Hillis Miller writes that *Under Western Eyes* is a tale of double identity in which one self, Razumov, rejects and betrays the other, Victor Haldin, and brings about his death.[33] So viewed, Conrad's story appears definitely Stevensonian in theme, especially in the late pages, where it reads like one of Stevenson's romances of pursuit. And it ends, we should note, with the hero, now mercifully deaf,

[30] *Bookman* [New York], IV (Oct. 1896), 166.

[31] *Joseph Conrad: Life and Letters*, ed. G. Jean-Aubry, 2 vols. (New York, 1927), II, 147.

[32] See Chap. V, note 2.

[33] *Charles Dickens: The World of His Novels*, pp. 274-275.

in full retirement from life, "not 'in the centre [of Russia],' but 'in the south,'" in "the suburb of some very small town, hiding within the high plank-fence of a yard overgrown with nettles."[34] In another work, Lord Jim is afflicted with a kind of paralysis, very familiar to us, at the moment when he confronts *his* evil double, Gentleman Brown. So is Axel Heyst, Conrad's unfortunate Will o' the Mill, when he sits helplessly across from Mr. Jones at the climax of *Victory*.

On the other side of the duality, Conrad's notion of the violent, hollow man, as exemplified by Kurtz of "Heart of Darkness," may also have derived from Stevenson. For in *The Master of Ballantrae* the narrator writes that he had moments when he thought of James Durie "as a man of pasteboard—as though, if one should strike smartly through the buckram of his countenance, there would be found a mere vacuity within." And the narrator goes on to note that "This horror (not merely fanciful, I think) vastly increased my detestation of his neighborhood" (xiv, 263-264).

We have already noted the similarity between Conrad's Kurtz and Attwater of *The Ebb-Tide*. In Stevenson's romance the protagonists could relate to their savage opponent in only two ways: by trying to murder him or by kneeling abjectly at his feet. These two solutions, and a third, inglorious resignation from life, are the sum of Stevenson's pessimism. It is important to note that in two of Conrad's greatest works, "The Secret Sharer" and "Heart of Darkness," the narrator-hero is able, at least momentarily, to fully accept his double with all his savagery and in spite of his violent crimes. On the other hand, Charles Darnaway of "The Merry Men" draws back from the identical vision, expressed even in the very same words—"the horror—the horror"—which Conrad's Marlow is

34 *Under Western Eyes* (New York, 1926), p. 379.

strong enough to embrace. Marlow remains loyal to Kurtz, while Darnaway piously rejects his uncle as an enemy to God.[35]

At the end of Stevenson's *The Beach at Falesá*, Wiltshire has remarried his native mistress, legally this time, and has pretty well accepted the loss of caste which this union implies. What he cannot fully make up his mind to, however, is the fact that his daughters are not white; he concludes his narrative in this troubled manner:

> But what bothers me is the girls. They're only half-castes, of course; I know that as well as you do, and there's nobody thinks less of half-castes than I do; but they're mine, and about all I've got. I can't reconcile my mind to their taking up with Kanakas, and I'd like to know where I'm to find the whites. (xv, 391)

The Beach of Falesá was published in 1892, three years before Conrad's first book, *Almayer's Folly*, which deals directly with this final problem of Wiltshire's. Conrad's story had been in the works for a number of years, and there is little question of an influence here, although the appearance and popularity of Stevenson's short romance may have encouraged Conrad to go on with his writing. But what *The Beach of Falesá* and other Stevenson books most certainly gave to Conrad was a British and an American audience interested in the South Seas and more than willing to accept the phenomenon of a serious, psychological writer of highly pitched adventure stories. How Herman Melville could have used such an audience fifty years earlier! Meredith had been leading fiction, even romantic fiction, in quite a different direction. So had Henry James. But with Stevenson in the South Seas, even James became interested in the exotic, and it was said of him that

[35] See Chap. IV, pp. 141-142.

he could have taken "a First in any Samoan subject."[36] He must have welcomed in Conrad a successor to his dead friend. Moreover, Conrad's reputation as a writer was not really assured until W. E. Henley, another of Stevenson's old friends, decided to publish "The Nigger of the *Narcissus*" in his influential magazine, *The New Review*.

In his first letter to Henry James, Stevenson marked out the direction he wanted English fiction to take:

> Of course, I am not so dull as to ask you to desert your walk; but could you not, in one novel, to oblige a sincere admirer, and to enrich his shelves with a beloved volume, could you not, and might you not, cast your characters in a mould a little more abstract and academic . . . , and pitch your incidents, I do not say in any stronger, but in a slightly more emphatic key—as it were an episode from one of the old (so-called) novels of adventure? I fear you will not; and I suppose I must sighingly admit you to be right. And yet, when I see, as it were, a book of *Tom Jones* handled with your exquisite precision and shot through with those sidelights of reflection in which you excel, I relinquish the dear vision with regret. Think upon it.[37]

Of course, Henry James did well to reject this advice, but others were just as right to take it. And with the fiction of Conrad and his followers, most notably with the romances of William Faulkner, the twentieth century, at least, has not had to relinquish Stevenson's dear vision. Moreover, Stevenson realized it himself in a number of his works—certainly in "The Merry Men," the *Strange Case*

[36] Stevenson's letter to Henry James, July 7, 1894, *Henry James and Robert Louis Stevenson*, p. 242.

[37] Dec. 8, 1884, *Henry James and Robert Louis Stevenson*, p. 104. The friendship between the men was so new at this point and the tone of the letter throughout is so polite, that the parody of James' style must be unconscious.

of Dr. Jekyll and Mr. Hyde, The Master of Ballantrae, and in the fragment of his masterpiece, *Weir of Hermiston.*

We are left, though, with a question, the same question with which we began. If Stevenson is so serious and so successful a writer as this study has tried to maintain, then why has he lost so much of his reputation? A few answers have already been suggested. For one thing, some of the essays, with their cloying optimism, give a misleading impression of Stevenson's mind, at least of his best mind, which he seems to have reserved for his works of fiction. More legitimate is the objection that his characters, though certainly drawn with sufficient complexity, are perhaps not full or rounded enough to satisfy the taste that the realists have cultivated in us. If we insist on real, flesh-and-blood men and women, such as we encounter on the street or in the works of the great realists, then the entire romance tradition, from Goethe to Faulkner, is more or less closed to us.

Another explanation for this loss of critical esteem came from Henry James, who suggested that our concern with the incidents of Stevenson's life has destroyed the interest we had in his works. And certainly when we try to balance the handful of critical books that have been written on Stevenson against the great number of biographies, James' theory that Stevenson "has *superseded,* personally, his books"[38] appears not so fanciful. The early biographers in particular, all close friends or relatives, tried to fatten the widow's estate by creating an ultra-saleable Stevenson, and the "barley-sugar effigy" they produced has proved unpalatable to a later generation which prided itself on its tough constitution. If this is so, then it is unfortunate, because the portrait these biographers drew has been well repudi-

[38] Letter to Edmund Gosse, 1901, "Introduction," *Henry James and Robert Louis Stevenson,* p. 46.

ated by the more responsible writers and scholars of Stevenson's life who have published in the last twenty years.

But the damage does not end here, for Stevenson was equally unlucky in his friends among the critics. However he is regarded, Stevenson was certainly the greatest writer of fiction that his country had produced since Walter Scott, and there is unfortunately, though understandably, an echo of "Whaur's yer Wully Shakespeare noo!" in much of the early Scotch praise which was accorded him. Because he could tell an interesting story, moreover, he also attracted questionable champions among critics who stubbornly and stupidly opposed all modern trends in fiction. As John Jay Chapman wrote:

> The doughty old novel readers who knew their Scott and Ainsworth and Wilkie Collins and Charles Reade, their Dumas and their Cooper, were the very people whose hearts were warmed by Stevenson. If you cross-question one of these, he will admit that Stevenson is after all a revival, an echo, an after-glow of the romantic movement; and that he brought nothing new. He will scout any comparison between Stevenson and his old favorites, but he is ready enough to take Stevenson for what he is worth.[39]

This tendency to regard Stevenson as a lesser Scott may have been all right, for the booksellers at least, in days when serious historians of fiction could write of Scott as the only English novelist "whose work can, without absurdity, be compared to Shakespeare's."[40] But in these times of more demanding tastes, when, to be well regarded, a writer must be not only a sage and a storyteller, but an artist, as well; when Scott himself must fight to stay in the canon

[39] "Robert Louis Stevenson," *Emerson and Other Essays* (New York, 1898), pp. 228-229.
[40] Edward Wagenknecht, *Cavalcade of the English Novel* (New York, 1944), p. 152.

and even Shakespeare is forced to concede a few care-
lessly written plays; then Stevenson's other loyalty, to the
more profoundly Romantic tradition, must be emphasized.
It must be stressed, moreover, because it is the truer and
more serious loyalty. As we saw at the beginning, Stevenson
did not base his art on the daydream literature of Scott,
but on the artistically and intellectually controlled romances of Victor Hugo, for whom "the moral significance,"
Stevenson wrote, "is the essence of the romance; it is the
organising principle."[41] Finally, this loyalty to the serious
romance tradition must be insisted upon because here Stevenson did most certainly bring something new, and here
he is far from being a mere afterglow. He enriched romantic prose fiction by informing its conventions with his
own particular vision, and by understanding its principles
and its past literature as perhaps no other romancer had
ever done.

[41] "Victor Hugo's Romances," *Works*, IV, 56.

INDEX

INDEX

A

Aeschylus, 112
Ainsworth, William Harrison, 245
Aldington, Richard, 148n
Allen, Walter, 187-88
Ampère, Jean Jacques, 21
Aristotle, 8
Arnold, Matthew, 100; *Culture and Anarchy*, 28
Aytoun, William, 138-39
Azam, Dr., 32

B

Ballantine, John, 25
Balzac, Honoré de, 16, 205n
Barbauld, Anna Letitia, 15
Barbey d'Aurevilly, Jules, 168n. *See also St. Ives*
Barrie, James M., 226, 239n
Barrymore, John, 148, 153
Baudelaire, Charles, 237
Beach, Joseph Warren, 116
Beckford, William, 234
Beeching, H. C., 199
Beerbohm, Max, 22
Bennet, Arnold, 229; *Old Wives' Tale*, 165
Binet, Alfred, 30, 31, 32, 32n, 33, 38n
Black, William, 84
Blackwood's Edinburgh Magazine, 26
Blake, William, 17-18; *The Book of Thel*, 71
Brodie, William, 121-22
Breuer, Josef, 32-33
Brontë, Charlotte, and the romance, 5, 13; *Jane Eyre*, 13, 178. *See also The Master of Ballantrae* ("Stevenson," WORKS); and Jane Austen, 15;

and doubles psychology, 27, 33, 178; *Villette*, 178, 201n
Brontë, Emily, 5, 27; *Wuthering Heights*, 13, 14, 36, 144. *See also Kidnapped* and *The Master of Ballantrae* ("Stevenson," WORKS)
brothers motif, 165-66
Brown, Charles Brockden, 8, 9; *Edgar Huntly*, 9; *Ormond*, 9; *Wieland*, 9, 25
Browning, Elizabeth Barrett, 196
Browning, Robert, 30; *The Ring and the Book*, 144, 202n; *Men and Women*, 201n
Buchanan, Robert William, 84
Buckley, Jerome H., 28, 122
Bulwer-Lytton, Sir Edward George Earle Lytton (Lord Lytton), 162; and doubles psychology, 28-29, 33; *Eugene Aram*, 26, 28, 71. *See also* "Markheim"; and Hamlet, 63, 71; and Hawthorne, 29; and Hogg's *Justified Sinner*, 26; *Leila*, 63; and the romance, 5, 15-17, 28, 34; *A Strange Story*, 28-29, 201n. *See also* "Olalla"; and Yeats, 234; *Zanoni*, 13, 17, 28
Bush, Douglas, 196
Byron, George Gordon, Lord, *The Corsair. See also Deacon Brodie*
Byronism, 107, 173, 174, 223

C

Cadell, Robert, 25n
Calvin, John, 23, 31, 90-91
Carlyle, Thomas, 28
Cervantes Saavedra, Miguel de, 7; Meredith on, 19; *Don Quixote*, 21

J

James, Henry, 4, 34, 232; and Conrad, 242-43; on Dostoyevsky, 128n; and doubles psychology, 33, 230-31; "The Jolly Corner," 230-31; and narrators, 144; "The Private Life," 231, 231n; on Stevenson, 3, 44, 78, 90, 94, 244
James, William, 30, 33; *Principles of Psychology*, 32n
Janet, Jules, 30, 33
Janet, Pierre, 30, 31, 32, 33, 74
Jenkin, Fleeming, 117
Johnson, Samuel, 8
Joyce, James, 229; *Ulysses*, 165, 230; *Finnegans Wake*, 230; *A Portrait of the Artist as a Young Man*, 230
Jung, Carl Gustav, 20
Jung-Stilling (Jung, Johann Heinrich), 29

K

Kafka, Franz, 179, 229
Kant, Immanuel, 20; and doubles psychology, 23-24, 28
Keats, John, 237
Keith, C., 149n
Kingsley, Charles, 28
Knopf, Alfred, 240
Knowlton, Edgar, 128
Knox, John, 131

L

Lang, Andrew, 3
Lawrence, David Herbert, 6, 204, 229; and Pan, 196; *Lady Chatterley's Lover*, 231; *Sons and Lovers*, 231
Leavis, F. R., 4, 6, 11, 36, 40
Levin, Harry, 6, 201n
Lewis, Matthew Gregory, and

the romance, 9-10, 22, 34; *The Monk*, 9-10; *The Bravo of Venice*, 10; *Romantic Tales*, 10
Lockhart, John Gibson, 26
Lytton, see Bulwer-Lytton

M

Macaulay, Thomas Babington, and villainy, 28
Macleod, Fiona (William Sharp), 84
Maeterlinck, Count Maurice, 237
Mann, Thomas, 229
Mansfield, Richard, 148, 148n
March, Frederic, 148
Mark Twain and Scott, 7n; and R. L. Stevenson, 79-80; and civilization, 114-15; *Pudd'nhead Wilson*, 166; *The Adventures of Huckleberry Finn, see Kidnapped*
Marlowe, Christopher, 237
Marryat, Frederick, *The Phantom Ship*, 189
Mataafa, 53, 53n
Maturin, Charles Robert, and the romance, 5, 10; *Melmoth the Wanderer*, 35, 136n-37n; *The Fatal Revenge*, 208n. *See also The Master of Ballantrae* ("Stevenson," WORKS), "The Merry Men"
Melville, Herman, 242; and the romance, 16, 17, 227; and "The Merry Men," 136n, 142; *Moby Dick*, 136n, 142, 163, 189; *Pierre*, 166, 201n-202n; and *The Master of Ballantrae*, 184
Mesmer, Franz, 26
mesmerism, 22, 26, 29, 31
Mesnet, Ernest, 32
Michel, Alfred, 155
Miller, J. Hillis, 21n, 26n, 240